12-25-93

To my
Sweetheart

a little history
of the great State
of Maine

I Love you so much

Ada

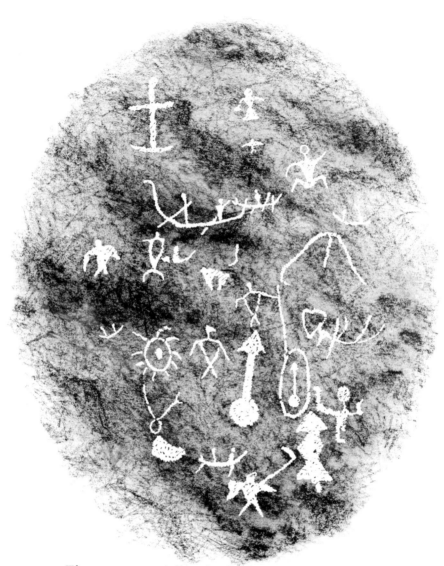

These are some of the petroglyphs at Embden, Maine, thought to have been carved by the Indians over several centuries on a rock ledge jutting out into the Kennebec River. Nobody knows the exact meaning of the figures. Stephen Laurent calls them Wanbanaki-awikhigan, *"Abenaki writing." Illustration by Suzanne A. Gabel.*

Dawn over the Kennebec

BY MARY R. CALVERT

The Monmouth Press
Monmouth, Maine

ISBN 0-9609914-3-3
Library of Congress Catalog Card Number
83-91227

Mfd. in the United States of America
First edition, revised 1986
Third printing

I dedicate this book to the memory of my father

STANLEY RENIER

who was born on the bank of the Kennebec River in Norridgewock and never lived more than five miles from it
in Madison.

He loved to read, and instilled in me a love of geography and history, especially that of the Kennebec valley and Maine.

He took my two brothers and me to the summit of
Mount Bigelow to count the lakes below; to the Chain
of Ponds to pick blueberries; to Embden Pond for fishing;
and for many miles through the woods to blaze trails and
to scale lumber in his woodlots.

They were experiences never to be forgotten.

ACKNOWLEDGEMENTS

The cover painting, *Gift of God*, was done by the famous marine painter Earle Barlow of East Boothbay, Maine. This beautiful painting was done expressly for this volume, and depicts George Popham sailing into the Kennebec River in his flagship *Gift of God* in 1607.

My husband deserves special thanks for his never-failing help and encouragement. I couldn't possibly list all the helpful things he has done to make this book possible, so I will just say, "Thank you, Francis."

My late cousin Lindon James Collins, of Rockwood and Skowhegan, pored over quadrangle maps and script for fully two years, locating places with obsolete Indian names and proofreading the draft of the Montresor, Chadwick and Finlay chapters. As an expert woodsman and guide, his help and advice were invaluable.

My dear friend Elizabeth Hamilton Hartsgrove of Bath helped in so many ways that I find them hard to list. An amateur archaeologist and collector of Indian artifacts and Maine histories, she spent hours searching for information and making notes for me. She also guided me to locations with which she is very familiar, around Moosehead Lake, Chesuncook, the West Branch of the Penobscot River and others, to take photographs.

Elinor Hamilton, her twin sister, famous during the 1930s and 40s as the "Wilderness Nurse" of Moosehead Lake, fed and lodged Elizabeth and me during these jaunts in her beautiful cottage at Seboomook. Elinor also delved into her past to give me information about Dr. Pritham of Greenville and her own adventures as a nurse in Great Northern Paper Company lumber camps. Both will have chapters in the next volume.

Ruth Lepper Gardiner, mapmaker, artist and musician of Southport, drew the perfectly detailed maps for this book. She put up with my changes, corrections and deadlines with good nature and a smile.

Stephen Laurent, Abenaki Indian and hereditary chief of the St. Francis tribe in Canada, gave me a great deal of information about the Abenakis. He proofread entire chapters, including the one on Indian place names. Mr. Laurent has made several tapes to demonstrate the sound of the Abenaki language, one copy of which has been given to the Maine State Museum. His wife Marguery, although not Indian, was also very helpful on points of Indian culture and literature. In the summer they jointly run an Indian shop near their home in Intervale, New Hampshire, where they are keeping the study of Indian culture alive.

Agnes Richardson Gott of Camden, Maine is a descendant of the famous "Old Louis" Annance of Greenville. She has given me a great deal of help in untangling the genealogy of the Gill-Annance family, founded by two English child captives back in the early 1700s. With her talent for storytelling and writing she made her childhood in Greenville come vividly to life.

My friend Alicia Roof of Largo, Florida gave me valuable assistance on part of the book done in Florida. She edited and typed script, and helped by her interest and encouragement.

Linda Griffiths of the Twin City Printery staff, holder of a BA from Oxford University and an MA from Berkeley, took me in hand and coached me in the mysteries of getting a book in print. She has edited the script, done a bibliography and index, selected the typeface and designed the pages and cover. Most of all I appreciate her interest and encouragement.

Virginia Barter of Boothbay Harbor, wife, mother, singer, selectman, and church worker, has somehow found time to turn my messy first drafts into beautifully typed script. All this has been done with infinite patience and good humor (and, I fear, some night work) to meet deadlines.

Dr. Bruce Bourque, research associate in archaeology for the Maine State Museum, was very generous with his time for conferences and help in the chapters on Indian history and the Red Paint People. Photographs and photocopies were made available to me.

Mrs. Sanford, special collections librarian at the Raymond Fogler Library at UMO, produced reams of materials I asked for, and often suggested things I didn't know existed. Her help in researching and in having materials photocopied was very much appreciated.

All the research librarians at the Maine Historical Society helped from time to time. They photocopied passages from old and rare books, searched for manuscripts, and brought out relics from the Indian village at Old Point, including Father Rasle's chest with the secret drawer, and the chapel bell.

Last but not least is Mr. White Nichols of Wiscasset, archaeologist and historian, who very kindly guided me to the petroglyphs on the Kennebec near Solon, to the site of the first settlement in Skowhegan, to Fort Halifax, and other interesting sites. He gave me much information on archaeological discoveries, and answered many of my questions on the ancient history of the Kennebec valley.

Paraphrasing a quotation from *Oliver Twist:* I thank you each and every one.

Contents

Essay on Bibliography

A mystery story could hold no more fascination than my search for information for *Dawn over the Kennebec*. The search took my husband Francis and me to the Room of Treasures at Chartres Cathedral in France; to the convent and museum of the Ursulines in Quebec City, conducted by Soeur Marcelle Boucher, curator of the convent archives; to Stephen Laurent, hereditary chieftain of the St. Francis tribe of Indians, Odanak, Canada, now living in New Hampshire; through him to an attic in Montreal, where some copies of his father's book, long out of print, were found.

I found several books written by Indians about the Abenakis and Penobscots. They are all out of print and difficult to find now. The Maine State Library, Maine Historical Society, Bowdoin Library and the special collections division of the Raymond Fogler Memorial Library, University of Maine, Orono, have some of them.

Since the Abenakis and other Maine Indians had no written language, researching their history is difficult. The only sources for information are conversations with descendants of the Indian tribes, who have been told legends and history by their grandparents and others; and reading the writings of people who have done so. Fannie Hardy Eckstorm of Bangor became well acquainted with many members of the Penobscot and Abenaki tribes in her travels around northern Maine with her father, a prominent lumberman in the early 1900s. She wrote two very important books for researchers: *The Penobscot Man* and *Indian Place-Names*. Although she wrote about place names of the Penobscot valley and the Maine coast, I found many I could use in my chapter on Kennebec valley place names.

THE SEARCH

Once an author decides upon the subject of "the Book," it is necessary to start the long process of research. Obviously, in the case of a history, the writer cannot have been present, and so must reconstruct past events through the eyes and writings of those who were there. Many accounts must be read, and those chosen which are verified by others, or, in the case of firsthand accounts, have the ring of truth.

For the first chapter of *Dawn over the Kennebec* I decided I would like to know what the very first meeting of the red man and the white man could have been like. What did the Indians think when they first realized that they were not alone in their, until then, isolated world?

For this information and further material on Indian life, language and customs, I hunted for books or manuscripts written by the Indians themselves. I was not sure I would find any about the Abenakis of the Kennebec valley with whom my book dealt. I enlisted the help of my friend Stephen Laurent of Intervale, New Hampshire, as he carries in his Indian shop not only Indian-made articles, but books about them. His father Joseph Laurent wrote the excellent *Abenakis and English Dialogues,* the first vocabulary ever published in the Abenaki language, comprising the Abenaki alphabet, key to pronunciation, and many grammatical explanations and synoptical illustrations showing the numerous modifications of Abenaki verbs. It gave also the etymology of Indian names of certain localities, rivers, lakes, etc. Through Mr. Laurent, I obtained for my collection a first edition of this valuable little book, now very rare. It was published in 1884, and the author was Abenaki chief of the Indian village of St. Francis, P.Q.

His son, Stephen Laurent, is an Indian scholar in his own right and has written an English translation of Father Rasle's French-Abenaki dictionary, which we hope will be published at some future date.

I also found two other books written by Indians: Henry Lorne Masta's *Abenaki Indian Legends, Grammar and Place Names* and Joseph Nicolar's *The Red Man.* I used a great many of Mr. Masta's place names in my chapter on place names, believing them to be more correct than those of later authors. Mr. Masta was a schoolteacher on the St. Francis reservation and started the first Protestant church there. There was a monument to his memory placed in St. Francis (now Odanak) a few years ago. The little book by Joseph Nicolar called *The Red Man* is the one I used for the opening chapter of *Dawn over the Kennebec.*

I was delighted when I found *The Red Man* in Isaac Davis' Antiquarian Book Store in Gardiner. Mr. Davis has been very helpful in searching for books to build up my collection over a span of five or six years. I realized at the beginning that it would be impossible to spend the time necessary to research the material for my book in libraries and historical societies. For one thing, they were all too far from my home, and would involve countless hours of reading and photocopying. I have succeeded in building a library large enough to take care of most of my research.

Joseph Nicolar, a Penobscot, had written just the book I needed for my introduction. I had already ascertained that the Penobscots and Abenakis were very close. They visited back and forth constantly. There was no language barrier, and their legends were no doubt the same or very similar.

It was 1893 when Mr. Nicolar wrote what I consider a jewel of a book about the legends and traditions of the red man. He was a descendant of what he called "that once numerous and powerful race," and his life had been spent in the researches of his people's past. He had talked for countless hours with the elders, hearing their stories of the legends passed down through many generations. After forty years he declared himself satisfied that no more could be found, as the traditional storytellers had all gone to the happy hunting grounds.

I found Mr. Nicolar's prose very easy to read and almost poetic at times, particularly when he described the awakening to life of the first man on earth, Klose-kur-beh, at the Creation.

> Nearer and nearer came the brightness toward his body until it got almost to a touching distance, and a feeling came into his flesh, he felt the warmth of approaching brightness, and he fell into a deep sleep.

And after he awoke:

> "Turning toward my right hand and facing the north, Behold! there was a high mountain seven rainbows high. To this I went, and up the mountain I walked; seven times my strength left me, and seven times the wind of the heavens fanned my brow, each time giving me strength to go on my way. Seven times I reached out my hand unto the seven rainbows and lifted myself on my feet, so that I was able to walk to the top of the mountain."

His description of the first coming of the white man to the red man's world is very moving.

The Indians thought it best, and it was so decided in council, that when the strange people came they should be greeted as friends, and if possible made brothers. They would be greeted with the word Nitch-ieh! meaning brother.

Father Sebastian Rasle lived with and ministered to the Abenakis of the Norridgewock village at Old Point for thirty-four years. Toward the end of his life Father Rasle acceded to the pleas of his brother and nephew to relate his manner of life and work among his parishioners in the wilds of Maine. In the face of charges that he encouraged the Abenakis in their fierce raids against English villages, it is only fitting that we allow him the privilege of stating his case. This he is well qualified to do and has done in his letters to his relatives, in which he would have no reason to tell anything but the truth.

Credit is due to the officials of the Society of Jesus that we have the writings of Father Rasle and other priests of the order. Father Rasle's writings make up an important part of the 1781 *Memoires of America,* occupying volumes six through nine. In his writings Father Rasle identifies himself with his savages to the extent of giving his recollections of their speeches in the form of direct address, after the manner of ancient historians; but it is quite evident that his account is very close to the spirit of the original orator.

A later edition of the *Jesuit Relations* was printed between 1896 and 1902, Reuben Gold Thwaite, editor. It consists of 73 volumes in the original French with translations in Latin, Italian and English. This set of books may be found in the Maine Historical Society, Maine State Library, Bowdoin College Library and the Raymond Fogler Library, University of Maine, Orono. On pages 133 to 229 may be found "Lettre du Pere Sebastian Rasle, missionaire de la compagne de Jesus dans la Nouvelle France à monsieur son frere."

The original handwritten manuscript of Father Rasle's French-Abenaki dictionary is in Harvard's Houghton Library. It was printed in 1833 by John Pickering. These first editions are quite rare. The Maine Historical Society owns one, and also the Maine State Library. I have been informed that the State Library has planned to have a few copies made of theirs so the original may be kept in a safe place and the copies made available for study. This project to preserve a valuable and historic document, the nucleus of all we know of the Abenaki language, and at the same time to place copies in the library for research, deserves high praise.

Colby College Library owns a volume of excerpts from the 73-volume *Jesuit Relations and Allied Documents*, edited by Mealing and published in 1963. They also have a photocopy of the Pickering edition of Father Rasle's dictionary for the use of researchers.

SOURCE MATERIALS USED FOR CHAPTERS ON THE INDIAN WARS

While it seemed at first that there was little material on these subjects, my search was rewarded with quite a variety of books and pamphlets. Since the Indians themselves had no written language it was necessary to learn what we could from the writings of the first white people who came in contact with them.

Verrazzano appears to have been the first explorer to take back news of the Maine Indians. On his return to Europe after his voyage of 1524 he wrote a long letter to Francis I of France, his sponsor for the voyage, describing his travels along the American coast, including the Maine shores. This letter was printed by Hakluyt in his first book *Divers Voyages Touching the Discovery of North America,* published in 1582. He published another book later which, to my surprise, has been printed by our own Maine Historical Society. The name of this book is *A Discourse Concerning Western Planting,* written in 1584.

It was in his letter to Francis I that Verrazzano gave the Maine Indians a bad name, and called the country where he found them "the Land of Bad People." Just so it would not be overlooked, he placed that name on his map.

Many years passed before another meeting was recorded between white men and the Kennebec Indians, and we discover this event in the annals of the Popham Colony, established at the mouth of the Kennebec, then called the Sagadahoc, in 1607.

The Sagadahoc Colony is the title of a very informative book published by the Gorges Society of Portland in 1892, edited and introduced by Henry Otis Thayer of Limington. In his introduction Mr. Thayer points out that for a long time the history of the Popham Colony had been pretty much of a mystery. However, there had been some very thorough research done by several historians, notably James Phinney Baxter, at the time of publication president of the Maine Historical Society. Thayer himself provided much information from his careful researches done during his long residence on the Kennebec River.

Two important discoveries were made in time to be included in *The Sagadahoc Colony*. The first was a journal of the colony, unknown until a few years before the book was written. Mr. Thayer wrote in his preface that the material was discovered by the Rev. B. F. DaCosta in 1875-1876 and was first published in the proceedings of the Massachusetts Historical Society in 1880. The manuscript reposed at that time, and as far as I know still does, in the Library of Lambeth Palace, London, England. Manuscript No. 806 is looked upon as the original and authentic record of the opening stages of the Popham Colony.

The Gorges Society thus decided to publish this manuscript as their contribution to Maine history. James Phinney Baxter traveled to England and supervised an exact transcription of the book, using the precise type and abridged forms of the original.

The second lucky discovery was a plan of Fort St. George published in Alexander Brown's *Genesis of the U.S.* The plan and the evidence derived from it was reviewed by the Maine Historical Society in 1891 at their annual field day. The conclusions on the main point of locality received ample, and to Mr. Thayer gratifying, approval. The original plan of the fort was discovered in an unlikely hiding place in Spain; we have to thank General E. Burd Grubb, and Señor Claudio Perez y Gredilla, the official in charge at Simancus, for the beautifully executed reproduction used in *The Sagadahoc Colony*.

This book, it seems to me, is the most authoritative one on the Popham Colony, with its complete bibliography and notes on every source used.

Other books of interest to the student of Kennebec history follow: *The Pioneers of New France in New England* by James Phinney Baxter. In 1894, Mr. Baxter came out with this book, its name very much like that of Francis Parkman's 1865 *Pioneers of France in the New World*. However, the two books are very different.

Parkman's book ends on Christmas day, 1635, with the death of Samuel de Champlain, founder and builder of Quebec. Parkman was one of the first historians to record the story of the early

French explorers in North America. Carefully researched and written in an interesting manner, it is a must for those who wish to understand the early French explorations and explorers.

Baxter's book is also well written and researched. He was a careful historian who made many trips to foreign countries to track down material. He was dedicated to the task of sorting out the sometimes biased accounts of the Indian wars to make sure that our English ancestors were not maligned. When you have a continuing war between the English and French, with the Indians lined up solidly behind the French whose Jesuit priests had brought them the word of God, had given up every comfort to live as the Indians did, and, in the case of Father Rasle, had refused to escape to Canada so he could die with them, you cannot fail to have extremely biased accounts of the conflicts. We have the accounts of the soldiers who sacked Norridgewock, the accounts of the French who heard the story from Indian survivors, and so on. When I first read Mr. Baxter's book I thought he was too biased in favor of the English, but after studying it further I began to sympathize with his concern for our English forefathers. They feared the Indians with good reason, and had forgotten that the first atrocities were committed by the earliest English explorers, who one and all kidnapped the savages to take back to Europe, some to slavery.

Other books that add to the story of the Kennebec Indians and the Indian Wars are:

Thomas-M. Charland, *Histoire de St. François-du-Lac.* This gives much background information about St. François-du-Lac, where many of the Kennebec Indians fled after English attacks. Among other subjects Charland gives an account of Major Rogers' sack of St. Francis from the French viewpoint. Many will have read Kenneth Roberts' account of this same event in *Northwest Passage.*

Thomas Church, *The History of King Philip's War, Commonly Called the Great Indian War, of 1675 and 1676.* A word about the author might prove interesting to the reader. Thomas Church wrote the history originally in 1716, a quarto. It was reprinted in Newport in 1772 in octavo. Samuel G. Drake, the editor of the volume printed in 1829, wrote that he never succeeded in finding one of the first editions, and thus copied from the second.

A preface was written by Colonel Benjamin Church, the hero of the account of King Philip's War written by his son Thomas.

The history of the war is detailed; it unfolds like a mystery story, gripping the imagination, even though the reader knows the outcome before he turns the first page. Sometimes gory, and maybe biased, it ends with a classic cops and robbers hunt through the woods of Massachusetts, ending with the death of the villain, King Philip.

Henry D. Kingsbury and Simeon L. Deyo, editors, *Illustrated History of Kennebec County, Maine.* This is a good history of Kennebec County and also famous for its excellent Indian History by Captain Charles E. Nash. Twenty authors furnished chapters. The cities of Augusta and Waterville are included in Kennebec County.

Mr. Kingsbury in his Preface gives a definition of history which I like:

> History is a record of human experience. Human acts are its sources, its forces, its substance, its soul. Individual life is its unit; collective biography its sum total.

L'Abbé J. A. Maurault, *Histoire des Abenakis.* Maurault's book was particularly useful. I learned from it that the Abenakis were not aborigines of Canada but of Maine. The first paragraph in his History reads:

> Quelques uns ont pensé que nos Abenaki sont des aborigines du Canada. C'est une erreur. Ces sauvages sont les descendants de la grande tribu des Canabas, qui residait sur la riviere Kenebec.

This book gives us good accounts of Druillette's voyages to Maine, his ministry to the Norridgewocks and other Kennebec tribes, his amazing friendship with John Winslow, Pilgrim agent at Cushnoc, and the story of the Gill-Annance family, descended from two child captives who elected to stay with the Abenakis and later married to found a numerous and important Canadian family. One of their descendants "Old Louis" Annance, moved to Greenville, Maine and became famous as the "White Indian" of Moosehead Lake.

To me the most important discovery in Maurault's book was the story of Mrs. Johnson's captivity among the Indians and French. I knew she had written a book about her terrible experiences during five years of captivity, but I had not found a copy. I later obtained her small book and was able to study it, as she wrote it in

English. It is a spellbinding tale, written in simple but powerful prose by a woman with little education, but with a tragic story to tell. *The Kennebeck Proprietors* by Gordon E. Kershaw gives us the interesting story of the settlement of the Kennebec valley sponsored by the great land company formed by a group of speculators in 1749. These men were wealthy Boston merchants and they sought to develop the wilderness areas bordering the Kennebec River. Theirs was not the first land company on the Kennebec; they revived the defunct claim of the Pilgrims, given by the Council for New England over one hundred years before. The aim of the Plymouth Patent group was to develop the fur trade with the Indians in order to pay back their English backers for the trip to America.

This book is necessary reading for those who wish to sort out the complicated land grants, patents, early deeds and land sales of the Kennebec valley. It is interesting reading, especially the chapter on the two forts built in 1754, Forts Western and Halifax, and the story of Governor William Shirley's forays into the wilderness of the upper Kennebec, searching for a rumored tribe of Norridgewock Indians and a French citadel at the Carrying Place. Governor Shirley was forced to retreat to Boston with the news that neither existed.

Indian Antiquities Of The Kennebec Valley by Charles C. Willoughby. The Maine Historic Preservation Commission and the Maine State Museum published a facsimile edition of Charles Clark Willoughby's paintings, which is a valuable addition to our knowledge of the Kennebec Indians. All types of Indian relics are pictured and described in detail, their uses given and locations where found.

Another fine book for readers interested in delving deeper into the study of archaeology is *Archaeology of Maine* by Warren K. Moorehead, Field Director, Archaeological Survey of New England. Mr. Moorehead gives careful reports of his explorations of Red Paint People graves, shell heaps, and interior village sites, including Moosehead Lake and the Kennebec valley.

I also used a small pamphlet written by Walter Brown Smith of the Lafayette National Park Museum in Acadia National Park for added information on the Red Paint People. *The Lost Red Paint People of Maine* is the title of the 45-page book, written in 1930.

The Red Paint People are Maine's great mystery. Who were they? Where did they come from? How did they live? and where did they disappear to? The only traces they left, that have been found so far, are some tools and piles of red ochre in their cemeteries. We wish we knew more!

My favorite source of information on the early explorations is *The European Discovery of America, the Northern Voyages* by Samuel Eliot Morison. The author was an amazing man, professor of history at Harvard, winner of two Pulitzer Prizes, for *Christopher Columbus, Admiral of the Ocean Sea* and for *John Paul Jones*. He was presented with the Balzan Foundation Award in History, the Presidential Medal of Freedom, the Emerson-Thoreau Medal for Literature, and the Francis Parkman Medal of the Society of American Historians. After Pearl Harbor he was commissioned admiral in the United States Navy, saw action at sea, and went on to write the masterful and exciting *History of the United States Naval Operations in World War II* in fifteen volumes, also available as a condensation in one volume.

In his *Northern Voyages* Morison wrote the story of the early explorers who discovered island after island, coming ever nearer to the continent of North America. We learn about St. Brendan and the Irish; Thorvald and Karlsevni; Eric the Red, Leif Ericsson; Cabot; Verrazzano; Cartier and Samuel de Champlain. To Champlain goes the honor of putting the fantastic legend of Norumbega to rest. Morison wrote:

> In September of 1604 after passing Mount Desert and Isle au Haut, Champlain sailed boldly up the Penobscot to the head of navigation at the site of Bangor. He reported no city, no precious metals, no streets lined with gold — nothing.

It is a pity that Morison's busy life did not permit him time to write his proposed "Later Northern Voyages."

The stories of the captives taken during the Indian wars were quite difficult to track down. I found some in town histories, such as the history of Wells and Kennebunk and the history of Gorham. Invaluable were:

True Stories of New England Captives Carried to Canada During the Old French And Indian Wars by Charlotte Alice Baker. This book was written in 1897 and reprinted in 1975 by Garland Publishing Co.

New England Captives Carried to Canada between 1677 and 1760 during the French and Indian Wars by Emma Lewis Coleman, published in 1925, Portland, Maine.

Emma Coleman was Miss Baker's assistant and secretary before the turn of the century, when they made many trips to Canada and searched many a church register to try to learn the fate of the captives. Her book was dedicated to Alice Baker, who in her preface gives her purpose in researching and writing the book.

> As often as I read in the annals of the early settlers of New England the pathetic words, "Carried captive to Canada whence they came not back," I have longed to know the fate of the captives.

To learn their fate she traveled to Canada several times, accompanied by Emma Coleman, trying at first to trace members of her own family, then widening the search to all she could find traces of.

The historian Francis Parkman wrote of Miss Baker's book, "We are all your debtors." However, the two-volume work of Miss Coleman is the more complete of the two, reflecting her further research and information which came to light between 1897 and 1925.

For information on Benedict Arnold's expedition to Quebec, I suggest the following books:

The most helpful was Kenneth Roberts' *March to Quebec.* Roberts told the story by reprinting the journals written by Arnold himself and several of his officers and soldiers. Thus we have, as it were, eyewitness accounts by men who were present on the march and the campaign in Quebec.

Another very interesting journal is included in this book. It is the detailed day-by-day account of the circle voyage from Canada to Fort Halifax, taken by Lieutenant John Montresor of the British Army in 1761. The famous Montresor map is shown, the one used by Arnold, which proved to have some serious omissions which could easily have caused the destruction of his army.

The second was *Arnold's March from Cambridge to Quebec* by Justin H. Smith. Mr. Smith published his book in 1903 and was at that time Professor of Modern History at Dartmouth College, and so he was eminently qualified to write this book, which he called "A Critical Study." He also reprinted Arnold's journal of the expedition. I found his facts checked out in general with Kenneth Roberts' conclusions made many years later.

During the time Mr. Smith was writing his book, another author was also working on the same subject. Neither one was happy about this situation and Justin Smith was naturally upset when John Codman published his *Arnold's Expedition to Quebec* in 1901, fully two years before Mr. Smith's book was ready.

Smith did take advantage of the situation by cramming his notes with contradictions of many of Mr. Codman's statements. In comparing the two books, I found the Codman book more interesting to read, but the Smith book more accurate. Codman recounts the fascinating story of Princess Jacataqua of Swan Island, who supposedly fell in love with the young and dashing Aaron Burr and accompanied him to Quebec. He gives us the unlikely story of Burr's and Jacataqua's meeting with a young British officer who promised to take care of the Indian girl in her coming confinement with Burr's child. Codman gives as a source for this wild story one of Burr's biographies; he does not mention which one. Kenneth Roberts labels the whole romantic tale a bit of local tradition. It is a shame, as it was a great story.

I cannot end this treatise without mentioning, and paying homage to, the town histories of Maine. Some of these were written by untrained writers, for one of the best reasons to write a book — the fact that no one else had done it.

The most amazing things can be found in many of them. J. W. Hanson wrote two in the middle 1800s: first, the history of Norridgewock and Canaan, called *The History of the Old Towns,* with a very good chapter on Indian history stressing the story of Father Rasle and the destruction of Norridgewock. His chapters on the settlement of the five towns included in the book are complete and interesting, giving many personal stories of the founding families. His *History of Gardiner, Pittston and West Gardiner* also has an Indian chapter and, again, the material on the early settlers and the setting up of the towns is excellent.

North's *History of Augusta,* Owen's *History of Bath,* Allen's *History of Dresden* (reprinted in 1977 by Jennie G. and Eleanor L. Everson), Emma Huntington Nason's *Old Hallowell on the Kennebec,* Louise Coburn's *Skowhegan on the Kennebec,* and the old classic by Ernest George Walker, *Embden Town of Yore* all add important parts to the jigsaw puzzle of Kennebec valley history over the years. For those interested in genealogy as well as history they are priceless.

AUTHOR'S NOTE TO THIRD PRINTING

Since writing *Dawn over the Kennebec* I have done further research which has confirmed my belief expressed on pages 57-59. I am now convinced that George Weymouth did indeed discover the Kennebec River in 1605.

My sources are Henry Wilson Owen's *History of Bath, Maine;* Samuel de Champlain's narrative of his explorations, translated by Charles Pomeroy Otis and edited by W. L. Grant in *Voyages of Samuel de Champlain, 1604-1618,* available in the State Library; and James Rosier's *True relation of the most prosperous voyage made this present yeere 1605, by Captaine George Weymouth, in the discovery of the land of Virginia: Where he discovered 60 miles up a most excellent river; together with a most fertile land,* Gorges Society edition of 1887, loaned to me by historian Arthur M. Griffiths.

In his *History of Bath* Mr. Owen wrote that Weymouth was beyond doubt the first Englishman to set foot on the soil of Bath. It was he who took back to England the first description of the river of Sagadahock, as the mouth of the Kennebec was then known. Weymouth's discovery resulted in the immediate project to plant a colony on the river he had described, and George Popham, following Weymouth's route in 1607, proceeded directly to the Sagadahock to start his colony.

More evidence that Weymouth discovered the Kennebec River is contained in Samuel de Champlain's relation of his own arrival at the "Quinibequy" (Kennebec) in July of 1605, just after the *Archangel* had departed. Champlain wrote:

While waiting [at the Kennebec], there came to us a captain called Anassou ... He told us that there was a ship, ten leagues off the harbor, which was engaged in fishing, and that those on her had killed five savages of *this* river, under cover of friendship. From his description of the men on the vessel, we concluded that they were English, and we named the island where they were La Nef [modern-day Monhegan] ... [Page 77, *Voyages of Samuel de Champlain,* emphasis added.]

Champlain's account verifies the fact that the Indians kidnapped by Weymouth were Kennebec River Indians.

The most important evidence that George Weymouth was indeed in the Kennebec River is the narrative written by James Rosier. He includes a detailed description of the river the Englishmen entered, argued by some to be the St. George:

The River it selfe as it runneth up into the main very nigh forty miles toward the great mountaines, beareth in bredth a mile, sometime three quarters, and halfe a mile is the narrowest, where you shall never have under 4 and 5 fathoms water hard by the shore, but 6, 7, 8, 9, and ten fathoms all along, and on both sides every halfe mile very gallant Coves, some able to conteine almost a hundred saile ... It floweth by their judgement eighteen or twenty foot at high water. [Pp. 138-139, Gorges Society edition.]

The St. George River is in fact an estuary or arm of the sea, about twelve miles long, with a very small winding stream running north from the Thomaston bridge. I don't believe that Weymouth in his rather bulky craft could have gone north of where the bridge now is.

Other circumstances used by historians to identify the St. George River can be applied equally well to the Kennebec. For example, while the vessel lay in the river, friends of the kidnapped Indians came in search of them, and their canoes came into the river from the east. They came, in other words, through the Sasanoa River, and the gut north of Arrowsic Island, a usual thoroughfare for the Indians of the Kennebec. This passageway into the Kennebec from the east is a peculiarity making the identification almost positive.

The historians who contend that Weymouth discovered the St. George River are no doubt correct. Weymouth made his headquarters on Monhegan Island for some time after his arrival, and he certainly went to the nearby mainland, which accounts for the relic with the name of Thomas King (the great fisherman) on it.

However, it would have been very peculiar if at that point he had returned to England. He didn't; he sailed a few miles westward to "Pentecost Harbor," and Boothbay Harbor fits his description of that very well. Fisherman's Island fits his anchorage there, from whence they went to the well protected harbor. I quote Rosier (page 101): "[The] Harbour ... [was] farre beyond our expectation, in a most safe birth [berth] defended from all windes ..." and, I can add, protected by islands.

The evidence seems conclusive. Let's give back to George Weymouth the honor of discovering the Kennebec River.

Mary R. Calvert, August 1992

Mount Kineo on Moosehead Lake, Maine. Photograph by the author.

The Legends

*as passed down by the Indians
from one generation to the next.*

THE NORRIDGEWOCK INDIANS called it Arransoak. It was the thoroughfare that linked them with neighboring tribes. Its waters provided a lifeline upon which they could travel in their swift and sleek birchbark canoes, to nearby waterfalls to spear salmon; to the great body of water Sebem, which we call Moosehead Lake, to secure Kineo flint for their arrowheads; and, after the white man came, downstream with loads of fine furs to be traded for European goods and wampum. Mount Kineo juts out into Moosehead Lake from the eastern shore, reaching almost to the opposite side at the point where Moose River makes its entrance. Kineo's position, on a slender promontory midway of the lake and at its narrowest part, is very marked. Seen from the south or east, it is a sheer wall of almost bare rock rising to a height of more than 760 feet above the waters of the lake. Under it the lake continues its descent for another two hundred feet. The Indians who lived there thought that the lake was bottomless under the cliffs of Kineo.

Kineo's sheer rock cliff is the most famous landmark of the area and has been so since the very earliest days. Indians from all over New England made the long trek to its base for Kineo flint from which to make arrowheads, tools, and utensils. According to geologists this superior "flint" is actually hornstone, a brittle, flintlike mineral, and Kineo has one of the largest masses of that substance in the world.

It is not surprising that Mount Kineo inspired many dramatic legends among the Indians. One of them concerns a man named Kineho, for whom the mountain is supposed to have been named. Kineho was reputed to be a famous warrior who had fought bravely to win many victories for his tribe, but was burdened with hatred in his heart towards even his own family, so he ran away and hid on a mountain top many days' travel from his home. After years of loneliness in his hideaway, and as he sat by his campfire one evening looking out across the lake, he saw a light flickering on the opposite hill. By the light of the moon he sped, in his canoe, to the opposite shore and quickly climbed to the top of the hill. There he found, beside the dying embers of a fire, his old mother Maquasso, quite exhausted by the long trip to persuade her son to return to his family and tribe. With her last breath she begged her son to go back; so Kineho buried her beside the smoldering embers of her fire, and, overcome with remorse, returned. Thus according to legend Mount Kineo and Squaw Mountain were named.

This legend may be found in a book of poems written by Frances Mace around 1880. "Old Louis" Annance of Greenville told another legend about the Moosehead area that goes like this:

In ancient times both men and animals grew to an immense size. The Indians thought moose in particular were too large, and sent a hunter to make them smaller. The hunter killed a big bull moose, Mount Kineo, and reduced its size by cutting slices from its body. The rock at the bottom of the mountain looks like a steak; streaks of lean and fat can be plainly seen in it. The hunter cooked his meat, and afterwards turned his kettle, Little Kineo Mountain, on its side to let it dry. So the moose grew smaller and smaller.

A variation of this story came from John Pennowit, a Penobscot Indian who passed most of his life of over eighty years in the Maine woods. He is probably the same man referred to by Thoreau as "John Pennyweight." Hubbard accepts his version as more correct than the others.

This legend says that there used to be a mighty warrior who was chief of the whole nation, and endowed with superhuman powers. While traveling through the forest one day, he came upon two moose; he hurriedly dropped his pack and started in pursuit of them. The smaller moose, Mount Kineo, was soon overtaken and killed. The chief, after boiling some of the meat, turned his kettle upside down so it wouldn't rust, took up the trail of the larger moose, and followed the latter all the way down to Castine,

The Legends

where he killed and dressed it. The heart, liver, and other entrails he threw to his dog, and they formed the long string of rocks that are there to this day. This legend has been preserved in the Indian name for Little Spencer Mountain, *Kokadjo,* meaning "kettle mountain."

Still another legend about Mount Kineo was told by Louis Annance to Dr. E. A. Thompson at Moosehead Lake in the summer of 1848. This legend was put into verse, and is here reprinted from a copy loaned to me by Louise Curney of Rockwood.

> Years ago no men but red men
>   Hunted by the Moosehead side;
> Years ago no men but red men
>   Roamed the forests far and wide.
> From the north and south they came here
>   In the spring and in the fall,
> The Penobscots, the St. Francis,
>   And the Norridgewocks and all.
>
> First they came in peace together,
>   Brothers in the hunt were they,
> But there soon came strife and discord,
>   Each upheld his right to stay.
> Bloody wars and cruel slaughters
>   Took the place of right and good,
> And the war cry and the death chant
>   Broke the stillness of the wood.
>
> The Great Spirit saw the strivings
>   Of his children, and was sad;
> Why this quarreling and bloodshed,
>   With so much to make them glad.
> He must send some great affliction
>   Which should be to them a sign
> That they all must cease their warfare,
>   And obey his will divine.

4

The Legends

So he sent to earth a monster,
  Sent a beast of wondrous might,
Claws it had that tore up oak trees,
  Teeth that split stones at a bite,
Muscles tough as strongest ash tree
  Wrapped about an iron frame,
Storm winds blew from out its nostrils,
  To the woods its eyes set flame;

And it killed around the lake shore
  Fox, and deer, and moose, and bear.
Killed the fish in lake and rivers,
  Killed the little birds in air.
In the forests 'round, the red men
  Found naught but the slaughtered game,
And they understood its meaning
  And their hearts were filled with shame.

So they promised the Great Spirit
  If he'd take the beast away
They would live in love and friendship,
  Live in peace. That very day
Came another awful monster,
  Larger, stronger than the first;
The earth trembled at his footfalls,
  At his growl the raincloud burst;

And around and 'round the lake shore
  It pursued the other fast,
While the water wild and foamy
  Rose in whirlpools as they passed.
'Round the lake they raced and struggled
  Over rocks and brooks and rills,
Till the first beast was exhausted,
  And his breathing shook the hills.

Then with one last mighty effort,
  Forth he sprang upon the beach,
While the woodlands all around him
  Echoed back the other's screech,

The Legends

And the other without pausing,
  With a strength no tongue can tell,
Sprang upon him, and together
  Both into the water fell.
And just when the water touched them,
  They became a mound of stone,
You can see it over yonder,
  Kineo, so sad and lone.
It will always stand, a warning
  To the nations old and new,
We must live and love as brothers,
  And be generous and true.

One part of this legend may indeed be true: the reported strife between Indian tribes in the Moosehead area. Tradition says that Moosehead was the scene of many fierce encounters when the Mohawks invaded the territory. They were the ancient enemies of the Abenakis and Penobscots. Thus the old Indian name of Wilson Pond was *Etas-i-i-ti,* meaning "where they had a great fight," or "destruction ground."

The Indians had legends, not only to account for the geographical features they knew so well, but also to account for their own origin as a people. Joseph Nicolar of Old Town recorded the story as learned over a period of forty years from the recitations of the tribal elders. These legends were passed down from father to son and mother to daughter for many generations. Nicolar's book is entitled *The Life and Traditions of the Red Man* and was written in 1893.

Klose-kur-beh, "the man from nothing," was the first person to come upon the earth. Legend says that he opened his eyes lying on his back in the dust, his head toward the rising sun and his feet toward the setting sun, the right hand pointing north and the left hand to the south. He had no strength to move any part of his body, yet the brightness of the day revealed to him all the glories of the whole world; the sun was at its highest, standing still, and beside it the moon without motion and the stars in their fixed places, while the firmament was of a beautiful blue.

A personage appeared before Klose-kur-beh, one like himself, standing at his right hand, his face toward the rising sun. In silence this personage raised his right hand in the direction of the sun, then passed it from there to the setting sun, and immediately a streak of lightning followed the motion of his hand from one side of the earth to the other. Immediately as the lightning passed, a sense of thought came to the first man and he stirred. His first thought was that he believed the person was able to bring strength to him. The Great Being answered his thought, saying these words:

"Thou doest well to believe in me. I am the head of all thou beholdest, and as thou believest, arise from thy bed of dust and stand on thy feet; let the dust be under thy feet and thou shalt have the strength to walk."

Immediately strength came to this first man; he arose and stood beside the Great Being. Turning toward his right hand and facing north, behold! he saw a mountain seven rainbows high. He was given directions for a long journey and told that at the end he would find companions, and to there abide. He started as the sun rose.

The Legends

The works of Klose-kur-beh were wonderful. He taught the Indians how they must live, calling them his children. He told them about the spiritual power, how it was in every living thing, and that it was the same power that had sent him to prepare the way on earth for the generations to come, to subdue all obstacles which are against the nature of mankind, and to reduce the earth to such a state as to become a happy land for the people.

When the first man was teaching his people, he pointed out to them where the Great Spirit existed: in the sun, moon, stars, clouds of heaven, mountains and even in the trees of the earth. Three of his teachings were held more sacred than any others: first, the power of the Great Spirit; second, the land that the Great Spirit gave them and that they must never leave; third, that they must never forget their first mother, but must always show the love they have for her, stopping all work during observances in her honor.

The name Klose-kur-beh needs explanation. The word *Klose-ki,* in the old Indian language, meant "simple" or "nothing." *Klose-ki-ner-quatt* is the word for "simple appearance," and *Klose-kur-beh* means "the man from nothing" or "the first man." In Nicolar's narrative he is careful to use the words of the traditional storytellers, who were so aware of their importance that they made a great effort to learn all they could of Klose-kur-beh's life and experiences.

None of these traditions located the country where these things took place, but it was agreed by the storytellers that it was in the eastern part of the red man's world. So firmly did the Indians believe this that they began to look for the appearance of other people from that direction.

After many moons had passed, some young warriors and an old man went on a hunting trip toward the eastern sea. One day, as a light snow fell, arriving at the seashore in a little cove where a small brook flowed into the sea, the Indians discovered a human footprint, then another and another. They began at the water's edge and went back to it around the brook of fresh water. The Indians could not discover a canoe, even in the distance or on the horizon. The tracks were very strange; the moccasins that made them must have been made of a hard substance; they were large and the toes pointed outward, instead of inward as Indian footprints did.

The old man began to weep, and on returning to the village he gathered the elders together to tell them what the hunters had seen. He explained his tears in this manner:

"Upon seeing the tracks in the snow I remembered all the warnings which have been given us, how a time is coming when we must look for the appearance of strange men appearing from the direction of the rising sun. I know that a great change must follow their coming that will put a bar to our happiness, and our destiny will be at the mercy of unknown events."

Everybody was told of the mysterious tracks, even the squaws and the little children, and soon the cause for them was apparent. From a high bluff overlooking the eastern sea, the Indians finally sighted a huge canoe, sails fat with wind, that moved the white men in the canoe swiftly southward.

It had happened just as the storytellers had said: the white man had come to the red man's world. The discovery was not looked upon as anything strange since it had been foretold by the old prophets. The Indians thought it best, and it was so decided in council, that when the strange people came they should be received as friends, and if possible made brothers. They would be greeted with the word *Nitchieh,* meaning brother.

The Indians

*The early history of the Abenakis,
including picture writing and relics.*

WHEN THE FIRST WHITE MAN stepped
off his ship onto the soil of the Ken-
nebec valley, he found it peopled by a race strange to
him, the red man. Each must have been surprised at
the appearance and manners of the other, and both
probably felt fear and curiosity. They looked, they
observed, they tried to communicate, and above all
they were wary. The long and painful process of
learning to come to terms with each other had begun.

The Indians who inhabited the Kennebec valley
were called Abenakis, meaning "the people of the
east." This name has been spelled in many different
ways, including *Abenaques, Abnakis, Abenaquiois,
Wapanachkis, Wabenakies,* and *Wobanakis.* According to Joseph Laurent, the word derives from *woban,*
"daybreak," and *ki,* "earth, land," or rather from *aki,*
which is a term used in composition for "land,
ground, region." Therefore an Abenaki is "a person
from the land where the sun rises," or, more simply,

11

The Indians

"an easterner."

The Abenaki nation was widespread, extending from present-day Vermont to the Penobscot River in Maine. They lived in peace with their eastern neighbors, the Etchemins (meaning simply "the people"), who lived in the area from the Penobscot River to the Atlantic. It is not certain just how many aborigines there were in Maine when the first Europeans arrived. However, J. W. Hanson, author of the excellent histories of Gardiner and Norridgewock, gives the number of Abenakis as 13,000 in the early 17th century. Of these he thought about 5,000 lived in the Kennebec valley.

These early Kennebec Indians were nomadic; they were forever searching for food, for materials to clothe themselves, and for shelter. They were lean and tough, great hunters and fishermen. They stored food in holes in the ground, and smoked and dried both meat and fish. They carried burning coals from one camping place to another, smoldering in a piece of decayed wood, enclosed in a clamshell sealed with clay. Their nights were spent wherever the day's hunting and fishing took them; when night fell they made camp and slept on the ground.

Having very few possessions, the Abenakis could quickly gather them up and move to better hunting and fishing grounds. If the move was more than a few miles, the journey was made by water in their birchbark canoes. These were light in weight and could be carried easily from one lake or stream to the next, or shouldered for the necessary portages around the many rapids and falls. With its vast network of waterways and chains of lakes, Maine was ideally suited for such travel.

Every spring, the Indians would plant corn, squash and beans in the intervales of the Kennebec River valley, made fertile by the annual spring freshets. This land was, and is, excellent soil for growing these crops. The quality and flavor of intervale corn is hard to beat, as the author can testify from personal experience. The low-lying lands along the river bends were so well worked by the Indians that the settlers who came later often found that no plowing or other processing was necessary.

After planting, the Indians went to the sea every summer by way of the many streams and rivers that served them as thoroughfares. Indians of the upper reaches of the Kennebec would travel down the length of the Kennebec via the East Outlet of Moosehead Lake, Indian Pond, the Forks, and thence to the sea south of Bath. There they found fish and clams, which were a welcome change from their winter diet of deer and moose, and often left evidence of their great feasts in extensive shell heaps that can be seen even today. They could also escape the black flies and mosquitoes that made the woods unpleasant in hot weather.

At harvest time, the Indians would travel north again, gather their crops, and prepare for winter. Many of their winter encampments were situated on the headwaters of the Kennebec and Penobscot rivers. The Indians chose their winter quarters near moose and deer yards so meat would be available; also they made use of the animal hides for many purposes.

The Abenakis in Maine were roughly divided into four tribes: the Sokokis on the Saco River; the Anasagunticooks, who lived on the Androscoggin; the Wawenocks, east of Merrymeeting Bay; and the Kennebecs, also called Canabis, on both sides of the Kennebec River. The Kennebecs in turn consisted of four subordinate groups, each with a chief or sachem who answered to the bashaba as the supreme ruler. This powerful leader lived on Swan Island where he had a fortified abode, which was built in a circular form with the entrance on the north, and possibly having an underground passage for escape when enemies approached. The four Kennebec clans were the Sagadahocs, their territory lying between Merrymeeting Bay and the Atlantic Ocean; the Cushnocs in the area of present-day Augusta; the Teconnets in the fertile region of the mouth of the Sebasticook River, one of the important tributaries of the Kennebec; and the Norridgewocks who lived at Old Point in the present town of Madison. Thus an Indian who lived in the village at Old Point would belong to the Norridgewock clan, the Kennebec tribe and the Abenaki nation.

The Wawenocks did not live on the Kennebec but their ties of friendship with the Canabis tribe link them closely together. Their territory extended from the lower Kennebec River to the St. George River and they were also the immediate subjects of the bashaba of Swan Island. John Smith reported that they were "active, strong, healthful and very witty," and said that they would paddle their canoes faster with five paddles than his own men could with eight. The Wawenocks were faithful to those they considered friends; in combat, though, they would fight to the death. The name Wawenock signified "very brave, fearing nothing."

The annual migrations of the Kennebec Indians, and their way of life, can be reconstructed to some degree by studying the physical evidence they left behind: the ancient shell heaps, the flint beds and the few artifacts found in old village sites and burying grounds. The Kennebecs often chose the mouths of streams or rivers for their camping grounds and for the graves of their fathers. Some known campsites along the Kennebec are at the mouth of Spencer Stream on Moosehead Lake; the Forks of the Kennebec and Dead rivers; the mouth of Austin Stream in Bingham; the present towns of Solon and Embden, just south of the bridge; Old Point in Madison, just north of the Madison-Norridgewock boundary; at the foot of the falls in Skowhegan; and, further south, the mouth of Cobbosseecontee Stream in Gardiner, and the mouth of Nehumkeag Brook in Pittston. Nehumkeag, it appears, was the site of a flourishing clan of the Kennebecs at the time Captain John Smith visited the area in 1614.

The mouth of the Cobbosseecontee was also well known to the Kennebec Indians, and many bones, tools, kettles, and arrowheads have been uncovered there. The stream also figured in an ancient legend

Indian artifacts found in the Moosehead Lake region by Elizabeth Hamilton Hartsgrove. Above: two round-bladed fish knives, two small points and a slate spear. Below: axe, white leaf knife, and broken projectile. These artifacts are in the collection of the Greenville Public Library, Greenville, Maine. Photograph by the author.

concerning the mysterious transformation of an Indian warrior into a sturgeon or *cabbassa,* thus accounting for the name of the stream.

The discarded tools found around these and other campsites help us to picture what Abenaki life was like before the Europeans came. Many of the pieces found at campsites were chipped out of flint or other types of stone. Spearheads were used for hunting game at close range, attached to a 3 to 5-foot shaft and thrown like a javelin. The smaller arrowheads, basically the same shape, were used for hunting moose, deer, bear and beaver. Indian knives, similar in size and construction to arrowheads, but with a keener cutting edge, look quite inefficient; but they were sufficient for skinning and dissecting animals, and were not meant for carving or cutting wood.

Stone drills are more rarely found; they were used for boring holes in wood, bones or soft rock such as slate. Scrapers are very small, curved chipped tools, often found in or around the shell heaps left by the Indians. They were used by the Indians for scraping hides for wearing apparel or coverings for their huts. Another type of stone tool sometimes found is the stone axe, made of a hard rock which had been chipped into shape and then ground down to form a cutting edge. These axes, like the knives, were not as durable as modern steel axes, but they were suitable for the tasks at hand.

Stone gouges are sometimes found, though they are not as common as arrowheads and knives. They were used primarily for hollowing out logs to make dugout canoes. Such canoes were made out of whole tree trunks, in a simple but time-consuming process. When an Indian decided to cut a tree, he cut the bark away at the trunk and let it stand for about a year. This caused the tree to die and the next step could be performed. He put a ring of clay around the tree just above where he wished to make the cut and built a fire to burn the wood, now well dried out. After the fire had burned itself out, he would then take his stone axe and cut away the charcoal. The burning and cutting would be repeated until the tree fell. Then the stone gouges would be used to hollow out one side. Some of these dugout canoes were long enough for 10 paddlers.

Birchbark canoes could be made much more quickly and were far more lightweight for long portages; however, they were not impervious to rocky stream beds. In the long trips through rapids and over carries choked with underbrush, the fragile bark became cracked. It would then be necessary to build a fire, heat pine pitch and caulk all the broken seams before proceeding.

Bones of birds and animals were used by the Indians as awls, bodkins, needles and other sewing implements. They would be worked down to a sharp point, and used to bore holes in bark or animal skins in order to lace these materials for clothing, birchbark containers, canoes and snowshoes. Bone fish spears were used by the Norridgewock Indians to catch the abundant salmon in the falls at Skowhegan and Madison. In the same spots can be found bone arrowheads, mostly broken, because they had been used to shoot game. When the animal was brought back to camp and the spear removed, the arrowhead was usually damaged and discarded.

Many Indian artifacts have been carefully preserved by such amateur archaeologists as Agnes Richardson Gott and Elizabeth Hamilton Hartsgrove, and may be seen in collections at the Greenville Public Library and the Maine State Museum. More detailed descriptions of the artifacts may be found in *A Report on the Archaeology of Maine* by Warren K. Moorehead, and in *Indian Antiquities of the Kennebec Valley*, by Charles C. Willoughby, a masterpiece of archaeological and artistic merit. Many artifacts have been destroyed either through carelessness or ignorance, and it is important for amateur archaeologists to notify the Maine State Museum if an Indian site is found.

At some sites traces have been found of a culture even earlier than the Abenakis, who inhabited Maine between 3,000 and 5,000 years ago. They are usually known as the Red Paint People, from the powdered iron ore called red ochre that is often found mixed in with their bones and stone tools. All the Red Paint sites found so far have been near or on streams or on the coast. On the Kennebec there are sites at Oakland, Waterville, Winslow and Kineo. The Red Paint People disappeared long before the advent of the Abenakis, who preserved no tradition of predecessors at all.

Another type of Abenaki relic that gives us a clue to their culture is their picture-writing. The only

The Indians

remaining examples of Kennebec Indian writing are carved on a long, low ledge jutting out into the river not more than a quarter of a mile below the Solon-Embden bridge, on the west or Embden side of the river. These are often called the Solon petroglyphs, even though they are in Embden. (This is one of several misplaced historical sites on the Kennebec, others being Caratunk Falls in Solon and the Norridgewock Indian village in Madison.)

More than half the thirty-foot ledge is covered with the strange drawings. Ethnological experts have been asked to translate the messages etched in the stone ledge, but everyone has failed, including experts from the Smithsonian Institution. However, scholars think the oldest drawings date back about four hundred and fifty years and were done by the Norridgewock Indians, whose village was only about ten miles downriver. The ledge may have been larger originally, because it was discovered in modern times by river-driving crews who were dynamiting the ledgy shores of the river to free the channel from obstructions which started log jams. Some of the ledge could have been broken off and lost before the river drivers noticed the strange writings.

The figures were cut, or rather pecked out, to a depth of one-quarter of an inch or more, with an awl or other tool, perhaps fashioned from Kineo flint, or from a dark slate-blue flint later seen by Arnold and his soldiers just below the falls in Madison. The labor and patience it took to peck away solid stone to produce the figures on this ledge is amazing, as it is estimated that hundreds of blows with the tool were necessary to complete even one of the pictures.

More than one artist did the work, and at least part of it was done after the Europeans arrived on Maine's shores. Many of the things pictured had been brought by the white men: a blockhouse, at least three crosses, a man with upraised arms. Other figures represent activities of the Indians: a canoe, a bow and arrow, a tomahawk, animals, birds and a bear skin. All of these excite our imagination and arouse our curiosity, but so far we don't know what message or messages the stone was meant to impart.

These petroglyphs are the most extensive Abenaki Indian writings we have in Maine and they may still be seen, although time and the action of the water are slowly taking their toll. In the spring the waters of the river lap constantly over the ledge and winds and rain beat against the incised figures. The Maine State Museum has a mural of the petroglyphs, so they may be studied there much more easily than by going down a woods trail to the river.

There is much evidence that the Abenakis also used birch bark for their maps and for communication over a distance. They had no written language and no alphabet until the Jesuit missionaries came in the seventeenth century, and so they invented a method of communicating their ideas by means of line drawing or pictures. These were most often done on the pure white birch bark which was plentiful in the Maine woods. Their pencil was a stick held over the coals of an open fire until the end was charred, or a piece of the coal itself. Both Father Druillettes and Father Rasle were to relate instances of the Abenakis' use of this picture writing. Almost none of the original birchbark maps and messages survive today, except for one nineteenth-century map drawn by Metallak, a famous Indian guide of the Rangeley Lakes region, and preserved by the Hamlin Memorial Library in Paris Hill.

Although the Maine tribes lived in peace with each other at the time the white man first arrived, they dreaded and feared their traditional enemies, the Iroquois and the Mohawks. The Mohawks, who lived in the present-day state of New York around Lake Champlain, Lake George and the Mohawk Valley, thought nothing of traversing the intricate waterways to Maine by way of the St. Lawrence, killing, burning and plundering all the way there and back. So they would go on the warpath, making the forest ring with their war whoops. Stealthily they struck and then returned waving bloody scalps as proof of their prowess. To seek revenge, the Abenakis had to travel a thousand miles, up the Kennebec to the St. Lawrence, up that river as far as the Richelieu, which would then lead the warring braves into the heart of the Mohawks' territory.

On the other hand, the Kennebec Indians treated the first European explorers in a friendly manner, both English and French. Unfortunately the English started to antagonize the natives almost as soon as they arrived on these shores. Weymouth's kidnapping of five prominent Indians and transporting them to England in the hold of his ship started a train of infuriating events. This was followed in 1614 by the kidnapping of 24 Indians by Thomas Hunt, a partner of John Smith, who enticed the Indians on board his ship to be taken to Spain and sold for slaves at $100 per head. To do John Smith justice, it must be pointed out that he had nothing to do with the kidnapping by Hunt, who was captain of his own boat and lingered after Smith left Monhegan for England. Smith said afterward that Hunt's vile act kept him from getting any more employment as a ship's master.

Some of the Weymouth captives were returned by the George Popham expedition in 1607. They had been well treated in England and taught to speak English, and so did not hold a grudge against the settlers. Samoset, a Hunt captive who escaped and got back to America on another ship, was disposed to help the Pilgrims and traveled to Plymouth from Monhegan Island to surprise them with the greeting "Welcome, Englishmen."

It is sad to relate, however, that the Popham colonists treated the Indians, who could have helped them through the first winter with corn and game, in a very shabby manner. In fact the acts of treachery were inexcusable. On one occasion the Indians were enticed with friendly overtures and invited to a celebration. During the festivities the settlers asked the Indians to show their strength by taking hold of ropes and pulling a cannon to another part of the grounds, during which powder was lighted and the charge went off, killing some and injuring others of the natives.

The Abenakis were brave and very much attached to their native soil, and also naturally courteous. They treated the first white men they met with kindness and hospitality, offering food to visitors even when it was scarce. For over fifty years the natives and the English lived peaceably together. One history of Gorham relates that for a long time the Indians and the settlers were neighbors and their children played together. Later, after the start of the Indian wars, the inhabitants would be heartbroken to recognize some of their former friends as members of the raiding parties.

Relations went from bad to worse when more English settlers started arriving and wanted to buy land, which the natives were very willing to sell according to their terms. The Indians soon caught on that a string of beads or a peck of corn was all they could expect for a valuable piece of property, with plenty of good fishing or hunting, their yardstick for the value of land. They were intelligent enough to resent such treatment.

A recounting of some of the early land deals proves that this was true. James Smith bought a tract of land from Robinhood in 1648. The price was one peck of corn on the first day of each November. The deed however states that the buyer received the exclusive privileges of hunting, fishing, fowling and other games. Robinhood, who had an eye for business, also sold Jeremysquam in 1649 and Woolwich in 1654 to

Edward Bateman and John Brown for insignificant amounts. On August 8, 1649, the land on both sides of the Kennebec from Cushnoc to Wesserunsett Stream, a tributary of the Kennebec in Skowhegan, was sold to William Bradford by Monquine, Ago-doademago and Tussucke.

That was not all by any means. The sachems of the Kennebecs, Kennebis and Abbagadusset, sold all the land on both sides of the river, proving that they expected buyers to occupy the land only as tenants in common. Obviously they did not expect to be driven off their land by their own tenants.

At the heart of the problem was the difference between what the two cultures meant by land owner-ship. The Indians owned the land in common, according to the legal definition, holding the soil as tenants in a state of nature. Any Abenaki had a right to use any land belonging to the Abenaki nation. They couldn't understand how one person could own a piece of land, as each Indian possessed an undivided portion of the territory of his particular tribe. Once we understand this point we can readily see why the Europeans and the Indians never agreed on just what a sale of land involved. The sachems made land sales with the understanding that they sold only what they themselves owned: the right to hunt and fish and to occupy the tract with others. When a purchaser died his rights reverted to the tribe. Since the white man had an entirely different idea of his rights as a purchaser, land titles and land owner-ship were to cause a great deal of trouble.

*Leif Eriksson was one of the first Europeans to look westward to
the New World. This statue of him, presented by the people of
the United States, stands in Reykjavik, Iceland. Photograph by
the author.*

Explorers and Settlement

*The French and the English race
almost neck and neck across the Atlantic.*

THE TENTH CENTURY SAW the first European explorers setting sail for the western hemisphere. Throughout the Middle Ages Europe was a busy and growing place, with kingdoms rising and falling in turn. Rulers were searching for ways to fill their coffers, always being depleted by the many wars. They were ripe for the stories of the greatest salesmen in history, who promised fabulous riches of spices and gold to be had by sailing westward through a shortcut to India, China and other lands of the Orient. For a long time no one guessed that a huge continent blocked the way.

In those days, America was still a sleeping giant, peopled with nomadic tribes who in turn hadn't the faintest idea from whence they came or what lay beyond their own tribal lands. They are now thought to have come from Siberia around 12,000 years ago during the last ice age, while there was still a bridge of land leading across to Alaska. The name Indians

27

The Vikings

was applied to them mistakenly by some of the early explorers, who thought they had truly reached the East Indies.

Among the many fishermen, explorers, and adventurers who reached Maine shores in the six centuries before the first permanent European settlement, it cannot be ascertained exactly who was the first white man to discover the Kennebec River. The list of possible visitors to Maine is long, and begins in the tenth century with the Vikings.

Erik Thorvaldsson, usually known as Erik the Red, was the first European to point the way westward. Pioneering in Iceland as a child, and belonging to an adventurous and seafaring people, Erik set sail as a young man to discover and explore the coast of Greenland. This took place in the year 982, more than 500 years before Columbus arrived in the West Indies, and was a remarkable feat of sailing and endurance. Erik is responsible for the name Greenland, unsuitably applied to the huge ice-capped island. The western fjord that he explored had green pasture land and birch and willow forests, and no doubt looked greener than the barren volcanic soil of Iceland, even with a backdrop of mountain glaciers. Also Erik intended to recruit settlers from Iceland to colonize the fjord, and certainly Greenland is a more attractive name than a truly descriptive one.

As the small Viking settlement on Greenland grew, curiosity arose as to lands that might lie to the west. A young man named Bjarni Herjulfsson sailed to the southwest and came back with stories of three new lands observed from the ship. Two of the lands he described as *Helluland* (Flat Rock Land) and *Markland* (Forestland). The third land, lying further south, Bjarni called *Vinland* or Land of Vines, presumably grapevines.

Sixteen years after Bjarni's trip, Leif Eriksson, the second son of Erik the Red, visited Bjarni Herjulfsson to hear the story of his voyage firsthand. He was so excited by the description of the new lands that he promptly purchased Bjarni's ship and made preparations to sail westward on his great adventure.

Leif Eriksson's party set out in the summer of 1001 in his *knarr* or roundboat. The voyage has been graphically reconstructed by Samuel Eliot Morison, Maine's admiral-author, in *The European Discovery of America*. He describes a knarr as a broad-beamed ship propelled by one large square sail, with lines made from walrus hide or braided from plant fibers. The knarr that Leif Eriksson sailed to Vinland had to be large enough to carry thirty people, several head of cattle and provisions for extended trips. There were long oars, worked through holes in the upper hull, for extra power or in case the wind failed. The compass did not exist,and would not be invented until the late twelfth century. Morison notes that no evidence has been found of a means of cooking on board, and that the crew must have subsisted on cold foods and beer or mead. Each sailor had his own sleeping bag made of sheepskin or cowhide. The hardships must have been great indeed on trips across the stormy and rough north Atlantic. However, life in the pioneer settlement in Greenland couldn't have been any bed of roses either.

The first land they encountered was Helluland, the land of the flat stones, which Leif judged correctly to be an inhospitable land. After landing and looking around a little, they raised anchor and left to sail further to the west. The next shore they visited was the one called Markland, land of forests, also named "Wonder Strands" in the Viking sagas, which described the land as "a thirty mile long beach of yellow sand, sloping back to a level sandy plain, with a fine black spruce forest as a backdrop for it all." Many streams wound through the forest and down to the sea.

According to the saga known as the Tale of the Greenlanders, "after sailing two 'doegr.' they landed on an island north of the mainland." From there they proceeded to the mainland where they went ashore in a spot where a stream flows out of a lake to the sea. They found grazing land for the cattle and a more hospitable climate than they had left in Greenland, and here they settled.

There were two other well-authenticated Norse voyages to North America after the famous one of Leif Eriksson. The first was that of Leif's brother Thorvald, who along with his crew spent the winter of 1004-5 at a place the sagas call *Leifsbudir* or "Leif's huts," subsisting mainly on fish. They explored the coast in the summer, spent the next winter at Leif's settlement, and again when summer came explored the coast further. On this trip they came upon some natives sleeping under skin-covered boats, and without even arousing them the Norsemen killed all but one, who escaped to sound the alarm to the remainder of his party. More aborigines arrived in a fleet and attacked the Norsemen. When they withdrew one Viking was dead: Thorvald Eriksson, the leader of the expedition. He was buried on the cape they called Crossness, as a cross was left to mark his grave. This battle was the first recorded contact between Europeans and American aborigines, scornfully called *Skraelings* in the sagas.

On their return to Greenland, the news of Thorvald's death caused consternation. Another expedition was planned; some said it was to bring Thorvald's body back to Greenland, but it seems also to have been an attempt to plant a permanent settlement in the New World. This expedition took livestock and provisions for an extended stay. The leader of the expedition was Thorfinn Karlsevni, who had married Gudrid, the widow of Thorvald Eriksson. She went with her husband, as did several other women. During their stay in the New World, a son was born to Karlsevni and Gudrid, whom they named Snorri. Snorri Karlsevnisson was thus the first white child born in America, in the autumn of 1008, over five hundred years before the birth of Virginia Dare.

After several voyages of exploration and more encounters with the hated Skraelings, the Vikings decided to leave. With their departure, the curtain fell on European exploration in North America for many

The Vikings

years.

Where did the Vikings go? There is only one authenticated site of a Viking settlement in North America, and that is at L'Anse aux Meadows, Newfoundland. Ancient foundations were discovered there in 1960 by a Norwegian archaeologist named Helge Ingstad, and after several years of digging it has been declared the first, if short lived, dwelling place of Europeans on the American continent. It is quite possible that the expedition to found a permanent settlement, under Thorfinn Karlsevni, came to L'Anse aux Meadows, where there were already some buildings waiting.

Did the Vikings come to Maine? Samuel Morison did not think so, but another student of the Norse voyages did. This was Frederick J. Pohl, whose entertaining book, *The Viking Settlements of North America*, was written after close study of the sagas as primary sources. Many events of Leif Eriksson's voyage are described by Morison and Pohl in a similar way; the great difference lies in the locations of the three lands, Helluland, Markland and Vinland. Morison does not believe the Vikings ever came south of Canada, while Pohl believes they settled as far south as Cape Cod.

Pohl points out that the sagas describe vineyards and birch trees growing in Vinland, the site of Leif's first winter settlement. Wild grapes do not grow on the northern coast of Newfoundland, but they do grow all along the coasts of Nova Scotia and Maine, and further south. From that fact and geographical clues, Pohl deduced that *Leifsbudir* was on Follins Pond, Cape Cod, although the artifacts found in this location are not impressive.

If Leif's settlement was located on Cape Cod, as Pohl argues, it was from there that Thorvald and his men set out to explore northeastward during the summer. A "fjord in mountainous land" described by them could then correspond to Somes Sound in Mount Desert Island, Maine. The party went ashore at this spot and Thorvald pronounced the land fair. The country about them was cleared, and must have been used for centuries by the Indians either as a camping ground or for raising crops. There is indeed a spot on Mount Desert Island called Jesuit Field as it was found cleared and ready for use when the Jesuit priests arrived in 1613 to minister to the Indians.

The description of the Skraelings does not help resolve the mystery. According to Morison and other writers, *Skraelings* means barbarians, weaklings, even pygmies, and the type of boat they used was a skin-covered kayak, which sounds more like Eskimos than Indians. Pohl, on the other hand, translates *Skraelings* to mean Shriekers or War-Whoopers, which could apply to Maine Indians as they were extremely noisy at their powwows and on the war path. Indian captives much later would tell about these raucous ear-splitting affairs when the yelling and shouting would continue for hours on end.

There are probably as many versions of the Norse landings as there are theorists, and one must try to decipher the riddle for oneself from the evidence. The

John Cabot

Maine coast theory got a slight boost a few years ago when an ancient Norse coin was found near Bar Harbor. It is certainly fun to try to answer the questions raised by the sagas; however, the historians will probably argue for years to come, and no definitive location for Vinland seems likely in the near future.

After the Norse voyages to the New World, five centuries passed before European curiosity was again stirred by the possibility of lands to the west. Toward the end of the fifteenth century, explorers and adventurers beseeched their rulers for patents of permission to explore, and for the financial backing necessary to launch an expedition. The contestants in the race for the New World included the kingdoms of Spain, France and England; the last two were most important in the discovery of Maine, but Spain represented a powerful threat at sea throughout the centuries of discovery.

The English claim to North America was founded on the voyages of John Cabot, an Italian who sailed under the rather grudging patronage of Henry VII of England. No money was forthcoming along with the royal permission to explore, so Cabot had to set out on his first voyage with only one rather small ship, named the *Mathew*. The voyage began at Bristol about the 20th of May, 1497, with the benefit of the compass, quadrant, traverse table and other newly invented aids to navigation, all of which the Vikings had lacked. Landfall was made on June 24, 1497, in northern Newfoundland, coincidentally only a few miles from L'Anse aux Meadows, site of the Viking settlement of 500 years before. Cabot, of course, knew nothing about the voyages of the Norsemen. He was rewarded on his return to England, and the territory was named New Found Land.

Cabot started on another voyage of discovery a year later, in early May of 1498. This time the king loosened up his purse strings and outfitted one ship; four more were financed by merchants of Bristol. The few facts known about this second voyage are tragic. One ship returned to Bristol. The other four were never heard of again, along with their crews and the dedicated explorer John Cabot. It was on this second voyage that England based her claim to the whole continent from the Atlantic to the Pacific. At that time they had no idea of the true extent of their claim.

England's claim was based on an international understanding that the discovery of a coast entitled the discoverer to the possession of that territory. However, another custom gave to the discoverer of a river the right to the territory drained by that river and its tributaries. At the same time that England was exploring the North American coast, France was discovering the St. Lawrence River; the series of majestic inland seas called today the Great Lakes; and the Mississippi River and its then unguessed-at tremendous watershed. These conflicting claims by two of the most powerful nations of Europe would lead to war after war, with resounding consequences for the Kennebec River valley and its inhabitants.

The first recorded visitor to Maine shores was sailing for France. This was the Florentine, Giovanni da

Giovanni da Verrazzano

Verrazzano, who, unlike earlier explorers, belonged to a noble family and had been well educated. A portrait of the time shows him to have had strong features, a dark beard and mustache, a Roman nose, and an air of confidence. By the age of 38 Verrazzano had established himself as a mariner and aspired to greater feats, such as finding a route to China by sailing westward.

Verrazzano appealed first for Italian backing for an expedition, but the French king, Francis I, turned out to be more sympathetic, and lent him a ship named *La Dauphine.* There were to be four ships in the fleet; however, two were lost in a storm before the expedition started, and the third, *La Normande,* sailed only as far as the coast of Spain before returning to France. *La Dauphine* was a seaworthy ship of one hundred tons and could carry a crew of fifty. This was twice the size of Cabot's *Mathew,* which had braved the Atlantic much further north than Verrazzano planned to go.

Verrazzano's expedition sailed from Dieppe on January 17, 1524. The first three weeks of the voyage were delightful. They sailed on the northern edge of the trade winds with a gentle wind blowing east-southeast. Then the wind changed and brought on a severe storm. Verrazzano wrote in his log: "With the divine help and merciful assistance of almighty God and the soundness of our ship, accompanied of the good help of her fortunate name, we were delivered." He altered his course to west by north and sighted land at or near Cape Fear, North Carolina. He did not stop here as he wished to explore a little to the south before turning northward. He had no intention, however, of going far enough south to meet the Spaniards.

The Florentine was still searching for a passage to the Pacific, as attested by a letter: "We sailed along this isthmus (the outer banks) in continual hope of finding some strait or northern promontory at which the land would come to an end, in order to penetrate to *quelli feleci liti Catay* (those happy shores of Cathay)." The will-o'-the-wisp dream of a shortcut to the Orient persisted for a very long time. It would not come true till nearly four centuries later, when a channel was forced through the isthmus of Panama.

The trip northward was long and eventful. At one place Verrazzano's party encountered an Indian, who thrust toward them what they took to be a burning stick. They had never seen or heard of tobacco, and so fired a round of blank shot to frighten him away. The stick, of course, was a peace pipe, offered to the strangers as a friendly gesture.

Another stop was at New York Bay on the 17th of April. The explorers anchored at the narrows which are today named after Verrazzano, as is the magnificent bridge that crosses them. From there *La Dauphine* proceeded northeast, sailing past Sakonnet Point and Cape Cod, and across Massachusetts Bay toward the coast of Maine.

It is thought that the ship entered Casco Bay first. Verrazzano described the country as pleasant and open, with high mountains visible inland. These must have been the White Mountains of New Hampshire.

Soon afterward Verrazzano came in contact with the Abenaki Indians. He described the site of the encounter as a high cliff where the Indians consented to trade with the white men in a small boat by letting a basket down to them. The latitude of this spot was 43°40'N, so that it must have been either Seguin Island, which seems unlikely, or Bald Head at the top of Small Point. The cliff here is steep and a small boat could easily have been rowed to the base, and a basket let down for the trading goods. The Indians were only interested in knives, fishhooks and tools. For these they put such small pelts and foodstuffs as they could spare in the basket.

The expedition had met Indians before, notably the Wampanoags at Newport Harbor, whom Verrazzano described with admiration. However, Verrazzano's opinion of the Indians of Maine is expressed by the name he gave to the country, "Land of Bad People." The Indians would not let the explorers come ashore, and if they came too close, the cliffs resounded with loud war whoops accompanied by a shower of arrows. In some manner, however, Verrazzano learned that the Indians' food was largely obtained by hunting and fishing and also by harvesting groundnuts, a protein-rich legume now extinct in Maine. Groundnuts *(Apios americana)* were to help save the Plymouth Colony during the first hard years, and no doubt they were one of the foods to be let down over the cliffs at Bald Head in the trading.

Giovanni da Verrazzano

The explorers' description of their reception by the Abenakis strongly indicates that they were not the first white men to visit there, and that the previous visitors had aroused hostility. Morison, describing the scene, wrote that the awkward method of trading was not the thing that bothered the white men most. It was the natives' uncouth manners. The Indians raised such a clamor with whoops, yells, raucous laughter and shouts that no attempt at communication could be made. As the crews left the Indians laughed and shouted all the more, at the same time making all sorts of disdainful and vulgar gestures. The Europeans left with derisive laughter in their ears and the sight of Abenaki braves turning their backs and exhibiting bare rear ends to show what they thought of the white men.

Quite reasonably, that part of Maine and her inhabitants did not make a good impression on these early tourists, and on the Verrazzano map there it is — "Land of the Bad People"!

Upon leaving the mouth of the Kennebec, Verrazzano sailed northeast again. He wrote of seeing many pleasant islands, with harbors and channels winding between them, which he compared to islands in the Gulf of Venice. It was the month of May and the weather was good. Shadbushes covered with white blossoms grew on the shore among the evergreens, as they still do. For the three largest islands Verrazzano encountered, he chose the names of the three princesses of Navarre, Anne, Isabeau, and Catherine. These islands were later known as Monhegan, Isle au

Giovanni da Verrazzano

Haut, and Mount Desert.

Verrazzano seems to have been the first to use the name *Oranbega* or *Norumbega*, which later writers applied to a fabled city on the Penobscot River. Mentions of this place are so shadowy that modern researchers believe it never existed. However, the name later was applied to all the land now comprising Maine. Verrazzano applied the name to a part of the coast near the "Daughters of Navarre."

The voyage continued to the east-northeast to cover the remainder of the Maine coast, and eventually the ship reached as far north as Newfoundland. Although Verrazzano had not found a shortcut to the Indies, he had performed the feat of exploring the American coast from the thirty-fourth degree of latitude to the fiftieth, with some short explorations inland. On his arrival home in Dieppe he was given a tumultuous reception, and on the same day wrote a lengthy letter to King Francis containing the first known description of the North American coast.

After Verrazzano, there was an interval of about eighty years before a European again visited the mouth of the Kennebec and told about his exploits. That does not mean that the Maine coast was empty of visitors, however. The fever of discovery was running high, and a number of explorers took pen in hand to describe what they had seen.

In 1556 Andre Thevet, a Frenchman and a writer of repute, took passage on a vessel that sailed along the entire eastern seaboard. He visited the coast of Maine and has left us a description of the Penobscot River:

"Here we entered a river which is the finest in the whole world. We call it Norumbega. It is marked on some charts as the Grand River. The natives call it Agoncy. Several beautiful rivers flow into it."

He goes on to describe an island, Alayascon (present-day Islesboro) where the party was received by a group of Indians with great kindness and hospitality. The French group stayed and feasted with the Indians for five days, and departed with good will on both sides.

The next known visitor was English. This was Sir Humphrey Gilbert, brother-in-law to Sir Walter Raleigh, who in 1578 received a grant from Queen Elizabeth of England of any lands he might discover in the New World. He was given full powers to explore and settle such lands. Unfortunately Gilbert's first voyage never got started. He was not a good organizer; his sailings were always late and without proper preparation. He quarreled with his officers and they disobeyed his commands, one of them even sailing off in his ship before Gilbert was ready. Twice storms forced the fleet back to home port. The voyage of 1578 was aborted, a failure.

A second voyage was started with high hopes on June 11, 1583. Gilbert's first objective was Newfoundland. Then he planned to sail southward to the coast of Maine, or Norumbega, as they called it, and start a settlement. Gilbert's intentions are recorded in a document that gives instructions for such a settlement in case of his death. He may have had a premonition that he would not return.

Humphrey Gilbert

Five ships, with 260 men, started the voyage. Morison lists the ships as the *Delight, Bark Raleigh*, the *Golden Hinde*, the frigate *Swallow*, and the frigate or pinnace *Squirrel*.

The trip was ill fated from the beginning. They were late in getting started, as Gilbert usually was, and especially late for making a north Atlantic crossing. The *Bark Raleigh* turned back only two days out of Plymouth Sound. The four remaining ships fought through a month of head winds and stormy seas. The *Swallow* left the fleet, and when she returned, Gilbert found that her master had been practicing a little piracy on the side.

When four ships entered St. John's Harbor in Newfoundland, they found Portuguese, Spanish and French fishermen already anchored there. Gilbert decided to take formal possession of the place for England. There being no objections from the fishermen, who even fired a salute in honor of the occasion, he claimed the country in the name of Queen Elizabeth. Of course Cabot had already claimed Newfoundland for England in 1497, but people had almost forgotten about the political events of a century before. So Gilbert made the deed doubly certain on August 5, 1583, which Newfoundland accepts today as the birth date of the British Empire.

The remainder of the voyage was disastrous. Only the *Golden Hinde* eventually succeeded in getting back to England. Her crew brought back the sad news of the loss of the other boats and men, and the death of their leader, Humphrey Gilbert. So ended the dream of colonizing Norumbega in the sixteenth century.

Before we leave this century, however, let us recognize a man who, though he never set foot in the New World, had perhaps more influence than any other person on the English explorers of Maine. This was Richard Hakluyt, a churchman and writer, who even today is quoted widely as an authority on the early English explorations. His lifelong goal was to inspire his countrymen to explore and settle North America.

Hakluyt's first book, *Divers Voyages touching the discovery of North America,* came out in 1582. It included the letters patent granted by Henry VII to John Cabot, so that no one would forget that Cabot had formally claimed Newfoundland in 1497 for England. It included his own translation of Sebastian Cabot's Northwest Passage attempt, Robert Thorne's writings urging a circumpolar voyage, and Verrazzano's letter to Francis I. Hakluyt added notes of his own, urging the benefit to England of colonizing the northern regions of America.

In 1584, while he was chaplain to the English ambassador in Paris, Hakluyt wrote *A discourse concerning Western Planting.* This little pamphlet, meant for lobbying at Queen Elizabeth's court, argued that English settlement of North America would help to spread the Anglican religion; strengthen England's trade status and provide her with overseas bases in case of a war with Spain; bring wealth into the country, employ "numbers of idle men," and

Gosnold & Pring

finally, that hardy perennial, lead to the discovery of the Northwest Passage to China. At the time Queen Elizabeth was fully occupied with the increasingly strained relations with Spain, and Hakluyt's pamphlet had no immediate effect. However, his discourse might be said to have provided the blueprint for exploration and settlement by England for the next two centuries.

The beginning of the seventeenth century saw a renewal of interest in the New World. Captain Bartholomew Gosnold set out with an expedition from England in 1602, bound for the northern part of North America. He is thought to have sailed to the southern coast of Maine around Cape Porpoise, then south to explore what is now the Massachusetts coast, including Martha's Vineyard. He wanted to plant a colony there but, according to reports of the trip, not one of his crew would consent to being left behind on that isolated shore; so the whole company sailed back to England.

The next year, 1603, Martin Pring made a voyage to the coast of Maine. The expedition was outfitted and provisioned by city officials and merchants of Bristol for a voyage of eight months. Two ships were supplied: the *Speedwell*, captained by Pring with a crew of 30, and the *Discoverer* with Captain William Browne and a crew of thirteen men and one boy.

The two vessels left Milford Haven on April 10, 1603, only a few days after the death of Queen Elizabeth and accession of King James I. They passed within sight of the Azores and arrived on June 7 at

The St. Croix Colony

Penobscot Bay. Captain Pring and his companions were delighted with the country full of great woods, and the safe moorings for their ships among the islands. The fishing was good, so the ships' larders were replenished. The men saw beautiful silver gray foxes on one of the islands, and therefore gave them the name "Fox Islands."

From Penobscot Bay they sailed in a southerly direction, passed the islands of Casco Bay and continued on to the Saco River. They returned to England in August, with valuable cargoes including a birchbark canoe as an example of native craftsmanship.

Immediately after the voyage of Martin Pring, the Kennebec River was at last definitely explored by Europeans. There is still doubt, however, as to who deserves the title of discoverer of the Kennebec. Was it the Englishman George Weymouth, or the Frenchmen Sieur de Monts and Samuel de Champlain? The evidence is unclear, and the subject still arouses controversy among scholars.

Of the two parties, the French were first to cross the ocean. Henry IV of France granted a royal patent on November 8, 1603, to the nobleman Pierre du Guast, Sieur de Monts. In the patent de Monts was appointed lieutenant governor of all North American territory between the 40th and 46th degrees of latitude, with authority to colonize and rule it at his discretion, and to subdue and Christianize the native inhabitants. The entire territory was called Acadia, and the present state of Maine was included in it.

Samuel de Champlain. Reprinted with permission from A
Pictorial History of the State of Maine, *edited by Thomas
Morgan Griffiths and Arthur Morgan Griffiths, 1970.*

46

The St. Croix Colony

Sieur de Monts fitted out two vessels and departed for America on March 7, 1604. The pilot and geographer for the expedition was Samuel de Champlain, a skilled navigator who had explored the St. Lawrence River the year before. The small fleet made an uneventful crossing. After making landfall in Nova Scotia, de Monts searched the coast for a suitable place for a settlement, and chose the small island of St. Croix in present-day Calais, Maine.

Champlain was given the duty of planning and laying out the new town, which he did at once. In the autumn of 1604 de Monts selected him to embark on an exploratory trip southward along the coast of Maine. With him in a small ship went a crew of twelve and two Indian guides. After a two-week delay because of fog in Passamaquoddy Bay, they sailed southwest, winding their way through the many islands of the area. When the ship arrived at an island known as Pematiq, Champlain, observing its rocky mountains, named it *l'Isle de Monts Deserts* — an apt description of Mount Desert Island, and possibly also a pun on the title Sieur de Monts. The ship anchored in the beautiful bay near Bar Harbor which we know as Frenchman Bay.

Champlain had friendly relations with the Indians he met. On a tour of Mount Desert Island he came across a group of them fishing and hunting for otters. They offered to pilot the Frenchmen to the Penobscot River, then known as the Norumbega. The party explored this river as far as Kenduskeag Stream where falls barred their way, just north of the present Ban-

The St. Croix Colony

gor. They continued down the coast and, according to historian James Phinney Baxter, attempted the exploration of the Kennebec River, but ran into bad weather which compelled them to return to St. Croix Island.

Snow fell, and moving blocks of ice surrounded the island that winter, so the colonists were unable to get to the mainland to hunt the abundant game there. They were forced to live on the salt meat they had brought from France. Because of this limited diet, scurvy broke out, and 36 out of the 80 men died of this dreaded disease and were buried in the ground of the New World.

Milder weather in the spring brought renewed hope to the survivors, and they decided to sail southward to look for a kinder environment for their little settlement. Sieur de Monts and Champlain hoisted anchor and set sail from St. Croix Island on the 18th of June, 1605.

On this voyage, besides the two leaders, there were some gentlemen, twenty sailors, and the Indian Panounias and his squaw. The explorers were quite willing to take the Indian woman as she was a native of the lower Kennebec, one of the people called Almouchiquois by the explorers.

After an eventful trip down the coast, the party reached the mouth of the Kennebec, and it was at this point that the river received the name it bears today. Champlain wrote that the Indian name for the place sounded like *Quinibequi* or *Kinibeki*, which he said they associated with the twisting, narrow passage between Bath and Sheepscot Bay. This stretch of water, today called Hell Gate on the Sasanoa River, was a ledgy passage through which the strong tides furiously boiled back and forth, endangering the Indians' frail canoes. In their mythology they associated the place with demons and disasters. The Algonquin word for serpent or monster was *Kinai-Bik* and this referred to the maelstrom which was and still is Hell Gate. Hockomock ("the bad place") is the name of a headland at Upper Hell Gate. At that time the Indians considered that the river had several mouths, and that the Sasanoa River and other nearby waterways were all part of the Kennebec. Champlain was the first European to apply the name to the present Kennebec.

The Frenchmen anchored the ship around three hundred yards from the river's entrance in five or six fathoms of water. Champlain described the place: "At the entrance there is an island [Seguin], quite high, which we have named 'La Tortue' [the Tortoise] and ·between this and the mainland are some scattered islands and rocks, covered at high water, but the sea breaks over them. The island of La Tortue and the river are SSE and NNW." They were delayed at this spot by fog until the 5th of July, when they began to explore. First they entered the Sheepscot River and proceeded to the site of the future Wiscasset. It is odd that they did not take the obvious route straight up the Kennebec. However, Champlain's description of the Sheepscot tallies with what is there: meadows, small streams and an island four leagues long, West-

The St. Croix Colony

port Island.

At one place they met some Indians in two canoes, with whom they were able to communicate through their Indian guide's wife. The Frenchmen were taken by the Indians to meet their chief, Manthoumermer. His wigwam was situated at what looked like the head of the river, probably Wiscasset. He was attended by twenty or thirty braves. After a shaky start, the meeting went well, and an alliance of sorts was established between the Indians and the Frenchmen. The next morning under the guidance of a party of Indians the explorers took another route westward, passing Hockomock Point and Hell Gate on their way to the Kennebec via the Sasanoa River. Their objective was a "large lake" (Merrymeeting Bay) which, they had heard, was the meeting place of all the neighboring Indian tribes.

The route along the Sasanoa was described by Champlain in his journal:

"Passing by some islands each of the savages left an arrow near a cape by which all must pass; they believe that unless they do this the devil will bring about some misfortune; they live in this superstition as well as many others. Near this cape we passed a fall of water, but it was not done without great difficulty, for though we had a fair and fresh wind and carried all the sail we possibly could, we were obliged to take a hawser ashore and fasten it to the trees and then pull with all our strength, and thus by main force and the favoring wind we got through. The savages who were with us carried their canoes along the shore, being unable to make headway with their paddles. After we passed the falls we saw beautiful meadow lands. I was much astonished at this fall because we had descended the river easily with the tide, but at the fall it was against us, but above the fall it ebbed as before much to our satisfaction."

Those of us who have gone through Hell Gate by boat cannot doubt that Champlain and his party were really there.

When the French expedition reached the main Kennebec River at Bath, they headed upstream as far as Merrymeeting Bay, which was described by Champlain:

"Pursuing our route we came to a lake which is three or four leagues long with islands in it. Here descend two rivers, the Quinibequy which comes from the northeast, and another which comes from the northwest, by which the Indians Marchim and Sazanon were to come; but having waited the whole day without seeing them we resolved to keep our time employed and so weighed anchor and came to the mouth of the river."

They proceeded to the mouth of the river by the main channel, anchoring near the present Fort Popham. Before leaving, Champlain recorded the Kennebec Indians' description of what he called "this noble river." They told him the Kennebec was the great route to the St. Lawrence River in Canada by way of the Chaudiere. They said also that not many Indians lived on the coast but were in the interior where they cultivated the soil. They no doubt meant the Norridgewocks, and other settled villages.

On the eighth of July the French ship sailed westward on a direct course for Cape Elizabeth, passing Casco Bay without entering. Champlain wrote about Casco Bay that it was full of islands, and beyond them to the west were mountains, where a savage chieftain lived whose name was Anela.

They visited various places in Maine and Champlain carefully described them all, including the natives and the way they lived. At the Saco River they entered and went ashore to visit the Indians and to look at their gardens. Both Champlain and Sieur de Monts were very much interested in the cultivation of maize. Champlain wrote that they planted three or four grains in one spot, then with the shell of the *signoe* they gathered some earth around them, and repeated the procedure about every three feet. No one has improved much on this method of planting corn, which the explorers called "Wheat of India." The implement used to hill up the earth was actually the shell of the horseshoe crab.

After leaving Chouacoet, which is what they called the Saco River and harbor, the little band of explorers sailed past the beautiful sand beaches of Kennebunk, Wells and York, finally anchoring off Cape Ann. Champlain made drawings, with meticulous detail, of all the harbors, inlets and beaches they went by. These sketches were to be the basis for the maps which it was his job to prepare as the Royal Geographer.

The party continued southward along the Massachusetts coast as far as Boston, and turned back north on July 25. After stopping at Chouacoet again to finally meet Marchim, the sagamore of Saco Bay, they continued to the mouth of the Kennebec.

Here they had a meeting with an Indian chief named Anassou, in which they learned, to their great surprise, that another party of Europeans had just departed. This incident is described in an address on Champlain given by General John Marshall Brown before the Maine Historical Society in 1875, called "Coasting Voyages in the Gulf of Maine." He in turn used Champlain's journal of 1613 as his source. Champlain wrote:

"[Anassou] told us that there was a vessel six leagues from the harbor which had been engaged in fishing, and the people on board had killed five savages of this river, under the pretense of friendship, and according to his description we judge them to be English, and named the island where they were 'Le Nef' [the hull of a ship] because at a distance it had that appearance." The island referred to was Monhegan Island, and the English party was the expedition commanded by George Weymouth on the ship *Archangel.* Anassou was mistaken in one detail: the five Indians had been kidnapped by Weymouth, not killed, and would be treated with relative kindness by the English. This was no consolation to their tribesmen and relatives, however.

Sieur de Monts and Champlain returned with their men to St. Croix Island. After the second winter at St. Croix the little colony was moved to the more fertile

George Weymouth

and pleasant Port Royal in Nova Scotia. This place figures prominently in the later history of the northeastern coast, and its name would be changed to Annapolis in honor of Britain's Queen Anne.

For the story of the English expedition of 1605, we must go back to the month of March, at a time when the French were dying of scurvy on St. Croix. The English had learned of Sieur de Monts' trip and the immense territory he had claimed for the king of France. They started moving, basing their right to explore on the old Cabot claim and Queen Elizabeth's grant to Sir Humphrey Gilbert. The Earl of Southampton and Lord Arundel outfitted a ship to patrol the coast, ostensibly to find a northwest passage to India. The true purpose was to keep an eye on the French and to prepare for the settlement of English colonies.

The *Archangel* sailed from England on the March 31, 1605, with George Weymouth in command. They reached Cape Cod on May 12 and sailed to the northeast, or, as we would later say, down east. On May 17 they sighted an island about six miles from the coast and cast anchor on the north shore. The anchorage was ideal, with abundant cod and haddock. Flocks of waterfowl hovered over the steep cliffs.

Weymouth went ashore and took possession of the island in the name of King James I of England, cousin and successor to Queen Elizabeth. He named the island St. George; it is now known as Monhegan.

The next stop was at a harbor they named Pentecost. Finding the soil extremely rich, they planted peas, barley, and other seeds, which in 16 days grew to 8 inches. This is the first recorded instance of Europeans cultivating a garden in Maine.

After extensive travels along the coast and much trading and communication with the Indians, Weymouth, by trickery and various wiles, kidnapped five Indians and locked them below deck. As Rosier, the historian of the voyage, wrote, "We shipped five savages and two canoes with all their bows and arrows."

After securing the captives the ship immediately made sail and headed westward. They sailed through some of the most beautiful of Maine's coastal scenery. They passed islands, craggy headlands, inlets, coves and forests as far as the eye could see, and finally entered a large river mouth.

Rosier noted that "the river as it runneth up into Maine nigh forty miles towards the great mountains, beareth in breadth a mile, sometimes three quarters, and a half at the narrowest. And there is never less than four fathoms of water hard by the shore and on both sides, every half mile very gallant coves."

Soon after entering the river, the *Archangel* cast anchor, and the captain with a crew of seventeen boarded a boat and rowed several miles upstream. They landed and, leaving six men to guard the boat, the remainder under command of the captain set out to explore some rather distant hills. They proceeded about five miles through what they described as exceedingly beautiful country without reaching the

George Weymouth

hills.

Their historian Rosier called the land good and fertile, resembling a stately park, with the hillsides covered with notable high timber trees suitable for masts of ships of four hundred tons and more.

The boat returned from the exploratory trip to find that an Indian canoe had approached, appearing from one of the numerous inlets on the east. It was propelled by many men with paddles. On board was the "Royal Ambassador," who conveyed an invitation to Weymouth to visit the Bashaba, the head chief.

Weymouth had been watched all the way up the river. The Indians had heard about the capture of five of their tribesmen and intended to try to rescue their friends. If they did not succeed, they would warn their people of the treacherous ways of the English so that no more captives would be trapped. Their pleadings were in vain, and they returned to the families of the captured men with a burning resentment against the English and a desire for vengeance. If Weymouth had wished to turn the Indians against him as one man, he could not have thought of a more successful method.

As it happens, Weymouth's purpose in capturing the Indians was not for monetary gain or for sale to slave traders. He wanted information to help the English make their plans for settlements. He treated the captives well and they became reconciled to their new life. Rosier recorded their names as Nahanada, Skitwarroes, Assecomet, Tisquantum and

Dehamida.

Upon returning to England, three of them were assigned to Ferdinando Gorges, and the other two, it is thought, went to Sir John Popham. Both these men gave great credit to the Indians for helping them understand the geography of the new country. They intended to return them to their homes, and at least three of them made it back. However, two were sent on a ship which was captured by Spanish pirates, and they probably were sold into slavery.

What was the great river described by Rosier? Not all scholars believe that it was the Kennebec. Henry S. Burrage, D.D., Maine State Historian in the nineteenth century, argued that the description given by Rosier actually fits the St. George River, and the distant hills seen by the men were the Camden Hills. In this case Pentecost Harbor would correspond to George Island Harbor and not to Boothbay Harbor, as some believe.

Other writers have said Weymouth captured the five men on the Pemaquid peninsula, giving no specific location. Anassou, meeting Champlain's party on the Kennebec River, described the captives as "from this river." I have wondered why, if the kidnapped Indians were residents of Pemaquid, they were later willing to be returned to the banks of the Kennebec, there to stay and act as interpreters for the Popham party.

If Anassou was right, it is quite possible that the Englishman George Weymouth discovered the Kennebec River, with the Frenchmen right on his heels.

George Weymouth

If the newer historians are correct in their theory that Weymouth did not enter the Kennebec, then the honor of discovery belongs to Sieur de Monts and Samuel de Champlain.

The region that Weymouth had visited became an absorbing subject of conversation in England. Rosier was an excellent writer, and his glowing accounts of the new land show him to be the forerunner of modern advertising writers. The coast of Maine was described as the most desirable spot for colonies in the New World. Rosier, perhaps our first and most eloquent Maine booster, said that "nowhere on earth could be found more sunny skies, a more genial clime or more fertile soil. The forests were of unspeakable grandeur, the water of crystal purity, and it was a luxury to breathe its salubrious air."

The river entered by Weymouth is described thus by Rosier: "Many who have been travellers in sundry countries, and in most famous rivers, affirmed them not comparable to this one. It is most beautiful, rich, large, secure harboring river that the world affordeth." He goes on to describe the lovely bays and islands, hills and vales, that they encountered in Maine.

Thus it seems that the Popham colony of 1607 was the direct result of the glowing accounts of Weymouth and Rosier. Again, if it was not the Kennebec Weymouth visited, why did the next expedition go unerringly to that spot? Did they think it was the Kennebec that Rosier described in such complimentary terms? Were the instructions not clear? Or were their navigators at fault?

The Popham expedition was backed by the Plymouth Company, the same organization that would later finance the Pilgrim settlement in 1620. The Plymouth Company was comprised of intelligent upper-class men of high ideals, who wished to plant colonies in this new-found Eden. Lord Popham and Sir Ferdinando Gorges, both important in the early history of Maine, were prominent members of the company. They would take civilization and religion, which they believed must go hand in hand, to the New World. They wanted to send to the shores of New England the farmer, the carpenter, and the schoolmaster, along with Christianity. James I made a grant to the company of all North American territory between the thirty-fifth and forty-fifth degrees of latitude, including all the islands within one hundred miles of the coast.

The spot picked out as ideal for a colony was the mouth of the Kennebec River, called the Sagadahock by the English. The name Sagadahock applied to the river below Merrymeeting Bay, and was derived from the Indian *Sunkerdahunk* meaning "river mouth." The English would call it by that name for more than a century. Later Champlain's name Kennebec was given to the entire river from its source to its mouth.

The first efforts to colonize were not successful. A ship was sent out with only thirty-one men on board, including the crew, a small number for such an ambitious undertaking. To be returned to their homes were two of Weymouth's Indian captives, namely

The Popham Colony

Dehamaida and Assecomet. According to the historian of the voyage the destination was the mouth of the Sagadahock; the date was May 1606.

England and Spain were at war. The far roving Spanish fleet overtook the ship and easily captured it with all on board. The two Indians, who thought they were to be reunited with their families, were taken back to Spain and sold as slaves, as was the Spanish custom. One of these men finally managed to escape and turned up later in America.

Another ship was sent out before news reached England of the loss of the first vessel. The second ship carried more colonists and supplies, but when they reached the Sagadahock without finding the first ship, they returned to England forthwith.

The third attempt at planting a colony on the Kennebec was successful, although the colony was short lived. This was engineered by Lord Popham, Chief Justice of England, a man of wealth and high rank. The expedition was under the command of George Popham, a brother of Lord Popham, and Raleigh Gilbert, one of his nephews. Two vessels set sail on the 31st of May, 1607, on a course for Monhegan Island.

The ship *Gift of God* was under the command of George Popham; the *Mary and John* had Raleigh Gilbert as captain. On board were one hundred and twenty farmers, with a large supply of tools and provisions. According to Williamson, they steered directly for Monhegan and then proceeded "to the mouth of a fair navigable river," called by the Indians

The Popham Colony

Sagadahock.

According to some accounts, they first went ashore on Erascohegan (now Parkers Island), or, according to others, Stage Island, landing on the northern shore, which is level and easy to reach. The southerly side was high, bleak and rocky. The adventurers went ashore and, after giving thanks to God for a safe passage, read their patent, their ordinances and laws. After these ceremonies were concluded, the settlers built a few simple houses, sank some wells, and started commerce with the Indians of the locality.

It was soon evident, however, that the ten-acre island was too small to support a successful colony and that it was too far from the mainland for easy trading. The embryo settlement was therefore moved to the west side of the Sagadahock River to a pleasant and convenient situation on the southeast bank of a creek, near what is now called Atkins Bay, which stretches west into the land half a league (1½ miles) and forms a peninsula at the southerly corner of the present town of Phippsburg.

During the autumn they established a settlement that was called the Sagadahock Colony. A large house and barn and a few cabins were constructed. These, with the addition of a fort called St. George (afterwards named Fort Popham), and a blockhouse with a store room, was the extent of the first recorded European settlement on the Kennebec River.

As soon as the safety and comfort of the settlers was assured as far as possible, the two ships lifted anchor and sailed off for England, leaving 45 colonists situ-

A view of the Popham Colony, founded in present-day Phippsburg, Maine in 1607. At left on the stocks is the pinnace Virginia, *the first ship built in the New World. Reprinted with permission from Griffiths'* Pictorial History of the State of Maine, *1970.*

ated between an unbroken wilderness on one side and the cold North Atlantic on the other. These people were braving an unknown climate with winter approaching, and they were surrounded by Indians who had reason to distrust and fear the English.

Luckily, there were with the colonists two of Weymouth's captives, Shetwarroes and Dehamaida. The good treatment they had received in England had allowed them to forgive, if not forget, their kidnapping. They gave friendly aid to the settlers and acted as go-between, insuring a warm reception by the neighboring natives.

Trade was started, and the Kennebec Indians were delighted with the knives and other items brought from England. One brave named Amenquin was so pleased with a straw hat and a knife that he took off a beaver mantle worth 50 or 60 shillings and presented it to the leader of the English colonists. Another favorite item was the red cloth the explorers brought with them. An Indian would trade valuable furs for a strip of cloth only a few inches wide which he would tie around his head like a red crown.

When the settlement was established, the colonists felt free to explore a little. Raleigh Gilbert and nineteen men embarked from the new fort on September 23, 1607 to become the first white men to penetrate the Kennebec River to its head tide at ancient Cushnoc, now Augusta.

They sailed all day the 23rd and the 24th until they landed and found a good "champion place" (camping ground) where they spent the night. The next day they proceeded further up the river until they came to a flat low island where they found a cataract or downfall of water which Raleigh said "runneth by both sides of this island very bold and swift." They were forced to haul their boat through this downfall with a strong rope, after which they ascended the river another league (3 or 4 miles) and spent the night.

That night a series of strange events began when a party of Indians called to them from the opposite shore in broken English. The Indians and the Englishmen talked back and forth for a time, and toward morning the Indians disappeared in the forest. In the morning they reappeared and came across the river in a canoe. There were a sagamore and four braves. The sagamore announced that his name was Sebenoa and that he was "Lord of the River Sagadahock." Raleigh invited them aboard the shallop and gave them some small gifts.

The Indians, it seems, had been watching the shallop's progress up the river, or had received the news from neighboring Indians, and naturally were concerned as to the purpose of the trip. The fact that they spoke broken English indicated that they had already had some communication with the English. This was quite possible, as English fishermen had been coming to the coast of Maine since the opening of the century, and the Indians of the interior had been in the habit of visiting the coast for fishing and seafood. Doubtless they picked up a little English in trading with the crews of the fishing boats.

After the Indians visited the shallop the cloak and

dagger maneuvers began. That involved sending one of the Englishmen as a hostage with the Indians in their canoe, and taking Sebenoa in the shallop with them. Then the chase began as the Indians paddled for dear life up the river, followed by the shallop. They were forced to land at the foot of another rapid and take off through the woods on foot, still accompanied by the sagamore, who was probably enjoying the whole thing.

Nash, in his *Indians of the Kennebec,* gives a good description of this unusual visit to the sagamore's village: "After a good tedious march they came indeed to the savages' houses where they found near fifty able men very strong and tall such as their like before they had not seen; all newly painted and armed with their bows and arrows. Howbeit, after that the sagamore talked with them and delivered back the hostage and used them all very friendly, as we did to them. They showed their commodities of beads, knives and copper, of which they seemed very fond."

The Englishmen left after more half-threatening acts by the Indians as they boarded their boat for the trip back down the river. Their goal of following the river to its headwaters was abandoned. The party returned to the camping place of the night before and there set up a cross; then they proceeded back to the colony.

Captain Gilbert's logbook and William Strachey's *Historie of Travaile into Virginia* are the sources for the description of this trip, and lead to the conclusion that it was definitely the Kennebec that Gilbert

The Popham Colony

ascended, and not the Androscoggin, as a few historians have suggested. It is difficult to believe that a seaman of Gilbert's caliber could have been deceived into hunting for the Kennebec River way over on the west shore of Merrymeeting Bay, and then proceeding southwestward, without catching on that he was not on the Kennebec, which was known to flow from north to south.

Historians believe that the explorers' first camping place was the plateau where Randolph now stands, and that the low flat island in the midst of a downfall of water was the place where the Augusta dam was later built. A picture and a good description of Cushnoc Island can be found in North's *History of Augusta* on pages 450-451. Both tally with Gilbert's description of the low flat island where they had to haul their boat over the rapids.

The second camping place was undoubtedly an intervale near Gilley's Point where many vestiges of Indian encampments have been found. The next morning after exchanging hostages, the Gilbert party continued until their shallop went aground in shallow water. This may have been in Bacon's Rips where the river falls about thirteen feet. The last stop of the explorers was the Indian village, which was probably in Vassalboro or Sidney; both locations have been goldmines of Indian artifacts, many of which are now in the Maine State Museum. Both Moorehead's *Archaeology of Maine* and Willoughby's *Indian Antiquities of the Kennebec Valley* give accounts of archaeological sites in the area Gilbert visited.

Sebenoa seems to have become lost in the hazy annals of the Indians, but his friendly welcome to the first white men to visit the upper Kennebec assures him a secure place in the history of the Kennebec valley.

The winter of 1607-08 was severe, as Maine winters often are, and one tragic event after another struck the colony. A fire burned the store house in midwinter, destroying most of the provisions. But that was not the worst. While the ship from the colony was in England, being outfitted for a return trip with more settlers and provisions, word was received of the sudden deaths of both Lord Popham and Sir John Gilbert, prime movers of the plans for the Sagadahock settlement.

When the ship arrived in America in the spring of 1608, bringing this sad news, it was met with the news that George Popham, the leader of the colony, had also recently died. All these setbacks proved fatal to the Popham colony. The discouraged settlers deserted the little village on the Kennebec and all returned to England.

When the Popham colonists left, some of them sailed home in a small ship they had built during the winter. This ship, called the *Virginia,* was the first ever built in North America. If things had gone well, its seems likely that the Popham colony would have been the first permanent settlement in what was then called North Virginia, predating the Plymouth colony by thirteen years.

John Smith

The failure of the Popham settlement proved discouraging to the English, and some years passed before more English settlers came to the Kennebec. After all, the colonists had branded the country around the Sagadahock as being "cold and in that respect not habitable by our nation." Ferdinando Gorges, for one, argued that as for the coldness of the country, he had had too much experience in the world to be frightened by such a blast, and that there were many kingdoms more northerly seated and many degrees colder. Still he failed to find supporters for a new expedition.

European travelers continued to come, however, to the Maine coast. The French were cruising along the coast soon after the Sagadahock colonists left. Also, Sir Francis Popham, son and heir of Lord Popham, sent a ship to Maine waters every year for trading in furs and fishing.

One of the parade of Europeans to sail the waters of the Kennebec was the famous Captain John Smith, the same man whose life had been saved so dramatically by Pocahontas in 1606. He sailed the coast in search of furs, got along very well with the natives, and filled the ship with valuable pelts for his return to Europe.

1614 saw Smith on the Kennebec bartering with the Abenakis there. He ran into Nahanada, one of Weymouth's returned captives, and found that he had been elevated to one of the "greatest lords of the country." About this time Samoset was kidnapped and taken to Europe. The circumstances are not clear; however, this explains why Samoset was later able to speak English and greet the Pilgrims at Plymouth with "Welcome, Englishmen." Williamson's *History of Maine* says that Samoset was one of the Indians kidnapped by a man named Hunt, who lingered after John Smith left, and later sold some of his captives as slaves. Some of the Indians were taken around the mouth of the Kennebec and surrounding areas, and some from Plymouth, Massachusetts. Samoset escaped, and when he appeared at Plymouth in 1621 he told the Pilgrims that he was a sagamore from Monhegan.

According to Williamson, Samoset and Squanto came back to America with Thomas Dermer, an explorer of the east coast as far north as Newfoundland. Dermer had become good friends with both Samoset and Squanto during their captivity in England. He found them both a great help in reconciling the hostile Indians along the coast. In Dermer's account he gives Samoset's dwelling place as the Sagadahock River.

Dermer left the two Indians at their homes and sailed for Virginia on June 23, 1619. The trip was ill-fated; nearing Martha's Vineyard the party was attacked by the Indian Epinau and a group of warriors. Several of the crew were killed in the battle, and Dermer himself was so severely wounded that he died in Virginia shortly after arriving there. His untimely death was a great loss to the cause of English settlement on the Maine coast.

However, even as the age of explorers was coming

to an end, the age of settlers was inevitably beginning. Both Smith in 1614 and Dermer in 1619 had attempted to start small settlements in the "Territory of Sagadahock," as they called the strip of land lying between the Kennebec and the Damariscotta rivers. The territory was only five leagues in width, including the Sheepscot River and the islands. According to Sullivan, early settlers included a Mr. Walter Phillips, who lived on the west side of the Damariscotta near the great or lower falls, and Thomas Gent, who lived at Sheepscot Great Neck, where there was a fort.

According to Prince, Monhegan seems to have had settlers continuously from 1622 until the first Indian war. Apparently Sir Ferdinando Gorges started a plantation there in early 1621, and a couple of months later there was a "settlement of some beginnings." Prince adds that not much hope of its prosperity could be entertained, since the settlers were fishermen blended with stragglers of crews such as those from Dermer's ship.

So although the annals do not record precisely in what year, or by what persons, homesteads were first formed on the Kennebec, on the Sheepscot, on the Damariscotta, or at Pemaquid, we may conclude that it must have been around 1623. The harbors, headlands and rivers had made this section extremely attractive to the Europeans, and even today one can see the remains of chimneys and vestiges of dwellings, marked with antiquity. Archaeological diggings have been going on for several years on the Pemaquid peninsula, near the harbor and Fort William Henry. The foundations of what appears to be a complete early seventeenth-century English village have been unearthed. Artifacts of pottery and other materials have been uncovered and reconstructed with the help of the Smithsonian Institution, and they may be seen in a museum at the site.

The first English explorations in the upper Sagadahock valley, however, were made by traders sent out by the infant Pilgrim colony in Plymouth, called then New Plymouth. These pioneers had learned of the profits to be gained by bartering with the Indians for necessities. The first trips were to Monhegan and Damariscove islands, which were attended with such success that a trip was planned to ascend the Kennebec.

The trip was made by Edward Winslow and a party from the Plymouth colony in the fall of 1625. They must have been pleased with what they found, for within a few years the Pilgrims had established a trading post at the head of tide at Cushnoc (present-day Augusta) for the express purpose of trading with the Indians. Another trading post was located at the mouth of the river, probably near George Popham's old fort in Phippsburg. A third was established in the present town of Richmond.

The Indians often brought fine furs to trade at these posts, particularly the beaver skins so prized by European fashion. The Pilgrims brought cloth, manufactured tools and utensils, which began to make some changes in the centuries-old Indian way of life. Both sides dealt in corn and wampum. Wampum consisted of blue and white beads, long and as large as a wheat corn, blunt at the ends. These could easily be punched with a hole at the end and strung to made handsome necklaces, as they possessed clarity and beauty which made them very much sought after. Some of the other goods bartered were coats, blankets, fruit, biscuits and trinkets.

As the Pilgrims wished to secure exclusive rights to the Kennebec trade, their agent, Mr. Allerton, applied for and secured a patent from the Plymouth Council in 1627. A further grant was made on January 13, 1629, later to be called the Plymouth or Kennebec Patent. It was intended to further trade and fisheries and to propagate religion. The boundaries of the Kennebec Patent, as finally settled, were the north line of Woolwich below Swan Island on the east bank of the Kennebec, through the south bend of Cobbosseecontee Stream on the western bank, extending northward for a width of 15 miles on each side of the Kennebec, to terminate on an east-west line that crossed the Wesserunsett River (a tributary of the Kennebec in the present town of Skowhegan).

Disputes over land titles arose early and it is easy to see why. The colonies of Massachusetts and New Plymouth, as early as 1633, passed laws forbidding land purchases from the natives without a license from the legislature. However, the sales continued, often to private individuals within the boundaries of tracts such as the Kennebec Patent. Add to this the Indians' habit of selling the same piece of land several times, which complicated things still further.

Woolwich was sold several times by the Indians, in 1649 to Christopher Lawson, and in 1654 to Edward Bateman and John Brown. Thomas Clark and Roger Spencer secured all of Arrowsic Island in 1660, the seller being a sagamore. In 1666 the sagamore Jack Pudding sold lands on the Montsweag River to the proprietors of the Boston Company and, in addition, lands on both sides of the Kennebec River, including the principal islands in the vicinity.

Abbagadusset sold Swan Island in 1667 to Humphrey Davie. However, Swan Island is mentioned at much later dates as being the seat of the Bashaba, the supreme Indian chief. It seems that they must have reserved land for their village. Some of the land disputes lasted for years, until the government of Massachusetts took over at the end of the seventeenth century and began to straighten things out.

The English approach to the Kennebec River in the seventeenth century was by acquisition of legal title to tracts of land, and settlement. The French approach to the Kennebec was rather different, as we shall see.

This cross at the top of the Father Rasle monument in Madison, Maine symbolizes more than a century of French Jesuit missions to the Kennebec Indians. Photograph by the author.

74

The Missionaries

*The Black Robes come down the
watery highways from Canada.*

THE FRENCH APPROACHED the Kennebec
River mainly from the north, rather
than the south. During the seventeenth century, they
showed no interest in settling the Maine wilderness
with transplanted French families. Instead they con-
centrated on winning the Abenakis over to their side
by sending Jesuit missionaries to them.

They were successful due to the efforts of the
priests, who left their native France filled with zeal
and dedicated to the goal of Christianizing the savages. Those who stand out for their work among the
Kennebec Indians are Father Biard, Father
Druillettes, the brothers Bigot, and Sebastian Rasle.
These men gave up the attractions of civilized life in
France and devoted themselves to bringing the word
of God to the natives.

Who could imagine that the intrigues of the
French court, and an unrequited love affair of Henry
of Navarre, would have anything to do with the

Pierre Biard

faraway Kennebec River? Truth is sometimes stranger than fiction. The truth in this case links King Henry and a virtuous French noblewoman to the little colony at Port Royal and the Abenaki Indians, through the travels and ministry of Father Pierre Biard of the Society of Jesus.

Even before Sieur de Monts left Port Royal, another French nobleman named Jean de Biencourt Poutrincourt, Baron of Saint-Just, asked for and received a deed of gift for that place, promising to return within two years with several families to cultivate and inhabit it. King Henry ratified the deed and approached Father Pierre Biard, then a theology teacher in Lyons, with the suggestion that he go to America with the proposed expedition as a missionary to the Indians and as priest of the colonists. Poutrincourt for some reason kept delaying the trip until the king became annoyed both at the delay and his refusal to include missionaries in the party. Poutrincourt finally sailed for Port Royal in February of 1610 without the two appointed missionaries.

When this news reached the ear of Madame de Guercheville in France, things began to happen. This remarkable lady, beautiful and chaste, had matched wits more than once with Henry of Navarre. When she was the young Mademoiselle de Pons, Henry had pursued her openly and persistently, to no avail. The lady married the Marquis de Guercheville instead, had two daughters, and later became a widow, as beautiful and charming as she had been in her younger days. She was now rich as well and lived in her magificent château situated on the river Seine a few miles below Paris.

One of the most charming stories about the French court is the one told by the Abbé Cloisy and translated in "The Bell of a Jesuit Mission" by Robert Jones, about the way in which Madame de Guercheville tricked the king, rejected his suit but retained his respect and affection. Finally, when the king gave up and married Marie de Medici, he placed his old flame near the bride as maid of honor. It was reported that he did so with these words: "Madame, I give you for a Maid of Honor a woman of honor indeed."

Madame de Guercheville dedicated her fortune to bringing religion to the natives of the New World. Father Biard referred to her as "ardently zealous for the glory of God and the conversion of souls." She purchased all rights and claims to de Monts' land in Acadia, and later obtained from the boy king Louis XIII, son of her former suitor, a grant of all the territory between the St. Lawrence River and Florida.

This lady made arrangements for Father Masse and Father Biard to embark on a small ship sailing from Dieppe in January of 1611, arriving at Port Royal on June 22. They found the little colony in trouble, even with the additional supplies brought by the ship. Poutrincourt sailed for France in the middle of the summer, leaving his son Biencourt in charge. In spite of short supplies, Biencourt decided to make some explorations along the coast.

Father Biard went along on this trip to act as chaplain to Biencourt and his crew, and also to meet the Indians, with a view to teaching them the gospel. Thanks to the reports of Father Biard, we can add to our store of knowledge of the Indians of the lower Kennebec, because they made the mouth of that river their first stop.

They passed Seguin Island and went directly to the fort that had been abandoned by the Popham colonists in the spring of 1608, a little over three years before. The Indians of the area told them that the English colonists had treated them with cruelty and were driven away in retaliation. The French believed this, although these statements were only partially true, as the failure of the colony was due to the extremely cold winter and the death of their leader, George Popham. The party spent three days at the fort, which the Frenchmen thought had been poorly located.

Then, abandoning their plan of continuing westward in search of food, they sailed up the Kennebec. About nine miles from the sea twenty-four Indian warriors paddled into view. These were called Armouchiquois by Father Biard, belonging no doubt to the Kennebec or Androscoggin tribe.

The Indians were very curious but did not at first come very close. They advanced and then retreated, observing the crew with their muskets, the cannons on the deck, the number of men on board — everything. As night fell they made camp on the opposite shore and, as was their custom, started singing, dancing and making a terrible racket that continued through the night. Father Biard in his relation wrote:

"We presumed that the songs and dances were invocations to the devil, and in order to thwart that accursed tyrant, I had our men sing some church hymns such as *Salve Regina, Ave Maris Stella* and others. The Indians seemed amazed and stopped to listen, then the others started again mimicking the savages." Biard said that it was like two choirs answering each other in concert and it would have been hard to tell the real Armouchiquois from the sham ones.

Biencourt had had the foresight to engage two Etchemin Indians of the St. John River as interpreters. He had taught them some French, and the Abenaki and Etchemin languages were closely enough related so that Biencourt was able to communicate with the Kennebec Indians to some extent.

The morning after the powwow and hymn singing the Frenchmen proceeded further up the river accompanied by the Indians. They became more friendly and told the white men that if they wanted corn *(piousquemin)* to turn to the right through an arm of the river and they would within a few hours reach the wigwam of the great chief Meteourmite. The Indians indicated they would be glad to act as guides.

Biencourt cautiously followed them through the channel, now traversed by the Woolwich-Georgetown bridge, entering Nequasset Bay where he met Meteourmite coming to meet him. The furious tides at Hell Gate gave them some trouble, Biard saying: "We thought we should hardly escape alive, our people crying out piteously that we were all lost." Passing Hockomock, "the bad place," they found themselves in calm water and nearing the sachem's tent.

Biencourt put on his uniform for the meeting and found the chief alone but with the wigwam surrounded by forty young braves, each with his shield, bows and arrows laid out on the ground before him. The Europeans were beginning to observe that the natives loved ceremony, fancy dress and oratory. When Biencourt met Meteourmite in his dwelling, the chief admitted that they were short of corn and could not spare any but were willing to barter some furs instead.

After the agreement for trade was made the Indians began boarding the Frenchmen's boat in a rush, never having seen so large a one before. More and more noisy natives crowded aboard until the frightened crew started pushing them back, fearing that the boat would sink. Biencourt admitted later that he was on the point of crying "Kill, kill," thinking that the savages were trying to capture their ship, only being held back by the fact that Father Biard was ashore, on an island, celebrating holy Mass. Any shooting on the ship would surely have caused the death of the priest, and probably the crew also, who were badly outnumbered.

Suddenly the Indians perceived the danger of imminent sinking and swarmed off the boat as fast as they had climbed aboard. Thirty braves were counted as they left and the boat slowly rose to its normal water line.

Father Biard appeared before the Indians of the

Kennebec in his priestly capacity twice during this trip. The altar improvised by him was the first to be used in a Catholic service on the Kennebec or nearby. He seems to have been on the Sasanoa River, perhaps near the Sheepscot, when he held the service on an island near Meteourmite's wigwam. Biard related that he prayed to God in their presence and showed them the tokens used in the service, which they kissed willingly and showed to their children whom they brought to Father Biard to be blessed. He taught them to make the sign of the cross and talked to them at length about Christianity. All this had to be interpreted by one of the Etchemins they had brought along, who, although he knew nothing about the Catholic religion, acquitted himself well, mimicking Father Biard's slow speech and dignified demeanor perfectly.

The Indians admired the priest for his peaceful, kindly character, so different from the rough sailors of the crew, and they embraced him and made all kinds of friendly advances. They led him to the largest of the huts of the village, which held about eighty people. There he knelt and recited some prayers. The Indians acted as if they understood all he said and at the pauses shouted in loud voices Ho, Ho, Ho! as if attending one of their powwows. After the service he gave them some small crosses and images and left, being the first — as far as we know — to bring the word of God to the Kennebec Indians.

After the founding of Quebec, the Jesuit order in France started sending priests to Canada to be trained for service with the natives of the New World. The first church and mission was on the St. Lawrence about four miles above Quebec City. A church was built there and in 1637 Father Masse, who had been with Father Biard in St. Croix, was made the resident pastor. Two years later a converted French courtier gave the mission twenty thousand livres and in return the mission was named for him, the residence of St. Joseph of Sillery. This was the place where the Jesuits came to learn the Indian language and receive wilderness training before going out to their ministries.

The first missionary to the Kennebec Indians, Father Gabriel Druillettes, arrived at this mission in 1643 and began his studies. After one year among the Algonquins of the St. Lawrence he was forced to take an easier post at the mission because of poor health and serious eye trouble. All this training however was getting him in condition to take on an even more burdensome post in the wilds of the Upper Kennebec.

In the same year that Father Druillettes was preaching at the mission at Sillery, a converted Indian of the St. Lawrence tribe named Charles Mejachkawat was sent to the Kennebec to pass the winter among the Abenakis at Norridgewock. He told the Indians there about the mission, and his beliefs which the Jesuits had taught him. During his visit he went to the trading post at Cushnoc where he entered into heated discussions with the Pilgrims, defending his faith with spirited oratory, and made no secret of the fact that he considered the Pilgrim fathers heretics!

Mejachkawat returned to Sillery in the spring accompanied by a chieftain of the Abenakis, who wished to be baptized in gratitude for help he had received from the Black-Gowns of Sillery on a trip there. He was christened with the name John Baptist. He was without doubt the first Abenaki chieftain to receive the rites of baptism. He started to return to his tribe alone and tragically fell into the hands of a band of marauding Iroquois and was cruelly put to death.

In August of 1646 a group of Norridgewocks went to Sillery to petition most earnestly for a priest to come to their village. On the 15th of August, they went before an assembly of the Black-Gowns and one delivered an oration, saying that they had been touched by the kindness of the Indian emissary who had visited them the year before, that they had been told of the beauties of heaven and the horrors of hell. They told the assembled church dignitaries that there were thirty men and six women of their tribe who wished to receive instruction in the Catholic faith.

The assembly voted to comply with the request of the pious Indians from the banks of the Kennebec and selected Father Gabriel Druillettes for the post. Father Druillettes accepted the appointment as a call from God and made ready to leave the comfortable mission at Sillery, where he had barely recovered his health and eyesight from his first difficult assignment.

There was not much to do; his baggage included only his missal, crucifix, articles of priestly apparel, a box of medicines and some bread and wine for celebrating Mass. All this was made into a pack that could be slung over the shoulders or laid in a canoe. He was to be accompanied on the journey by the already converted Christian chief Negabamat and some other Abenaki braves. The voyage was started by ascending the turbulent Chaudiere River about ninety miles to its source in Lake Megantic. From there the small group crossed the trail that led over the Height of Land and by way of Dead River to the Kennebec.

The priest reached Old Point and the village of the Norridgewocks around the middle of September, much to the joy of the inhabitants. After staying with them for a week, he started again going down river and stopping at Indian villages along the way to preach and to seek converts. The village at the mouth of the Sebasticook was visited, and from there Father Druillettes proceeded to Cushnoc. When he arrived at the Plymouth trading post he was warmly received by John Winslow, the agent, who invited him to be his guest in the trading house; though very simple, it was quite a contrast to the huts of the natives where the priest had been passing the nights since leaving Sillery.

Father Druillettes was the first white man to come down the Kennebec from Canada and to approach Cushnoc from the north. He was French and Winslow English, but the language barrier did not prevent them from becoming close friends, a friendship which was to last a lifetime. Hatch wrote, "By signs and pantomimes and the spirit of Christian kindness that knows all languages, the host and guest soon became mutually intelligible, and with the help of Indian interpreters were able to understand each other."

Staying only a short time, the priest with an Indian guide continued down the Kennebec to its mouth, visiting more Indian villages along the way to nurse the sick and pray with the dying, to become the first white man to traverse the entire length of Kennebec waters from Canada to the sea. This historic trip down the length of the Kennebec was made in 1646. His companion and guide was the faithful Noel Negabamat.

They returned to Cushnoc where Druillettes presented his commission as a missionary from the Jesuit superior in Quebec to Winslow. As it was in French, the Plymouth agent could not read it, but he laboriously copied the document in his own hand to carry back to his headquarters in Plymouth. In the meantime the agent gave him permission to start a mission within the limits of the Plymouth lands and lent him much assistance.

The place chosen for the mission was a place near the river a league above the trading post, which was afterwards known as Gilley's Point — the same spot mentioned in Raleigh Gilbert's account of his meeting with the Indians in the summer of 1607. There was a village here of around fifteen large cabins at the time Father Druillettes arrived, and the Indians made a chapel built of planks for his use. The new chapel in the wilderness was named *La Mission de l'Assomption au pays des Abenaquiois,* or "The Mission of the Assumption in the land of the Abenakis." Father Druillettes labored here among the Indians until the May 20, 1647, when he returned to Sillery accompanied by thirty Indians who went to request the early return of their patriarch to their village. This petition was not granted and they returned much disappointed.

Father Druillettes would return to the small chapel at Cushnoc only for another short visit. His main work, after this voyage, was among the Abenakis of the Norridgewock village. There he established a mission, built a chapel and ministered to the receptive Indians. His ten years there involved him in many hardships and adventures.

One story tells how Father Druillettes, in January 1647, accompanied the Norridgewocks on their winter hunt to *Kasebem,* the "great lake of the north," now known as Moosehead. When they arrived they divided themselves into many groups, to better wage war against deer, elk and beaver. The white Father traveled with one party, following wherever they went.

In the spring when the hunting was over, the entire band assembled at a prearranged meeting place on the shore of the lake. Here the sorcerers who clung to the old Indian beliefs, and had not been converted by the Jesuit, lost face as it was seen that the party who had traveled with the priest had had a very successful hunt, had recovered from sicknesses, and had avoided the ambushes of the ever marauding Mohawks.

The Norridgewocks and their pastor gathered at the outlet of the lake, where there was much feasting and dancing to celebrate the end of a successful hunt. The canoes were made ready for the trip down the Kennebec River to their village at Old Point.

Father Druillettes made another trip down the Kennebec in 1650, visiting the native villages and meeting again his good friend John Winslow at Cushnoc. This trip was partially political: his mission was to try to persuade the governors of Plymouth, Massachusetts and New Haven, Connecticut to join with the Canadians in repelling the Mohawks, who for many years had been hunting and killing the Abenakis, even invading their villages. In addition, the Mohawks and Iroquois had tortured and massacred six missionaries of the Society of Jesus. The governors promised to cooperate to the fullest in the project.

The last voyage of Father Druillettes from Quebec to the Norridgewock village was the most difficult of all. An Etchemin guide led the party astray and they landed over on the St. John River instead of the Kennebec. Lack of food, bad weather, and a treacherous guide made the trip a nightmare before they succeeded in reaching the village at Old Point, twenty-three days after leaving Quebec. The chief, Oumamanradock, welcomed the famished travelers warmly and chastised the Etchemin guide for his treatment of the priest. The culprit admitted his guilt belatedly, saying, "I was a dog to have treated the

Black Gown so badly."

Druillettes spent a dreary cold winter at Norridge-wock among his parishioners, and at the beginning of March 1652 he departed for Quebec. He was fatigued with his labors and the hard winter he had passed, but could not have imagined that the trip back to Canada would be even more harrowing than when he had come. The party started out on snow-shoes; their food ran out; some of the hardy Indians died from exhaustion and all feared they would die of hunger and cold. Finally they were forced to boil their moccasins and then the priest's gown, which was made of mooseskin, and on such fare they finally reached Quebec on April 8. These were typical of the hardships which the Jesuit fathers endured uncom-plainingly to bring the word of God to the natives of the New World.

For several centuries it seemed that the good works of the beloved Black Gown at Cushnoc had been forgotten, as all traces of the chapel and village have long since disappeared. However, three hundred and thirty-four years later, on May 31, 1980, a memorial was dedicated on the approximate site of the simple house of worship built by the Indians. This is a replica of the original chapel with three explanatory murals that give the history of the mission. The memorial was dedicated by the Abenaki Assembly, Knights of Columbus of Augusta, and blessed by Bishop Edward C. O'Leary. It stands for all to see on the lawn of the Knights of Columbus building, on Riverside Drive just north of Augusta.

This replica of Father Gabriel Druillettes' chapel stands on Riverside Drive just north of Augusta. Within are several interpretive panels, including a portrait of the Jesuit missionary to the Abenakis. Photographs by Linda J. Griffiths.

The Bigot Brothers

Thirty years passed before the Norridgewock Indians were to have spiritual leaders again, in the persons of Vincent and Jacques Bigot. Like Druillettes before them, and Father Rasle who was to come after them, the two brothers had left affluent homes in France to devote their lives to Christianizing the Indians of Canada and Maine. They, like the others, accepted the primitive life of the Abenakis as their own, living in birchbark wigwams or rude wooden huts, sleeping on bearskins, and (one of the hardest sacrifices for the cultivated Frenchmen) eating the same foods. They often traveled with their Indian guides, sleeping on the ground under their canoes and eating whatever lake and forest could provide.

In the 1670s and 80s, after the first Indian war, so many Abenaki refugees fled to the Sillery mission on the St. Lawrence that it became overcrowded, and a new refuge was built on the opposite side of the river and named the Mission of St. Francis de Sales. The brothers Bigot were given charge of the new parish of around 500 souls. These Indians became known as St. Francis Indians and the village eventually became a Canadian reservation. It is clear, however, that the inhabitants were originally Abenakis from the Kennebec valley in Maine.

Vincent and Jacques Bigot were not content to sit in their mission all the time, and made many trips to the Kennebec and Penobscot rivers to minister to the natives. Jacques spent most of his time on the Penobscot, where he started a church around 1687 with the encouragement of the Baron Castine, who had married an Indian woman and was accepted as a leader by the Penobscot tribe. Vincent took a more active interest in the Norridgewocks, visiting them often, building a chapel, and reviving the mission after thirty years of inactivity.

Father Vincent Bigot's name surfaces in the history of the village in his rescue of the little white captive, Esther Wheelwright, from the Indians at Norridgewock. Esther had been captured in Wells in 1703 at the age of seven, and taken by her captor to the Norridgewock village, where she lived in the wigwam of her master with his squaw and other children. The priest saw the pale, ragged, listless child when he visited the mission to preach, teach the catechism, and take care of the sick. He started his campaign to rescue her by talking to her Indian captor. "The English rose is drooping, the forest life is too hard for her," he said. Her master replied: "The little white flower must not be plucked up. Let her grow up among the pine trees, to deck by and by the wigwam of some young brave."

Time went by slowly for Esther, but she proved an apt pupil under the tutelage of the kind Father Bigot, and soon she could say her credo and her catechism in both French and Abenaki. She seems to have forgotten English by this time. Father Bigot persevered in his attempts to free her from her captor, and finally, in the autumn of 1708, had the great happiness of transporting the now twelve-year-old girl to Canada, where he placed her in the tender care of Governor and Madame de Vaudreuil. This was not the end of the story for the remarkable Esther Wheelwright; but her story must wait until another chapter.

When the Comte de Frontenac sailed to Canada in the summer of 1689, there was on board his ship another young Jesuit priest. Father Sebastian Rasle, born January 28, 1657 in the province of Franche-Comté in eastern France, was destined to become famous as the last religious leader of the Norridge-wock Indians on the Kennebec, and also as a student of their language and author of the first French-Abenaki dictionary. The job, once started, would be lifelong, and would in the end take his life in a violent fashion.

Father Rasle came of a good family and was well educated. His first post after leaving college was as an instructor of Greek at Nîmes in southern France. It was there that he heard of the need for more missionaries for the far-flung Indian parishes under the jurisdiction of St. François du Lac in Canada. He decided to take up the challenge of the primitive life of the New World.

Rasle's first task when he arrived in Canada was to pass what he called an apprenticeship of two years in the parish of St. Francis. First he studied the Abenaki language by passing interminable hours with the Indians in their smoky wigwams. (The Indians loved to smoke, and did so almost continuously, even the women and children being addicted to the habit.) When he could converse with them he started to learn their ways of life and how to handle himself in the wilderness. He became expert at handling their birchbark canoes on the turbulent waters of the St. Lawrence. The first time he saw snowshoes, he wondered if he could ever master the art of walking in such awkward-looking footgear; but he did, surprising his Indian tutors with his agility and speed.

Rasle's first post was as missionary to an Indian village in far-off Illinois. His trip there was long and dangerous in the extreme. The party ran out of food because of scarce game and were reduced to eating lichens from the rocks to sustain them. This was called rock tripe, which had very little nourishment. The most that could be said of it was that it was slightly better than nothing. However, his life work was not to be among the Illinois tribes. He was recalled to Quebec after two years to prepare himself for his next job.

The assignment for which Father Rasle was destined was to the Norridgewock village on the Kennebec River. It was during the throes of King William's War in 1695 that Father Rasle set out on the voyage. He traveled down the ancient Indian trail of the Chaudiere, Dead River and Kennebec as far as the mouth of the Sandy River. On the point of land opposite, he found the village of the Norridgewocks, usually spelled *Nanrantsouak* by the French.

The Indian village to which Father Rasle came was located about a mile down river from the falls then called Norridgewock Falls, and eighty miles from the sea, at the southern tip of the present town of Madison. The village itself was beautifully situated on a broad flat intervale of 250 acres, with cornfields ascending the rolling hills that rose from the meadows of the intervale. A large bend in the river at this point caused it to flow on three sides of the village. Today the woods have taken over on the river bank and grown up the slopes of the surrounding hills, but the site is marked by a clearing on which stands a monument to Father Rasle, as well as the cemetery of the Sebastian Rasle Catholic Church of Madison. Both are surrounded by a handsome grove of pine trees.

Father Rasle set to work at once. First he had a chapel built and furnished it with the objects needed for the celebration of Mass. He was an artist and painted pictures of religious subjects to decorate the house of worship. There was also a small bell of which the natives were very fond; they vied with each other to ring it to see if it would sing as sweetly in their hands as in the Father's.

A poem of John Greenleaf Whittier, "Mogg Megone," includes a romantic description of Nanrantsouak after Father Rasle had lived there a few years:

On the brow of a hill, which slopes to meet
The flowing river, and bathe its feet;
The bare-washed rock, and the drooping grass,
And the creeping vine, as the waters pass,
A rude and unshapely chapel stands,
Built up in that wild by unskilled hands,
Yet the traveller knows it a place of prayer,
For the holy sign of the cross is there:
And should he chance at that place to be,
    Of a Sabbath morn, or some hallowed day,
When prayers are made and masses are said,
Some for the living and some for the dead,

Well might that traveller start to see
   The tall dark forms, that take their way
From the birch canoe, on the river shore,
And the forest paths, to that chapel door;
And marvel to mark the naked knees
   And the dusky foreheads bending there,
While, in coarse white vesture, over these
   In blessing or in prayer,
Stretching abroad his thin, pale hands,
Like a shrouded ghost, the Jesuit stands.

Rasle himself took pen in hand to describe his experiences among the Indians after many years at Nanrantsouak. His point of view is, of course, that of the French side during the course of the turbulent war against the English. However, in view of charges that he hated the English and urged his parishioners to attack the settlements on the lower Kennebec, it is only fitting that we allow him the privilege of stating his case.

Rasle's description of the everyday life of the Norridgewocks is contained in two letters, written to his brother and his nephew in France. They have been preserved, along with writings of other Jesuit priests, by the officials of the Society of Jesus, who gathered all the reports and letters written from America with the purpose of keeping them safe for future generations. The finest editors were employed with the assistance of the king of France, and the remarkable literary monument, consisting of twenty-six volumes by 1781, was published. Father Rasle's writings make up an important part of the section "Memoires of America" which comprises volumes 6 through 9.

The preface reads: "Compelled in some sort to

become savages with these barbarians in order to make of them first men and then Christians, they learned their language, lived as they lived, ran the woods with them, and in fine lent themselves to all that was not evil, that they might bring them to hear, to love, to esteem and to practice that which is good." The translation used here was done by Mr. E. C. Cummings in a paper given to the Maine Historical Society on December 9, 1892. His lecture was entitled "The Mission of Father Rasles as Depicted by Himself."

Excerpts from the letters of Rasle follow:

At Nanrantsouak, this 15 October, 1722

Honored Sir, My Dear Nephew: — The peace of our Lord: —

For more than thirty years that I have lived in the midst of forests and with savages, I have been so much occupied with instructing them, and forming them to Christian virtues, that I have scarcely had the leisure for writing frequent letters, even to persons who are the most dear to me. I cannot, however, refuse you the little detail of my occupations which you ask of me. I owe this as a recognition of the friendship which makes you interest yourself so much in what concerns me.

I am in a district of that vast extent of country which lies between Acadia and New England. Two other missionaries are occupied, like myself, with the savage Abenakis, but we are far apart from one another. The savage Abenakis, besides the two villages which they have in the midst of the French colony, have three other considerable villages situated upon the bank of a river. The three rivers flow into the sea to the south of Canada between New England and Acadia.

The village where I dwell is called Nanrantsouak; it is situated upon the bank of a river which reaches the sea thirty leagues from thence. I have built here a church which is suitable and very well appointed *(tresornée)*. I have held it a duty to spare nothing, either for its decoration, or for the beauty of the ornaments which serve in our holy ceremonies. Altar-cloths, chasubles, copes, consecrated vessels — all in it is proper, and would be so esteemed in our churches of Europe. I have made myself a little clergy of about forty young savages, who assist at divine service in serge and in surplice. They have their several functions as well for the service of the holy sacrifice of the Mass, as for the chanting of the divine office for the benediction of the holy sacrament, and for the processions which are made with a great concourse of savages, who often come from afar to find themselves there. You would be edified with the fine order they observe, and with the piety they evince.

Two chapels have been built about three hundred paces from the village, one dedicated to the most holy Virgin, and where her statue is seen in relief, is high up the river; the other, dedicated to the guardian angel, is low down the same river. As they are both the one and the other on the path which leads either into the woods or into the fields, the savages never pass that way but they make their prayer. There is a holy emulation among the women of the village as to who shall best adorn the chapel of which they have the care, whenever the procession is to move thither. All that they have of jewelry or of pieces of silk or of India stuff *(d'indienne),* and of other things of this nature, is employed for adornment. Our abundant light contributes not a little to the decoration of the church and the chapels. I have no occasion to be sparing of wax, for the country here supplies me with it in abundance. The isles of the sea are bordered with wild laurels, which in autumn bear berries nearly resembling those of the juniper. The boilers are filled with them and they are boiled with water. As the water boils the green wax rises to the surface and remains above the water. From three bushels *(un minot)* of this berry is produced about four pounds of wax; it is quite pure and beautiful, but not soft or plastic. After many trials I have found that by mixing with it an equal quantity of tallow — beef, mutton or elk — beautiful candles can be made, firm and excellent for use. With twenty-four pounds of wax and as much tallow, two hundred candles can be made of the length of more than a foot. An infinity of these laurels is found on the shores of the sea. A single person could easily collect twelve bushels of the berry in a day. This berry hangs in clusters from the branches of the tree. I have sent a branch to Quebec with a cake of the wax; it was found excellent.

All my neophytes are present without fail twice every day at

Sebastian Rasle

the church: — in the early morning to hear Mass and at evening to assist at the prayer which I make at the going down of the sun. As it is needful to control *(fixer)* the imagination of the savages, too easily distracted, I have composed some prayers of a nature to make the august sacrifice of our altars enter into their minds; they chant them or else they repeat them in an audible voice during the Mass. Besides the preaching which I make for them Sundays and feast days, I pass few working days without making them a short exhortation for the purpose of inspiring a horror of the vices to which their tendency is strongest, or for strengthening them in the practice of some virtue.

After Mass I teach the catechism to the children and young people. A great number of aged person are present at this service and answer with docility the questions put to them. The rest of the morning to midday is set apart for hearing all who have anything to say to me. 'Tis then they come in crowds to impart to me their pains and their anxieties, or to communicate to me the matters of complaint they have respecting their associates, or to consult me touching their marriages or other personal affairs. I have to instruct some, to console others, to re-establish peace in families at variance, to calm troubled consciences, and to correct some others with reproofs tempered with sweetness and charity.

In the afternoon I visit the sick, and go through the cabins of those who need some special instruction. If they hold a council, a thing which often happens among savages, they send one of the chief men of the assembly to ask my assistance as to the result of their deliberations. I repair at once to the place where the council is held; if I judge that they take a wise part, I approve it; if, on the contrary, I find something to say to their decision, I unfold to them my opinion, which I support by solid reasons, and they conform themselves to it. My advice always shapes their resolutions.

It only remains to refer to the feasts to which I am called. Those invited bring each one a plate of wood or bark; I give the benediction upon the meats; in each plate is placed the morsel prepared. The distribution having been made I say the grace *(les graces)*, and each retires, for such is the order of their feasts.

In the midst of these incessant occupations you would hardly know how to believe with what rapidity the days glide away. At times I have hardly the leisure to say my prayers and to take a little rest during the night; for discretion is not the virtue of savages. For some years, however, I have made it a rule not to talk with anyone from evening prayer till after the next morning Mass, and I have forbidden them to interrupt me during that time, at any rate except for some reason of importance, as for example to assist one dying, or for some other matter that cannot be put off; so that I have in this time leisure for prayer and for rest after the fatigues of the day.

When the savages go to the sea to pass some months in the pursuit of geese, bustards and other birds, which they find in abundance, they build on an island a church which they cover with bark, and near which they set up a little cabin for my residence. I am careful to take along a portion of the ornaments, and divine service is attended to with the same decency and the same concourse of people as at the village.

You see, my dear nephew, what are my occupations. As to what concerns me personally I assure you that I neither see, nor hear, nor speak, anything but savage. My food is simple and light. I have never been able to acquire the taste for the meat and the smoked fish of the savages; my nourishment is nothing but Indian corn, which is pounded and of which I make every day a kind of porridge that I cook with water. The only relish *(adoncissement)* that I add to it is in mingling a little sugar to correct the insipidity of it. There is no lack of sugar in these forests. In springtime the maples hold a liquor sufficiently like that which the sugarcane *(cannes des îles)* contains. The women busy themselves with gathering this in vessels of bark, as it is distilled from the trees; they boil it and obtain from it a good enough sugar. The first produced is always the best.

The whole Abenaki nation is Christian and full of zeal for the maintenance of its religion. This attachment to the Catholic faith has hitherto caused the nations to prefer our alliance to the advantages they might realize from the English, their neighbors. These advantages are of great interest to our savages; the facility they have of treating with the English, from whom they are at a distance of only one or two days' journey, the convenience of the way, the great cheapness they find in the purchase of the merchandise they require — nothing is more capable of attracting them. On the other hand, in going to Quebec more than fifteen days are required for reaching the place; they must fortify themselves with subsistence for the journey; they have various rivers to cross and frequent carries to make. They are sensible of these inconveniences, and they are by no means indifferent to their own interests. But their faith is infinitely more dear; and they conceive that if they should be detached from our alliance they would find themselves soon without a missionary, without sacraments, without sacrifice, almost without any exercise of religion and in evident danger of being plunged again in their original unbelief. Here is the bond which unites them with the French. It is in vain that they are pressed to break it, be it by the snares that are laid for their simplicity, or by acts of violent aggression, which cannot fail to irritate a community intensely jealous of its rights and of its liberty. These beginnings of misunderstanding cease not to alarm me and to make me fear the dispersion of the flock which Providence has confided to my care for so many years, and for whose sake I would willing sacrifice that which remains to me of life. Here are the different artifices to which they have recourse for detaching them from our alliance.

The governor of New England sent, some years since, to the region down river, the cleverest of the ministers of Boston, with the object of establishing a school and teaching the children of the savages and supporting them at the government's expense. As the allowance of the minister would increase in proportion to the number of his scholars, he omitted nothing for the purpose of attracting them to himself. He went to seek them, he caressed them, he made them little presents, he pressed them to come and see him, in fine he tasked himself with many unavailing efforts during two months without being able to gain a single child. The disregard with which they treated his caresses and his invitations did not discourage him. He addressed himself to the savages themselves. He put various questions touching their belief; and from the responses which were made to him took occasion to turn to ridicule the sacraments, purgatory, invocation of saints, beads, crosses, images, the lights of our churches, and all the practices of piety so sacredly observed in the Catholic religion.

I deemed it my duty to set myself against these first sowings of seduction. I wrote a candid letter to the minister, in which I pointed out to him that my Christians had knowledge enough to believe the truths which the Catholic church teaches, but that they had not the skill to dispute about them; that since they were not clever enough to resolve the difficulties which he proposed, it was apparently his design that they should communicate them to me; that I seized with pleasure the occasion he offered me of conferring with him, either by word of mouth or by letters; that I therefore sent him a memorandum *(memoire)*, and begged him to read it with serious attention. In this memorandum of about a hundred pages I proved by Scripture, by tradition and by theological argument, the truths which he had attacked by sufficiently dull jestings. I added in finishing my letter that, if he was not satisfied with my proofs, I looked to him for a refutation precise and based upon theologic reasons, not upon vague argumentations that prove nothing, still less upon injurious reflections which are not in character for our profession, and do not comport with the importance of the matters with which it is occupied.

Two days after having received my letter he departed on his return to Boston, and he sent me a short reply which I was obliged to read several times in order to comprehend the sense, so obscure was the style, and the Latinity so extraordinary. I gathered, nevertheless, by dreaming over it, that he complained that I attacked him without reason; that zeal for the salvation of souls had moved him to show the way to heaven to the savages; that for the rest my proofs were ridiculous and childish. Having dispatched to him at Boston a second letter, wherein I took up the faults of his own, he replied at the end of two years, without entering at all upon the matter in question, that I had a surly and captious spirit, such as was the mark of a temperament prone to anger. Thus ended our dispute, which sent away the minister and rendered abortive the design he had formed of seducing my neophytes.

This first trial having met with so little success, recourse was had to another artifice. An Englishman asked permission of the savages to establish on the river a kind of warehouse for the purpose of making trade with them, and he promised to sell them his merchandise much cheaper than they could purchase it even in Boston. The savages who were to find this to their advantage, and who would spare themselves the trouble of a journey to Boston, consented willingly. A little while after, another Englishman asked for the same permission, offering terms yet more advantageous than the first. To him equally the permission was accorded. This easy assent of the savages emboldened the English to establish themselves along the river without asking their consent. They built houses and raised forts, three of which are of stone.

This proximity of the English was agreeable enough to the savages so long as they were unaware of the net that was laid for them, and attended only to the convenience they enjoyed in finding whatever they might want with their new neighbors. But at length seeing themselves little by little, as it were, surrounded by the habitations of the English, they began to open their eyes and to be seized with distrust. They demanded of the English by what right they established themselves, and even constructed forts on their lands. The reply that was made them, namely that the king of France had ceded their country to the king of England, threw them into the greatest alarm; for there is no savage nation that endures otherwise than impatiently that anyone should regard it as in subjection to any power whatever. It will call itself the ally of a power but nothing more. Therefore the savages immediately sent a deputation to M. the Marquis of Vaudreuil, governor-general of New France, to assure themselves if it were true that the king had actually so disposed of a country of which he was not the master. It was not difficult to calm their anxieties; one had only to explain the articles of the treaty of Utrecht that concerned the savages, and they appeared content.

About this time a score of savages entered one of the English habitations, either for trade or for rest. They had been there but a little while when of a sudden they saw the house surrounded by a band of nearly two hundred armed men. "We are dead men," cried one of them, "let us sell our lives dear." They were already preparing to hurl themselves upon this troop, when the English, apprised of their resolution, and aware from other experiences of what the savage is capable in the first excess of fury, tried to pacify them by assuring them that they had no evil design, and had come simply to invite some of them to visit Boston for the purpose of there conferring with the governor on the means of maintaining the peace and good understanding which ought to prevail between the two nations. The savages, somewhat too easily persuaded, deputed four of their compatriots to repair to Boston; but when they arrived the conference with which they had been deluded led to the holding of them as prisoners.

You will be surprised, no doubt, that such a mere handful of savages should think of standing up against a force so numerous as was that of the English. But our savages do numberless acts of much greater hardihood. I will mention only one which will enable you to judge of others.

During the late wars a party of thirty savages was returning from a military expedition against the English. As the savages, and especially the Abenakis, do not know what it is to secure themselves against surprises, they fall asleep as soon as they lie down, without thinking even of posting a sentinel for the night. A party of six hundred English, commanded by a colonel, pursued them, even to their encampment, and finding them sound asleep he surrounded them by his men, assuring himself that not one of them should escape him. One of the savages having waked and discovered the English troops, at once gave the alarm to his comrades, crying out according to their wont, "We are dead men, let us sell our lives dearly." Their resolution was instantly taken. They at once formed six platoons of five men each; then, hatchet in one hand and knife in the other, they rushed upon the English with such furious impetuosity, that after having killed sixty men, the colonel in the number, they put the rest to flight.

The Abenakis no sooner learned how their compatriots had been treated in Boston, than they bitterly complained that the law of nations should be so violated in the midst of the peace which was enjoyed. The English answered that they held the prisoners only as hostages for the wrong that had been done them in the killing of some cattle of theirs, and that as soon as this loss should be repaired, which amounted to two hundred francs in beaver fur, the prisoners should be released. Although the Abenakis did not concede the justice of this claim for indemnity, they did not fail to pay it, unwilling to incur the reproach of having abandoned their brothers for so small a consideration. Still, notwithstanding the payment of the contested debt, the restoration of their liberty was refused to the prisoners.

The governor of Boston, apprehensive that this refusal might force the savages to have recourse to a bold stroke, proposed to treat this affair amicably in a conference. The day and place for holding it were arranged. The savages presented themselves with Father Rasle, their missionary. Father de la Chasse, superior-general of these missions, who at that time was making his visit, was present also. But Monsieur, the governor, did not appear. The savages augured ill of his absence. They adopted the plan of giving him to understand their sentiments by a letter written in Savage, in English, and in Latin, and Father de la Chasse, who is master of these three languages, was charged with writing it. It might seem of no use to employ any other than the English language, but the Father was pleased that the savages on their part should make sure that the letter contained nothing but what they had dictated, and that on the other hand the English should be placed beyond the possibility of doubting the faithfulness of the English translation. The purport of this letter was: 1. That the savages could not understand why their compatriots were kept in their confinement after the promise had been given of setting them at liberty as soon as the two hundred francs in beaver fur should be paid. 2. That they were not less surprised to see that their country was taken possession of without their consent. 3. That the English would have to depart from them as soon as possible and to set the prisoners at liberty; that they should expect their answer in two months, and that if after that time satisfaction should be denied them they would know how to do justice to themselves.

It was in the month of July of the year 1711, that this letter was taken to Boston by certain Englishmen who had been present in the conference. As the two months passed without the coming of any response from Boston, and as moreover the English ceased to sell to the Abenakis powder, lead and means of subsistence, as they had done previously to this dispute, our savages were disposed to resort to reprisals. It required all the influence which Monsieur the Marquis of Vaudreuil could exert upon their minds to induce them to suspend for a little while yet their entrance upon active measures of hostility.

But their patience was pressed to the last extremity by two acts of hostility which the English committed toward the end of December, 1721, and at the beginning of the year 1722. The first was the carrying off of Monsieur de Saint Castine. This officer is

Plate I: Mount Kineo, seen from Rockwood across Moosehead Lake. It rises almost eight hundred feet from the lake's surface.

Plate II: Misery Pond in Misery township, near Moosehead Lake.

Plate III: Dead River, shown here, is actually the west branch of the Kennebec River.

Plate IV: Wyman Lake, thirteen miles long, was formed by a hydroelectric dam built on the Kennebec River at Moscow.

(Plates I-IV are photographs taken by the author.)

a lieutenant of our troops. His mother was an Abenaki, and he has always lived with our savages, whose esteem and confidence he has merited to such a degree that they have chosen him for their commanding general. In this character he could not avoid taking part in the conference of which I have just spoken, where he exerted himself to adjust the claims of the Abenakis, his brethren. The English made of this a crime. They sent a small vessel toward the place of his residence. The captain took care to conceal his force with the exception of two or three men whom he left upon the deck. He sent an invitation to Monsieur de Saint Castine, to whom he was known, to come on board his vessel to partake of refreshments. Monsieur de Saint Castine, who had no reason for entertaining suspicions, repaired thither alone, and without following. But hardly had he appeared when they set sail and brought him to Boston. There he was kept on the prisoner's stool and interrogated as a criminal. He was asked among other things for what reason and in what capacity he had been present at the conference which was held with the savages; what signified the uniform *(l'habit d'ordonnance)* in which he was dressed, and if he had not been deputed to this assembly by the governor of Canada. Monsieur de Saint Castine replied that by his mother he was Abenaki; that he passed his life among the savages; that his compatriots having established him as chief of their nation, he was obliged to enter into their assemblies for the purpose of there upholding their interests; that in this capacity alone he had been present at the last conference; that for the rest the dress which he wore was not a uniform as they imagined; that indeed it was suitable and well enough trimmed *(garni)*, but that it was not above his condition, independently even of the honor which he had of being an officer of our troops.

Monsieur our governor, having learned the detention of Monsieur de Saint Castine, wrote immediately to the governor of Boston to make complaint on his behalf. He received no reply to his letter. But about the time the English governor had reason to expect a second remonstrance, he restored his liberty to the prisoner, after having kept him shut up for five months.

The enterprise of the English against myself was the second act of hostility which succeeded in irritating to excess the Abenaki nation. A missionary can hardly fail of being an object of hatred to these gentlemen. The love of religion which he seeks

Sebastian Rasle

by all means to plant in the heart of the savages, strongly binds these neophytes to our alliance, and withdraws them from that of the English. Also they regard me as an invincible obstacle to the design which they have of spreading themselves over the lands of the Abenakis, and of appropriating little by little this territory which is between New England and Acadia. They have often tried to carry me away from my flock, and more than once a price has been set upon my head. It was toward the end of January of the year 1722 that they made a new attempt, which had no other success than to manifest their ill will in regard to me.

I had remained alone in the village with a small number of old and infirm people, while the rest of the savages were at the chase. This time appeared favorable for surprising me, and with this purpose they sent a detachment of two hundred men. Two young Abenakis who were hunting along the seashore learned that the English had entered the river. Immediately they turned their steps in that direction to observe their march. Having discovered them at ten leagues from the village, they came on before, traversing the land, to give me warning, and to hasten the retirement of the old men, the women and children. I had only time to swallow the consecrated wafers *(consumer les hosties)*, and to pack in a little box the sacred vessels, and to make my escape to the woods. The English reached the village at evening, and not having found me, they came the next day to seek me, even to the place of our retreat. They came within gunshot when we discovered them. All that I could do was to bury myself with precipitation in the forest. But as I had not time to take my snowshoes, and as moreover there remained to me much weakness from a fall, in which some years before I had the thigh and the leg broken, it was not possible for me to fly very far. The only resource that remained to me was to hide myself behind a tree. They at once ran through the various footpaths made by the savages when they went in search of wood, and they came within eight paces of the tree which covered me, and where naturally they ought to have perceived me, for the trees were despoiled of their leaves; nevertheless, as if they had been held back by an invisible hand, they all at once retired upon their steps, and took again the route to the village.

Thus by a special protection of God I escaped their hands.

106

They pillaged my church and my little house. By that means they almost forced me to die of hunger in the woods. It is true that when my adventure was known in Quebec provisions were immediately sent me. But they could not arrive otherwise than late, and in the meantime I saw myself deprived of all succors and in an extremity of want.

These reiterated insults drove our savages to the conclusion that they had no more answer to look for, and that it was time to repel violence and to make open force succeed to pacific negotiations. On their return from the chase and after having put their seed into the ground they took the resolution to destroy the English habitations recently constructed and to remove to a distance from their abodes those restless and formidable neighbors, who little by little were gaining a foothold upon their lands and were planning to reduce them to slavery. They sent a deputation into different villages of the savages to get them interested in their cause and to engage them to lend a hand under the necessity that was upon them of making a just defense. The deputation had its success. The war song was chanted among the Hurons of Lorette and in all the villages of the Abenaki nation. Nanrantsouak was the place appointed for the assembling of the warriors in order that they might agree together upon the plan of operations.

In the meantime the Nanrantsouakians moved down the river; arrived at its mouth they took away three or four little buildings of the English. Then coming up the same river, they pillaged and burnt the new houses which the English had built. They nevertheless abstained from all violence toward the inhabitants, they even allowed them to depart to their homes with the exception of five whom they kept as hostages till their compatriots detained in the prisons of Boston should be restored to them. This moderation of the savages did not have the effect which they had hoped. On the contrary an English party, having found sixteen Abenakis asleep on an island, opened a general fire *(décharge)* upon them by which five of them were killed and three wounded.

Thus we have a new signal of the war which is likely to flame forth between the English and the savages. The latter look for no support from the French, by reason of the peace which reigns between the two nations; but they have a resource in all the other savage nations, who will not fail to enter into their quarrel and to take up their defense.

My converts, touched by the peril to which I found myself exposed in their village, often pressed me to retire for a while to Quebec. But what will become of the flock, if it is deserted by its shepherd? There is nothing but death which can separate me from it. In vain they represent to me that in the event of my falling into the hands of their enemies the least that can happen to me is to languish the rest of my days in a hard prison. I shut their mouths with the words of the apostles which the divine grace has deeply graven upon my heart. Have no anxiety, I say to them, as regards me. I fear not the threats of those who hate me without my having deserved their hatred, and I esteem not my life longer dear to myself, provided I finish my course and the ministry of the word which has been committed to me by the Lord Jesus. Pray Him, my dear nephew, to strengthen in me this sentiment which comes only from His mercy, that I may be able to live and die without ceasing to labor for those lost and neglected souls which are the purchase of His blood, and which He has deigned to commit to my care.

I am, etc.

A second letter, to Rasle's brother, followed in the next year:

At Nanrantsouak, the 12th October, 1723.

Honored Sir, and Very Dear Brother: —
The peace of our Lord: —

I cannot longer refuse to comply with the affectionate entreaties which you make in all your letters, that I would inform you somewhat in detail of my occupations and of the character of the savage peoples, in the midst of whom Providence has placed me for so many years. I do this the more readily that in yielding to the desires so urgently expressed on your part I shall be satisfying your tenderness more than your curiosity.

It was the twenty-third of July, 1689, that I embarked at La Rochelle, and after a voyage of three months sufficiently fortunate, I arrived at Quebec the thirteenth of October, of the same year. I applied myself at first to learning the language of the savages. This language is very difficult; for it is not enough to study the terms and their signification, and to secure a supply of

Chapel bell and strong box belonging to Father Sebastian Rasle at the Norridgewock village at Old Point, Madison, Maine. Both objects are now in the collection of the Maine Historical Society, Portland, Maine. Photographs reproduced by permission of the Maine Historical Society.

Sebastian Rasle

words and phrases; it is necessary also to know the turn and arrangement of words and phrases which the savages employ, and this one can catch only by constant intercourse and communication of thought with these people. I went, therefore, to dwell in a village of the Abenaki nation, situate in a forest which is only three leagues from Quebec. This village was inhabited by two hundred savages, nearly all Christians. Their cabins were ranged almost like mansions in towns. An inclosure of stakes, high and compact, formed a kind of wall, which gave them protection from the incursions of their enemies.

Their cabins are very readily set up; they plant some poles which are joined at the top, and cover them with great pieces of bark. The fire is made in the center of the cabin, and they spread rush mats all around, upon which they sit during the day, and take their rest during the night.

The clothing of the men consists of a coat of skin or else of a piece of red or blue cloth. That of the women is a covering which reaches from the neck to the knees, and which they dispose quite neatly. They wear another covering upon the head, which comes down to the feet, and which serves them as a mantle. Their stockings only reach from the knee to the ankle. Moccasins made of elk hide, and lined with fur or woolen, take the place of shoes. This footgear is absolutely necessary for the proper adjustment of snowshoes, by means of which they walk easily over the snow. These snowshoes, made of lozenge shape, are sometimes more than two feet long and a foot and a half wide. It did not seem to me that I could ever walk with such machines. When, however, I made the attempt, I found myself all at once so skillful, that the savages could not believe that I was using them for the first time. The invention of the snowshoe is one of great utility to the savages, not only for running over the snow, with which the earth is covered a great part of the year, but especially for engaging in the chase of beasts, and above all of the elk. These animals, larger than the largest oxen of France, go only with difficulty over the snow; so that it is not difficult for the savages to overtake them, and they often kill them with a simple knife at the end of a staff. They get nourishment from their flesh, and having well dressed the skin, in which they are clever, they find a market for it with the French and English, who give them in exchange coats, blankets, kettles, guns,

110

hatchets and knives.

To give you an idea of a savage, picture to yourself a tall man, active, of tawny complexion, without beard, with black hair and teeth whiter than ivory. If you will see him in full dress, you will find as the sum total of his finery what is called wampum *(rassade)*. It is a kind of shell or stone, that is fashioned in the form of little kernels, some black and others white, which they string and combine so as to represent various figures very regular, which have a decorative effect. It is with this beadwork that the savages bind and braid their hair over the ears and at the back of the head; they make of it pendants for the ears, collars, garters, girdles of the width of five or six inches; and with this kind of ornaments they hold themselves in much higher esteem than does a European with all his gold and jewels.

The occupation of the men is the chase and war; that of the women is to stay in the village and there with bark to make baskets, workbags, boxes, porringers, plates, etc. They sew the bark with roots and make various articles of furniture very neatly wrought. The canoes in like manner are made of a single piece of bark, but the largest of them can hardly hold more than six or seven persons. It is with these canoes made of a bark, which has scarcely more than the thickness of a crown-piece *(ecu)*, that they pass arms of the sea, and navigate the most dangerous rivers and lakes of four or five hundred leagues in circuit. I have made many voyages in this way without having run any risk. Only it once happened that in crossing the river St. Lawrence I found myself suddenly enveloped in blocks of ice of an enormous size, and the canoe was crushed. At once the two savages who were conducting me cried out, "We are dead men, it is all over with us, we must perish." Nevertheless making an effort they leaped upon one of the floating masses of ice. I did the same, and after drawing out the canoe we brought it to the extreme edge of the ice. There we had to betake ourselves again to the canoe to reach another mass of ice, and so from one ice pack to another we reached at last the river bank with no other damage than that of being well drenched and benumbed with cold.

The savages have a peculiar tenderness for their infants. They place them on a little piece of board covered with a cloth and with a little bearskin, in which they wrap them, and this is their

111

Sebastian Rasle

cradle. The mothers carry them on their backs in a way that is comfortable for the infants and for themselves.

Hardly do the boys begin to walk ere they try their hand in the use of the bow. They become so adroit at the age of from ten to twelve years, as seldom to miss killing the bird at which they shoot. I have been surprised at this, and should have found it hard to believe if I had not been a witness of it.

What shocked me most when I began to live with the savages was to see myself obliged to take my meals with them; nothing more disgusting. After having filled their boiler with meat, they let it boil at most three-quarters of an hour, after which they take it from the fire; they serve it in porringers of bark and distribute it to all who are in their cabin. Each one bites into the meat as one would into a morsel of bread. This spectacle did not give me much appetite, and they very soon observed my repugnance. "Why do you not eat?" said they. I replied that I was not in the habit of eating meat in this way without adding to it a little bread. "You must conquer yourself," they rejoined; "is that so difficult for a patriarch who knows how to pray perfectly? We overcame ourselves certainly — we on our part — in order to believe what we do not see." No more place for deliberation after this. It is necessary to conform oneself to their manners and their usages, in order to deserve their confidence and gain them to Jesus Christ.

Their meals are not regulated as in Europe. They live from hand to mouth. So long as they have wherewith to make good cheer, they profit by it without troubling themselves as to whether they shall have something to live upon in the days to come. They are passionately fond of tobacco; men, women, girls, all smoke almost continually. To give them a morsel of tobacco is to do them a greater pleasure than to give them their weight in gold.

Early in June, and when the snow is nearly all melted they plant their *skamgnar,* which is what we call corn of Turkey or corn of India. Their way of planting it is to make with the fingers or with a little stick different holes in the ground, and to throw into each eight or nine kernels, which they cover with the same earth that they have dug out in making the hole. Their harvest is reached at the end of August.

It is among this people which passes for the least gross of all

112

our savages that I served my missionary apprenticeship. My principal occupation was the study of their language. It is very difficult to learn, especially when one has no other masters than the savages. They have several vocal elements which they utter only from the throat without making any movement of the lips; *ou*, for example, is of this number, and therefore in writing we mark it by the figure 8 in order to distinguish it from other elements. I passed a part of every day in their cabins to hear them talk. I had to bring an extreme attention to combine what they were saying and to conjecture the meaning of it.

Sometimes I hit the mark, but oftener I was in error, because not being fashioned to the use of their guttural letters, I uttered half the words, and so afforded them occasion to laugh.

At last, however, after five months of continual application, I came to understand all their terms; but that did not suffice for expressing myself according to their taste. I had still a long way to make to catch the turn and genius of the language, which is totally different from the genius and the turn of our languages in Europe. To shorten the time, and put myself sooner in a condition to exercise my functions, I made choice of some savages who had the most wit and who spoke the best. I repeated to them rudely certain articles of the catechism, and they rendered me in all the delicacy of their language. I soon placed them upon paper also, and by this means I made for myself in no very long time a dictionary, and a catechism which contained the principles and the mysteries of religion.

It cannot be denied that the language of the savages has real beauties, and a certain something of energy not easily defined in the turn and manner in which they express themselves. I will give you an example. Were I to ask you why God had created you, you would answer me, that it is to know him, love him and serve him, and by this means merit eternal glory. Let me put the same question to a savage, and in the turn of his language he will answer me thus: The great Spirit has had thoughts of us; would that they might know me, that they might love me, that they might honor me, for then I would make them enter into my illustrious felicity. So if I were to say to you in their style that you would have much difficulty in learning the savage language, this is how I should have to express it: I think of you, my dear brother, that there will be a deal of trouble in learning the

113

Sebastian Rasle

savage language.

The language of the Hurons is the master speech of the savages; and when one possesses that, in less than three months he can make himself understood by any of the five nations of the Iroquois. It is the most majestic and at the same time the most difficult of all the savage languages. This difficulty arises not only from their guttural letters, but still more from the diversity of accents; for often two words composed of the same characters have significations totally different. Father Chaumont, who has dwelt fifty years among the Hurons, has composed a grammar of their language, which is very useful to those newly arrived at this mission. Nevertheless, a missionary is happy when, even with this aid, he can after ten years of constant labor express himself elegantly in this language.

Each savage nation has its peculiar language: thus the Abenakis, the Hurons, the Iroquois, the Algonquins, the Illinois, the Miamis, etc., have each their language. One has no book for learning these languages, and even if one had, it would be sufficiently useless. Usage is the only master that can instruct us. As I have labored in four different missions among savages, namely, among the Abenakis, the Algonquins, the Hurons, and the Illinois, and have been obliged to learn these different languages, I will give you a sample, that you may perceive the slight relation that exists between them. I have chosen a stanza of a hymn on the Holy Sacrament, which is commonly chanted during the Mass at the elevation of the Holy Host, and which begins with these words: *O Salutaris Hostia.* Here is the translation in verse of this stanza in the four languages of as many different nations.

IN THE ABENAKI LANGUAGE.

Kighist 8i-nuanur8inns
Spem kik papili go ii damek
Nemiani 8i k8idan ghabenk
Taha saii grihine.

IN THE ALGONQUIN LANGUAGE.

K8erais Jesus teg8senam
Nera 8eul ka Stisian
Ka rio vllighe miang
Vas mama vik umong.

Sebastian Rasle

IN THE HURON LANGUAGE.

Jes8s 8to etti xichie
8to etti skuaalichi-axe
I chierche axera8ensta
D'aotierti xeata-8ien.

IN THE ILLINOIS LANGUAGE.

Pekiziane manet 8e
Piaro nile hi Nanghi
Keninama 8i 8 Kangha
Mero 8inang 8siang hi.

Which means in English:

O saving Sacrifice, who art continually offered up, and who givest life, thou by whom man enters into Heaven, we are all assaulted, now strengthen us.

The village where I live is called *Nanrantsouak*, and is located in a region which is between Acadia and New England. This mission is about eighty leagues from *Pentagouet*, and a hundred leagues is reckoned as the distance from *Pentagouet* to Port Royal. The river of my mission is the largest of all those which water the lands of the savages. It should be marked upon the map under the name of *Kinibeki*, which is what has led some Frenchmen to give these savages the name of *Kanibals*. This river reaches the sea at *Sankderank*, which is but five or six leagues from *Pemquit*. After having ascended forty leagues from *Sankderank*, one arrives at my village, which is upon the height of a point of land. We are not at the distance of more than two days' journey at most from the habitations of the English. It requires more than fifteen days to reach Quebec, and the journey is very painful and very difficult. It would be natural that our savages should conduct their trade with the English, and there are no advantages that the English have not pressed upon them to attract and gain their friendship. But all these efforts have been fruitless, and nothing has availed to detach them from the alliance of the French. The sole bond which has so closely united them to us is their firm attachment to the Catholic faith. They are convinced that if they should give themselves over to the English, they would soon find themselves without a missionary, without sacrifice, with sacrament, and almost without any exercise of religion, and that little by little they would be plunged again into their original unbelief. This firmness of our savages has been put to all sorts of trial on the part of these formidable neighbors without their ever having been able to obtain any concession.

At the time that war was on the point of being kindled between the powers of Europe, the English governor recently arrived in Boston, asked of our savages an interview by the sea, on an island which he designated. They consented, and begged me to accompany them, that they might consult me respecting the crafty propositions which might be made, in order to make sure that their answers should involve nothing contrary either to religion or to the claims of the king's service. I accompanied them, and it was my intention simply to confine myself to their quarters, for the purpose of aiding them with my counsels, without appearing before the governor. As we were nearing the island, to the number of more than two hundred canoes, the English saluted us by a discharge of all the cannon of their vessels, and the savages replied to this salute by a corresponding discharge of all their guns. Then the governor appearing upon the island the savages landed there with precipitation, and thus I found myself where I did not wish to be, and where the governor did not wish that I should be. When he perceived me, he came several steps towards me, and after the ordinary compliments he returned to the midst of his people, and I to my savages.

"It is by order of our queen," he said to them, "that I come to see you. She desires that we live in peace. If any Englishman should be imprudent enough to do you wrong, do not think of avenging yourselves, but address your complaint immediately to me, and I will render you prompt justice. If it should happen that we should be at war with the French, remain neutral, and do not involve yourselves in our differences. The French are as strong as we are, so let us together settle our own quarrels. We will furnish you with all the articles you need; we will take your furs, and we will give you our merchandise at a moderate price." My presence interfered with his saying all that he intended, for it was not without design that he had brought a minister with him.

When he had ceased speaking, the savages retired to deliberate together upon the response they had to make. During that time the governor, taking me aside, said, "I entreat you, sir, not to move your Indians to make war upon us." I replied to him that my religion and my character of priest engaged me to give them only counsels of peace.

I was going on to speak still, when I saw myself all at once surrounded by a score of young warriors, who were afraid the governor was intending to have me carried away as a prisoner. Meantime the savages came forward and one of them replied to the governor as follows: "Great Chieftain, you tell us not to join ourselves to the Frenchman, supposing that you declare war against him. Know that the Frenchman is my brother; we have the same prayer, he and I, and we are in one cabin with two fires, he at one fire and I at the other. If I see you enter the cabin on the side of that fire where my brother, the Frenchman, is seated, I observe you from my mat where I am seated at the other fire. If in watching you I become aware that you carry a hatchet, I should have the thought, what does the Englishman mean to do with that hatchet? Then I rise upon my mat to consider what he will do. If he raises the hatchet to strike my brother, the Frenchman, I take mine, and I run to the Englishman to strike him. Is it possible that I could see my brother struck in my cabin, and remain quiet upon my mat? No, no, I love my brother too much not to defend him. So I say to you, Great Chieftain, do nothing to my brother, and I will do nothing to you; remain quiet on your mat, and I will remain at rest upon mine."

Thus ended this conference. A little while after, some of our savages arrived from Quebec, and announced that a French vessel had brought the news that war had broken out between France and England. Thereupon our savages, after having deliberated according to their custom, ordered the young men to kill the dogs for making the feast of war, and so finding out those who were willing to engage. The feast took place, they raised up the boiler, they danced, and there were found two hundred and fifty warriors. After the feast they set apart a day for coming to me and confessing. I exhorted them to be as much attached to their religion as they were in the village, to observe well the laws of war, not to practice any cruelty, not to kill any one except in the heat of the combat, to accord humane treatment to those who gave themselves up as prisoners, etc.

The way these people make war causes a handful of their warriors to be an object of more dread than would be a corps of two or three thousand European soldiers. After they are entered into the hostile country they divide themselves into different parties, one of thirty warriors, another of forty, etc. They say to some, "to you is given this hamlet to eat" (it is their expression) — to others, "to you is given this village," etc. Then the signal is given to strike all together, and at the same time in different regions. Our two hundred and fifty warriors distributed themselves over more than twenty leagues of country, where there were villages and hamlets and houses. On a given day they fell all together upon the enemy in the early morning; in a single day they made a clean sweep of English possessions, they killed more than two hundred, made a hundred and fifty prisoners, and on their side had only a few warriors wounded very slightly. They returned from this expedition to the village, having each two canoes loaded with the booty they had taken.

So long as the war lasted they carried desolation into all the lands pertaining to the English, they ravaged their villages, their forts, their farms, they drove away an immense number of cattle and made more than six hundred prisoners. Hence these gentlemen, persuaded with reason that in keeping my savages in their attachment to the Catholic faith I was drawing closer and closer the bonds which united them to the French, have had recourse to all sorts of shifts and artifices for detaching them from me. There are no offers or promises that they have not held out, if they would deliver me into their hands or at least send me back to Quebec and take in my place one of their ministers. They have made several attempts to surprise and capture me; they have gone so far even as to promise a thousand pounds sterling to the one who should bring them my head. You are well assured, my dear brother, that these menaces have no power to intimidate me or to abate my zeal; — too happy if I should become the victim of them, and if God shall count me worthy to be loaded with chains and to shed my blood for the salvation of my dear savages.

At the first news which came of the peace made in Europe, the governor of Boston sent word to our savages that if they would come together in a place which he pointed out to them, he would confer with them on the present posture of affairs. All the savages repaired to the place indicated, and the governor spoke to them thus:

"Men of *Naranhous,* I inform you that peace is made between the king of France and our queen, and that by the treaty of peace the king of France cedes to our queen Plaisance and Portrail, with all the lands adjacent. So, if you are willing, we shall live in peace, you and I; we were in peace formerly, but the suggestions of the French have caused you to break it, and it is to please them that you have come to kill us. Let us forget all these wretched affairs, and cast them into the sea, that they may appear no more, and that we may be good friends."

"It is well," replied the orator in the name of the savages, "that the kings should be in peace, I am very glad of it, and I do not find it painful either to make peace with you. It is not I that am striking you these twelve years past, it is the Frenchman who has availed himself of my arm to strike you. We were in peace, it is true, I had even thrown my hatchet I know not where, and as I was at rest upon my mat thinking of nothing, the young men brought me a word which the governor of Canada sent me, by which he said to me: 'My son, the Englishman has struck me, help me to get revenge for it; take the hatchet, and strike the Englishman.' I who have always listened to the word of the French governor, I search for my hatchet, I find it at last all rusty, I put it in order, I hang it in my girdle to come and strike you. Now the Frenchman tells me to lay it down; I throw it very far, that no one may see any more the blood with which it is reddened. So, let us live in peace, I agree to it.

"But you say that the Frenchman has given you Plaisance and Portrail which are in my neighborhood, with all the lands adjacent: he shall give you all that he will; for me I have my land which the Great Spirit has given me for living, as long as there shall be a child of my people, he will fight for its preservation." Thus all ended amicably; the governor made a great banquet for the savages, after which each one retired.

The happy accompaniments of peace and tranquillity which they were beginning to enjoy, caused the thought to spring up in the minds of the savages of rebuilding our church, that had been ruined in a sudden irruption which the English made while they were absent from the village. As we are far away from Quebec, and much nearer Boston, they sent thither certain of the principal men of the nation to ask for some laborers, with promise of liberal pay for their work. The governor received

119

Sebastian Rasle

them with special demonstrations of friendship, and made them all sorts of caresses. "I will myself reestablish your church," said he, "and I will deal with you more favorably than did the French governor that you call your father. It should be for him to rebuild it, since it was he in a sort that occasioned its ruin in leading you to strike at me; for on my part I defend myself as I can, while as for him, after serving himself of you for his own defense, he abandons you. I will do better by you; for I will not only accord you laborers, I will also pay them myself, and bear all the expense of the edifice you desire to construct. But, as it is not reasonable that I, who am English, should secure the building of a church without also placing there an English minister to take care of it and to teach religion in it, I will send you one with whom you will be content, and you shall send back to Quebec the French minister who is in your village."

"Your speech astonishes me," replied the deputy of the savages, "and I wonder at the proposition which you make to me. When you came here you had seen me a long time before the French governors; neither those who preceded you nor your ministers have ever spoken to me of religion *(la prière)* or of the Great Spirit. They saw my furs, my skins of beaver and elk, and this alone is what they thought about. This is what they looked after with eagerness. I could not furnish them enough, and when I brought them a great quantity, I was their great friend and that was all. On the contrary, my canoe having gone astray one day, I lost my way. I wandered a long time in uncertainty, until at last I came to a landing near to Quebec, in a great village of the Algonquins, where the black-robes teach. Hardly had I arrived when a black-robe came to see me. I was loaded with furs, the French black-robe did not even condescend to look at them. He spoke to me at first of the Great Spirit, of paradise, of hell, of prayer, which is the only way of reaching heaven. I listened to him with pleasure, and I had so strong a relish of his talk that I stayed a long time in this village for the purpose of hearing him. In fine, religion pleased me, and I engaged him to instruct me further. I asked for baptism and I received it. Then I return to my country and I tell what has happened to me. They envy my happiness and desire to share it, they go to find the black-robe and to ask of him baptism. It is thus that the French have conducted themselves towards me. If after that you had seen me you had spoken to me of religion, I should have had the misfortune of praying as you do; for I was not capable of finding out if your prayer was good. Thus I tell you that I hold to the prayer of the French. It suits me, and I will keep it even till the earth burns and comes to an end. Keep, therefore, your laborers, your money, and your minister — I say no more about them. I will speak to the French governor, my father, to send them to me.''

In effect, Monsieur, the governor, had no sooner learned the ruin of our church, than he sent us laborers for rebuilding it. It is of a beauty which would make it esteemed in Europe, and I have spared no effort for its decoration. You have been able to see by the details which I have given in my letter to my nephew, that in the depths of these forests and among these savage peoples divine service is performed with a great deal of propriety and dignity. It is to this that I give very great attention, not only while the savages remain in the village, but even all the time they are obliged to abide by the seashore, whither they go twice every year to find there something to live upon. Our savages have so far depopulated their country of beasts, that for the last ten years neither elks nor roebucks are found. Bears and beavers have become very scarce. They have hardly anything to live upon but Indian corn, beans and pumpkins. They crush the corn between two stones to reduce it to meal; then they make a porridge of it, which they sometimes season with fat or with dry fish. When the corn fails they search in their tilled fields for potatoes, or else for acorns, which they value as much as corn. After having dried them they bake them in a kettle with ashes, to take away their bitterness. For myself I eat them dry, and they take the place of bread for me.

At a certain time they betake themselves to a river not far distant, where for a month the fish come up the stream in so great a quantity that fifty thousand barrels could be filled in a day, if there were enough hands to do the work. There is a kind of large herrings very agreeable to the taste, when they are fresh. They are pressed together against each other to the thickness of a foot, and they are drawn up like the water itself. The savages dry them for eight or ten days, and they live on them during all the time that they are putting seed into their lands.

It is not till springtime that they plant the corn, and they do

Sebastian Rasle

not give it the last dressing till towards Corpus Christi day. After this they deliberate as to what part of the sea they shall resort to for seeking their sustenance till the harvest, which as a rule does not come till a little after the Assumption. After deliberation had they send to invite me to come to their assembly. As soon as I appear one of them addresses me in this manner in the name of all the others. "Our father, what I say to you is what all whom you see here say to you; you know us, you know that we are destitute of food. Hardly have we been able to give the last tillage to our fields, and we have no other resource to the time of harvest but to go and seek food at the seashore. It would be hard for us to leave our worship behind, therefore we hope that you will be pleased to accompany us in order that while seeking for our living we may not break off our prayers. Such and such individuals will embark you, and what you will have to carry shall be distributed among the other canoes. This is what I have to say to you." No sooner have I replied *kekikberba* (this is a savage term which means, I hear you, my children, I accord that which you request), than all cry out together *8ri8rie*, which is a term of thanks. Very soon after they leave the village.

On arriving at the place where we are to pass the night, poles are planted at suitable distances from each other in the form of a chapel; they encompass it in a grand tent of ticking, and it is open only in front. I always have to bring along with me a beautiful plank of cedar four feet in length with what is needed to hold it up, and it is this which serves as an altar, above which there is placed a canopy quite appropriate. I adorn the interior of the chapel with silk stuffs very beautiful; one rush mat tinted and well wrought, or else a grand bearskin, serves as a carpet. This is brought all ready, and it only needs to lay it down as soon as the chapel is in order. At night I take my rest upon a carpet; the savages sleep in the air in the open country, if it does not rain; but if there falls a shower or snow, they cover themselves with pieces of bark which they bring with them, and which are rolled up like linen cloth. If the journey is made in winter, the snow is cleared away from the space which the chapel is to occupy, and it is set up as at other times. In it each day there is made morning and evening prayer, and there I offer the holy sacrifice of the Mass.

When the savages have come to their final halting-place, they employ the next day in raising a church, which they make secure and shapely with their pieces of bark. I bring with me my plate, and all that is needful for adorning the choir, which I have draped with beautiful Indian and silk stuffs. Divine service takes place in this church as in the village, and in effect they form a kind of village with all their cabins made of bark, which they set up in less than an hour. After the Assumption they quit the sea, and return to the village for their harvest. They have then what they can live upon very poorly till after All Saints, when they return a second time to the sea. It is at this season that they make good cheer. Besides the great fishes, the shellfish and the fruits, they find bustards, geese and all sorts of game, with which the sea is all covered in the region where they encamp, which is parted into a great number of little islands. The hunters, who leave in the morning for the chase of geese and other kinds of game, kill sometimes a score at a single discharge of a gun. Towards the Purification, or at the latest, towards Ash Wednesday, there is a return to the village, it is only the hunters, who disperse themselves for the chase of bears, elks, roebucks and beavers.

These good savages have often given me proofs of the most sincere regard for me, especially on two occasions when I found myself with them at the seashore, they took a lively alarm on my account. One day while they were busy in their chase, the rumor got abroad of a sudden, that a party of English had made an irruption into my quarters and had carried me off. At the very hour they assembled, and the result of their deliberation was, that they would pursue this party till they had overtaken it, and that they would take me out of its hands, though at the cost of their lives. At the same instant they sent two young savages to my quarters at a sufficiently advanced hour of the night. When they entered my cabin, I was occupied with composing the life of a saint in the savage tongue. "Ah, our father," they cried out, "how glad we are to see you!" "I likewise have much joy at seeing you," I replied, "but what is it that brings you here at a time so startling?" "It is to no purpose that we have come," they said to me, "we were told that the English had carried you off; we came to take note of their tracks, and our warriors will not be slow in coming to pursue them, and to attack the fort, where, if the news had been true, the English would no doubt have had

Sebastian Rasle

you shut up." "You see, my children," I answered, "that your fears were not well founded; but the friendship which my children testify toward me fills my heart with joy, for it is a proof of their attachment to religion. Tomorrow, immediately after Mass, you shall go as quickly as possible to undeceive our brave warriors, and save them from all anxiety."

Another alarm equally false threw me into great embarrassment, and brought me into danger of perishing by hunger and misery. Two savages came in haste to my quarters, to warn me that they had seen the English at half a day's distance. "Our father," they said, "there is no time to lose, it is necessary for you to retire, you risk too much by remaining here; for our part we will await them, and perhaps we will make our way in advance of them. The scouts leave at this moment to watch them. But for you, you must go to the village with these men whom we bring to conduct you thither. When we know that you are in a place of safety, we shall be at ease."

I departed at the dawn of day with ten savages, who served me as guides. But after some days of travel, we found ourselves at the end of our scanty provisions. My guides killed a dog which followed them, and ate it; they were soon reduced to some sacks of sea-wolf skin *(a des sacs de loups marins),* which they likewise ate. This was something I could not taste. Sometimes I lived upon a kind of wood which was boiled, and which, when it is cooked, is as tender as radishes half cooked, excepting the heart, which is very hard and is thrown away. This wood had not a bad taste, but I found extreme difficulty in swallowing it. Sometimes also they found attached to trees some of those excrescences of wood which are white like great mushrooms; these were cooked and reduced to a kind of broth, but they were a long way from having the taste of broth. Sometimes the bark of the green oak was dried at the fire, and then peeled, and porridge was made of it, or again they dried those leaves that grow in the clefts of rocks, and which are called rock-tripe; when these are cooked they make a porridge very black and disagreeable. Of all these I ate, for there is nothing which hunger will not devour.

With such nourishment we could only make small progress in a day. We arrived, nevertheless, at a lake which had begun to thaw, and where there was already four inches of water upon the ice. It was necessary to cross it with our snowshoes, but as these

124

snowshoes are made with strings of hide, when they were wet, they became very heavy, and made our march much more difficult. Although one of our people went forward to examine the way, I sank suddenly to the knees, another who was walking at my side presently went down to the waist, crying out, "My father, I am a dead man." As I approached to lend him a hand, I sank down still deeper myself. In fine, it was not without much trouble that we got out of this danger, owing to the embarrassment which our snowshoes occasioned us, of which we could not deprive ourselves. Still I ran less risk of drowning than of dying of cold in the midst of this half-frozen lake.

New dangers awaited us the next day at the passage of a river, which we had to cross on floating masses of ice. Happily we succeeded in this, and at last arrived at the village. The first thing was to unearth a little Indian corn which I had left in my house, and of which I ate, hard as it was, to appease the first cravings of hunger, while those poor savages gave themselves to every sort of movements to make good cheer for me. And really the repast which they proceeded to get ready for me, although frugal, and as it might seem to you not very appetizing, was according to their ideas a veritable banquet. First, they served me a plate of soup made of Indian corn. For the second service they gave me a morsel of bear-meat with some acorns, and a cake of Indian corn cooked under embers. Finally, the third service, which formed the dessert, was an ear of Indian corn roasted before the fire, with some kernels of the same corn parched under embers. When I asked them why they had made me such good cheer, "Ah, what, our father," they answered, "there are two days that you have had nothing to eat; could we do anything less? May it please God that we shall often be able to entertain you in the same manner."

While I was dreaming of recovering myself from my fatigues, one of the savages who were encamped upon the seashore, and who did not know of my return to the village, caused a new alarm. Having come to my encampment, and not finding me or those who were encamped with me, he had no doubt that we had been carried off by a party of English; going on his way to carry the news to those of his quarter, he arrived at a river bank. There he took the bark of a tree, upon which with coal he drew the English around me, and one of them cutting off my head. (This is all the writing the savages have, and they communicate among themselves by these sorts of drawings as understandingly as we do by our letters). He then put this kind of letter around a stick which he planted on the bank of the river, to give news to those passing by of what had happened to me. A little while after some savages who were passing by in six canoes on their way to the village, took notice of this bark; "See there a writing," they said, "let us find out what it says." "Alas!" they cried out, as they examined it, "the English have killed those of our father's encampment *(quartier)*, and as for him they have cut off his head." They instantly took out the braidings of their hair so as to leave it negligently tossed about over their shoulders, and sat down before the stick till the next day without saying a word. This ceremony with them is the mark of the greatest affliction. The next day they continued their journey to within half a league of the village, where they halted, when they sent one into the wood near by in order to see if the English had not come to burn the fort and the cabins. I was reciting my breviary as I walked along the fort and the river, when the savage arrived opposite me on the other bank. As soon as he perceived me, he cried out, "Ah, my father, how glad I am to see you. My heart was dead, and it is alive again at beholding you. We saw a writing which said that the English had cut off your head. How glad I am that it was a lie." When I proposed to send him a canoe for crossing the river, he replied, "No, it is enough that I have seen you. I turn back now to carry the agreeable tidings to those who are waiting for me, and soon we will come and rejoin you." They came, in fact, that very day.

I trust, my very dear brother, that I have done justice to what you desired of me by the sketch *(precis)* I have now given you of the nature of this country, of the character of our savages, of my occupations, my labors, and the dangers to which I am exposed. You will judge, without doubt, that it is on the part of the English that I have most to fear. It is true that for a long time they have conspired for my destruction. But neither their ill will nor the death with which they threaten me can ever cause me to separate myself from my long-tried flock. I commend it to your devout prayers, and am with the most tender attachment, etc.

Father Sebastian Rasle lived among the Norridge-

wocks, ministering to their spiritual needs, until the massacre of 1724 by the British, at which time he was shot down along with most of his parishioners. He was deeply mourned by the survivors of the raid and buried under the altar of the village chapel. Soon thereafter, the few surviving Norridgewocks left Nanrantsouak never to return, and thus ended the Norridgewock village at Old Point. Close to this spot today stands a monument inscribed in Latin, which translates as follows:

"Rev. Sebastian Rasle, a native of France, and a missionary of the Society of Jesus, at first preaching for a few years to the Illinois and Hurons, afterwards, for thirty-four years, to the Abenakis, in faith and charity a true apostle of Christ, undaunted by the danger of arms, often testifying that he was prepared to die for his flock; at length, this best of pastors fell amidst arms, at the destruction of the village of Nanrantsouak, and the ruins of his own church, in this very place, on the 23rd day of August, A.D. 1724.

"To him and to his deceased children in Christ, this monument was erected by Benedict Fenwick, Bishop of Boston, and dedicated on the 23rd day of August, A.D. 1833. To the greater glory of God."

The Maine Historical Society in Portland has some treasures from Father Rasle's chapel at Old Point. These were taken by the English in two different raids on the village, the last raid bringing about its destruction and the death of Father Rasle. The artifacts are Father Rasle's strongbox, with its secret compartment, his crucifix and breviary, and the chapel bell.

And thereby hangs a tale.

The bell is not large nor did it hang in the belfry of a grand church, but rather it called the faithful to a tiny chapel in the Maine woods, high up on the Kennebec River. It was the only Old World sound in a primitive land until Colonel Moulton arrived at the head of two hundred British soldiers. At Norridgewock on that tragic day in 1724 the surprised Indians heard the muskets ring out and saw Father Rasle killed and scalped, along with many Indians. The soldiers marched off through the woods after putting the torch to the village, carrying with them some of the priest's possessions, but not the bell.

According to Convers Francis, in his "Life of Sebastian Rale, Missionary to the Indians," the legend goes on like this:

After the departure of the English troops, the survivors returned, finding nothing but smoking ruins and dead bodies. An Indian boy, perhaps one of the acolytes of the church, helped bury Father Rasle, then searched the ashes for a memento of the beloved priest. He saw the bell and took it with him as he fled with the other survivors up the river. As long as he lived he could never be persuaded to disclose where it was hidden; to all questions he answered, "The bell is safe, maybe Indian want it sometime." There it lay for eighty years and more while the Indian boy grew old and died, never revealing his secret. One night, around the year 1808, a furious storm roared down the valley, uprooting a huge pine tree, long a landmark on that part of the Kennebec. And there was the old chapel bell lying exposed, as if nature in her own good time had decided to return it. A woodsman rescued it and in time it reached the Maine Historical Society, where it joined Father Rasle's other possessions. The legend and stories I heard in Madison always said the bell was discovered under a pine tree; however, the script on the bell mentions a hemlock. Both trees grow in the area, although pines were and still are more abundant.

The sign that hangs on the bell at the museum reads as follows:

> Bell from Father Rasle's chapel at Norridgewock, Maine
> Chapel burned August 24, 1724
> This bell was found in the spring of 1808, about a mile from the chapel on the western side of the Kennebec River under a decayed hemlock tree. Weight 64 pounds. Gift of John Ware.

Thus ended the procession of French Jesuit missionaries southward along the Kennebec.

DEATH OF RASLES.

Father Sebastian Rasle meets his death and the Norridgewock Indian village is destroyed at the hands of Jeremiah Moulton's men in 1724. See pp. 171-175. Reprinted from William Allen's History of Norridgewock, *1849.*

130

The Indian Wars

*The conflagration that reduced Maine
to ashes and decimated the Abenakis.*

THE WARS BETWEEN the English settlers and the Indians of the Kennebec valley covered a period of 85 years between 1675 and 1760. By the time the last one ended, the rumblings of discontent heralding the American Revolution could be heard. The six Indian wars are usually referred to as:

King Philip's War, from June 24, 1675 to the treaty of Casco on April 12, 1678. This war was fought entirely between the Indians and the English colonists. The French were not involved.

King William's War, from August 13, 1688 to the treaty of Mare Point (Brunswick) on January 7, 1699. This was between the French and English with the Indians as allies of the French. Father Rasle arrived in Norridgewock at the beginning of this conflict.

Queen Anne's War, from August 1703 to the treaty of Portsmouth, July 11, 1713. Soon after Queen Anne ascended the British throne, she declared war on

France, and when the news reached America the French and Indians took up arms and the colonists again prepared to defend themselves.

Lovewell's War, from June 13, 1722 to Dummer's treaty, December 15, 1725. Important events of this war were the destruction of Norridgewock and the death of Father Rasle.

The *Spanish* or *Five Years' War,* from July 19, 1745 to the treaty of Falmouth on October 16, 1749.

The *French and Indian War,* from April 1755 to the treaty of Halifax, February 22, 1760, and Pownal's treaty, April 29, 1760.

At the beginning of King Philip's War in 1675 there were thirteen English settlements in Maine, with a total population of about six thousand. Widely scattered in farmhouses and small hamlets, mostly on the middle and southern coast, the colonists were in a very vulnerable position. The settlements were: Kittery (the first town, incorporated in 1652), York, Wells, Cape Porpoise (Kennebunkport), Saco, Scarborough, Falmouth, Pejepscot (Brunswick), Sagadahock and Kennebec (Georgetown), Sheepscot (Newcastle), Damariscotta, Pemaquid (Bristol), and Monhegan. There were also a few families on Swan Island, and at the mouth of the Androscoggin on Merrymeeting Bay. By 1699 there would be only four English settlements left in the state, at York, Wells, Kittery and and the Isles of Shoals. The rest of the original thirteen were destroyed in the wars.

King Philip's War started in Massachusetts, but

soon spread northward to the Kennebec region. King Philip was the nickname given to Metacomet, son of Massasoit, the good friend of the Plymouth colonists. After Philip became sachem of the Wampanoag Indians, he stayed on good terms with the English for some time; when the war started in 1675 there had been peace for 27 years, although at times it had been rather uneasy.

The event that lit the fuse of King Philip's War was the execution of three Wampanoags by the English. An Indian by the name of Sassamon who had been very friendly with the Plymouth colonists acted as a spy and advised them of King Philip's plots against them. Philip, learning of Sassamon's treachery, ordered three braves to hunt for Sassamon and put him to death, which they did. It was these three Indians that the Plymouth court tried for murder and executed. That act, added to other intrusions into the Indians' domain, set the feet of thousands of Indians on the warpath.

Messengers were sent to other New England tribes asking for help in the forthcoming war against the English. Philip's campaign to gain allies was successful and he was said to have an army of more than 3,000 braves. The first raid of the war was at Swansey on June 24, 1675. The depredations came thick and fast after the first one, with the English trying to build forts for the protection of the settlers. This only gave the cunning Indians more time to make surprise attacks before disappearing into the surrounding forests and swamps. The Indian form of warfare gave them an enormous advantage in attacking the wilderness settlements. A brave would lurk behind every tree and rock and they could move as silently as the night, to suddenly burst out upon the doomed settlers in terrifying war paint and with bloodcurdling war whoops.

A young Englishman of courage and experience was assigned the job of tracking down the elusive enemy. This was Colonel Benjamin Church, who would later play an important role in the Kennebec campaign after the war spread to that area. Col. Church and his men started immediately on the job of hunting down King Philip and his warriors.

An unequal chase started with the Indians outnumbered, although doing much damage and killing along the way. It took Col. Church and his men fourteen months to track down Philip and maneuver him into an ambuscade from which he could not escape. Philip and his warriors had hidden in a swamp on Mounthope neck when he was shot by an Indian who had joined Church's militia. The renowned King Philip fell forward into the mud of the swamp. On Church's orders he was beheaded, and the head was returned to Plymouth along with others garnered on the campaign for a bounty payment of thirty shillings each.

King Philip was hunted down and killed in August of 1676. This did not stop the savage war; it only served to scatter his warriors to the four winds. Many of them retreated to Maine to join the Abenakis there. Among them was a savage and cruel trio with the biblical names of Simon, Peter and Andrew. They were anything but apostolic, however. They had escaped from the ambush when Philip was killed, fleeing to Maine where they had insinuated themselves into many a council, urging the Maine Indians on to more and more deadly attacks on the settlers. They were complete villains and were responsible for many of the atrocities committed on raids during the remainder of the war.

The Maine Indians needed no urging, however, as they had many wrongs of their own to avenge against the English. One of their leaders, Squando, had a special reason for revenge. Squando was sagamore of the Sokokis (Saco Indians), a close ally of the Kennebec Indians, and had been antagonistic toward the English for some time. One day Squando's squaw was paddling down the Saco River in a canoe with her infant son when she was confronted by some rough sailors from an English ship. The sailors decided to find out whether an Indian baby is born knowing how to swim. They grabbed the child and tossed it into the cold water before the mother could stop them. She dived into the river and brought the infant to shore, but he died soon afterward from exposure. Naturally the parents blamed the sailors for the death of their child, and Squando from that day on used all his influence and efforts to rouse the Indians against the English. Squando himself claimed to have been visited by God who told him to fight the hated English to the bitter end.

Not only was Squando panting to go on the warpath because of the loss of his son, but his friend and ally Tarumkin was eager to join him; an insult to one was considered an insult to the other. Tarumkin was sagamore of the Anasagunticooks of the Androscoggin River. A third ally was Robinhood, or Ramegin, elected grand chief of the Kennebecs in 1675. Robinhood lived on the east bank of the Kennebec between present-day Woolwich and the sea, a place called *Neguasseg* by the Indians. He was the most friendly to the English of the three and was reluctant to take up arms against them. Robinhood refused to join with King Philip in the first war even though his friend Squando had been injured.

At the outbreak of the war, a committee of peace was appointed by the English to try to keep the war from spreading to the Kennebec. They journeyed up the river, and when they met five Androscoggins and seven Kennebecs they persuaded them to hand over their guns and ammunition. Later Benjamin Shurte of Pemaquid, who had been able to keep the Kennebecs on a somewhat friendly basis, talked to a group, trying to persuade them to remain neutral.

Squando however called the Sacos together and held war dances, which the settlers knew meant trouble. The first act against the English was the sacking of a house at the mouth of the Androscoggin River on Merrymeeting Bay. This is perhaps understandable, as a man named Purchase had lived there and cheated the Indians in trades for fifty years. The next occurrence was in Falmouth, where Thomas Wakely and his family were killed. During the following months seventy-two settlers were slain between the Piscataqua River and Casco Bay. These raids were carried out by the Sacos and Androscoggins.

The safety committee on the lower Kennebec, aided by Benjamin Shurte, were putting forth every effort to keep the war from spreading to the Kennebec Indians. Mr. Shurte had won the confidence of the local Indians by his fair treatment, and he invited the sagamores to Pemaquid for a meeting. He listened to their troubles, which were serious. Since they had had their firearms taken from them, the Indians had been unable to hunt and were near starvation, asserting that some of their tribesmen had actually died of hunger. They were in a miserable state. Mr. Shurte was presented with a wampum belt and given a captive English boy to be returned to his family.

Shortly after this conference an Indian runner arrived in Pemaquid, bearing an invitation to a grand council to be held in Teconnet (Waterville) for the purpose of drawing up a treaty of peace. Mr. Shurte bravely started out, and when he reached the Kennebec Mr. Davis of the committee of safety joined him for the trip upriver. They were greeted by a large gathering of Indians, including five important chieftains: Hopegood and Assiminasqua of the Kennebecs; Madockawando and Mugg of the Penobscots; and Tarumkin of the Androscoggins. There was one key figure missing, and that was Squando of the Sacos. He could never be talked into forgiving the English for the death of his infant son.

The talks started with the Indians giving their

version of events. Assiminasqua, who lived at the confluence of the Sebasticook and Kennebec rivers and was noted for his sage counsel, was selected as orator. He said, "We must tell you we have been in deep water. You told us to come down and give up our arms and powder or you would kill us; so to keep peace we were forced to part with our hunting guns, or to leave both our fort and our corn. What we did was a great loss; we feel its weight."

Mr. Shurte replied, "Our men who have done you wrong are greatly blamed; if they could be reached they would be punished. You all know however how well you have been treated at Pemaquid. We come now to confirm the peace. We wish to see Squando and hear Tarumkin speak."

Tarumkin assured the Englishmen he "loved the clear streams of friendship" and for himself chose the shades of peace. Seven Androscoggins echoed his sentiments, along with Hopegood and Mugg. But no treaty could be made without Squando. The commissioners were anxious and suspicious that if the weapons were returned to the Indians they might be used against them.

Madockawando, the Penobscot spokesman, abruptly rose and brought the meeting to a close with these words: "Where shall we buy powder and shot for our winter's hunting when we have eaten up all our corn? Shall we leave Englishmen and turn to the French? Or let our Indians die? We have waited long to hear you tell us, and now we want Yes, or No." Clearly the Indians felt that their only alternatives were starvation or war.

A few weeks after the council some Kennebecs and Androscoggins set out on their first raid, on the 13th of August, 1675. They chose the trading fort of Richard Hammond, situated at the head of Long Reach, just below the Chops or outlet of Merrymeeting Bay. They had a grudge against Hammond, as they said he had made them drunk and then cheated them. Hammond, Samuel Smith and John Grant were killed, and sixteen people were taken captive. A young girl escaped and ran through the woods at night to give the alarm to Sheepscot, thus saving that settlement.

The same night the raiding party, flushed with their success, stealthily approached and surprised the garrison on Arrowsic Island. The scene was horrible as thirty-five people were either killed or captured. Among the wounded was Captain Davis, who had accompanied Mr. Shurte to Teconnet on the ill-fated attempt to make peace. He barely escaped capture and death by hiding in a crack of the ledges on the shore.

The destruction wrought on this night in August was only the beginning of the raids that caused widespread devastation and drove the English from the banks of the Kennebec. The stories of killings, burnings and of women and children taken as captives are heartrending.

One story concerns Robinhood's son Hopehood, or Wohana, who unfortunately for the settlers proved to be quite unlike his more peaceful father. Hopehood's grudge against the English arose from his having been a prisoner in Boston for some time. He was hated and feared by all the white residents of the region, and when he became chief of the Kennebecs he drew them into the war in spite of his father's attempts to keep peace. He was fearless and vengeful and treated his prisoners barbarously. He himself would meet a violent end, killed by a party of Indians from Canada who mistook him for a Mohawk.

Early in King Philip's War, Hopehood led an attack on a house in Berwick with fifteen people inside, all women and children. As he tried to break down the door, a courageous young woman held it and succeeded in fastening the latch, giving the others time to escape. Hopehood broke the door with his axe and knocked the girl on the head, leaving her for dead. The Indians and their leader chased two of the children who were slower than the rest, killed one and took the other captive. Amazingly the brave young lady who held them at bay recovered.

In another raid, the peninsula of Casco Neck was laid desolate; thirty-four persons were either killed or carried into captivity. The families or remnants of families who were left were absolutely destitute, with winter just around the corner. When the news reached Boston, a ship was sent to the starving, homeless survivors huddled on Cushings Island.

After the raid, eleven Indians proceeded northward with their captives. They followed the route that was to become so familiar to white captives: up the Kennebec River, across the Great Carry to Dead River, across the Boundary Mountains into Canada to the Chaudiere River, and on to Quebec, where the captives could be sold as servants. The remainder of the Indians prepared to attack again.

The Indians, about a hundred strong, attacked at night and stealthily. Expert at paddling their canoes without a sound, they made a landing on the southeastern point of Arrowsic Island. Scattering, they concealed themselves until the strategic moment, when they crept through the gate and with hideous war cries surprised the terrified inhabitants. A hand to hand struggle ensued, but the Indians from the first had the advantage. Some of the settlers tried to escape in canoes, and about a dozen persons succeeded in escaping to the mainland, but thirty-five settlers were killed or carried away into captivity. The Indians left after putting all dwellings to the torch, leaving a scene of complete desolation.

Most of the inhabitants of the area fled to Monhegan Island, which they thought they could defend more easily than their scattered homes and small villages. From there they watched fearfully as smoke arose over the burning buildings of Pemaquid, New Harbor and several islands. In five weeks' time, sixty miles of the Maine coast was left bare of buildings and population, and all settlers had fled from the Kennebec valley.

Two other Indians, although they were not Kennebecs, attended the Teconnet council and played important parts in the later Indian wars. Madocka-wando actually lived on the Penobscot but joined with the Kennebecs so often in battles against the English that he might be considered one of them. His daughter was the wife of the Baron de St. Castine. Madockawando was serious in his speech and bearing. He had great native intelligence and, like Squando, said he had had supernatural visions and revelations. He was a brave and powerful chief, and was a friend of the English until they despoiled his crops because of injurious acts by other Indians. Then he became one of the most dreaded of the sagamores, and York and Saco were destroyed on his orders. At the end of King Philip's War Madockawando held sixty English captives. According to one historian, he was the mildest man ever to cut a throat!

Mugg was Madockawando's chief minister and right-hand man. He should not be confused with Mogg of the Norridgewocks, who played an important part in later wars. Mugg had lived with an English family for a time and had learned their language and habits, and so was invaluable in negotiations with the colonial authorities. His totem was a seal, and it was affixed as a signature drawing to several treaties. Mugg was an active participant in many raids on the lower Kennebec which were extremely brutal, although his name is not connected to any particular instances. Williamson describes this very influential sagamore as having alternately brightened and shaded his own character so that even the most skillful pencil would find it difficult to draw its true portrait. To the English this remarkable man was sometimes friend and sometimes foe; to the Indians he was counselor, peacemaker, warrior or emissary as the occasion demanded. Mugg was an effective orator in Indian and English, had good judgment and was inclined to seek peace. He was killed during a raid at Black Point (Scarborough) in the spring of 1677 by the English, who at first thought they had killed the hated Simon.

King Philip's War lasted for three long years, with three hundred English killed or dead in captivity. The region was devastated and the Indians reduced to poverty. No one knows how many of their warriors were killed. Finally, on April 12, 1678, a treaty of peace was signed by the sagamores of the Kennebec, Androscoggin, Penobscot and Saco rivers. It was a great day for both red and white men; all were heartsick and tired of war.

The final act of the drama was the return of the captives who had to be brought back from their miserable lodgings in the scattered Indian villages. Only then was the war really over for their waiting relatives.

King William's War erupted in Maine in the spring of 1688, barely 10 years after the treaty of Casco ended King Philip's War. This time the French were the aggressors in the struggle between two powerful kings, William III of England and Louis XIV of France. The French would have as allies all the Indian tribes of Maine, who would again practice a type of warfare the English didn't understand: skulking behind trees, creeping silently across fields, never coming out in the open until they burst forth with their horrible yells, swinging their hatchets and surprising and terrifying the settlers.

The events that ignited the second Indian war happened over on the Penobscot River. The arrogant Governor Andros of Massachusetts decided to go to Maine to humble the Indians and show them who was in command. He would inform them that they were in the territory of the king of England, and that French Acadia did not extend west of the St. Croix River.

The governor had chosen to give this message to Castine the younger, son of the Baron de St. Castine and a Penobscot Indian woman, and grandson of the powerful chieftain Madockawando. Young Castine, mentioned by Father Rasle in his letters, lived with his mother's people and was himself a chief of the Penobscots, a young man of stature and very much respected by his Indian tribesmen. In addition to being a chief sagamore of his tribe, he held a commission from the French king. He was described as having a sweet disposition and as magnanimous and peaceful; even the English recognized his worth.

When Governor Andros arrived before Castine's fort and house he found no one there. The governor's party broke into the house and proceeded to empty it of furniture, guns, ammunition and other valuables, which were loaded on the waiting frigate.

Young Castine was upset on his return at finding his house sacked, but being a mild-mannered person he was not disposed to make trouble. However, his tribe felt differently and immediately started to make raids on the English to get revenge. The governor, realizing tardily that he had stirred the Maine Indians to a frenzy with his high-handed raid, started feverishly to build forts and set up garrisons throughout Maine. By the time war was formally declared between France and England on December 7, 1689, the Indians of Maine had been skirmishing for more than a year in retaliation for the sacking of Castine's home.

The French Jesuit missionaries were an important part of France's efforts to win the Indians over to their side, and it was at the beginning of King William's War that Father Sebastian Rasle was assigned to the Norridgewock village on the Kennebec. The village was in a strategic location for French and Indian raids against the English. It was secluded from the enemy, and located at the crossroads of lines of communications by water: the Kennebec trail to Canada, and the upper Androscoggin via Sandy River and a maze of smaller streams and portages. We cannot know for certain how Father Rasle used his influence over the Indians concerning the war in which he found them embroiled. We do know the English blamed him for the depredations of the Norridgewocks; however, the evidence would indicate that he tried to influence them to seek a peaceful solution for their differences.

After the arrival of Father Rasle, the different tribes began merging to carry on the war against the English more effectively. First the Wawenocks, then the Sokokis and the Androscoggins joined the Kennebecs, and fought side by side with them in the following wars. The Penobscots under the leadership of the Castines, father and son, kept their tribal identity, as they have continued to do up to the present day.

After the conquest of Nova Scotia by William Phips in 1690, the Comte de Frontenac needed all his soldiers in Canada to protect the home front, and the Maine Indians were left more or less to themselves. The English took advantage of the situation to renew their attacks on the Indians. Major Benjamin Church was again summoned into service and put in charge of 300 soldiers. His orders were to proceed to Casco and Pejepscot to kill or drive from the country any Indians there, and also to ransom or rescue any English captives found.

Church landed at Maquoit and marched with his men, before dawn, toward the fort at Pejepscot on the west side of the Androscoggin River at the lower falls. The Indian Doney saw them and alerted the village, crying, "Englishmen! Englishmen!" There was no resistance and the Indians fled in all directions, some even jumping into the river and drowning.

Church recovered the English captives, who were in a wretched state, nearly starving. In turn he took some Indian prisoners, including the wives of Kancamagus and Warumbee and many Indian children. The wives of the sagamores were sent on board Church's boat, along with some of the children, on the squaws' solemn promise that eighty English captives would be restored. Williamson adds that it is painful to relate, and nowise creditable to the usual humanity of Major Church, that the remainder of the females and many children were put to the sword or the tomahawk. Although Church had made a good record in King Philip's War, even the government of Massachusetts did not condone what he did on this expedition.

Two old women were spared and given a message to transmit to the sagamores. It was: "You will find your wives and children at Wells."

In October, ten sagamores proceeded to Wells, where they were very pleased to have their squaws and children returned to them. Their orator made the following speech: "The French have made fools of us. We will go to war against you no more. We are ready to meet your head-men at any time and place you appoint and enter into a treaty." Sure enough, on the 20th of November, 1690, a truce was signed by commissioners from Massachusetts and six sagamores.

Ten English captives were released. According to Williamson, the Indians were very reluctant to part with Mrs. Hall, who wrote very well and had acted as their secretary. It seems a little incongruous that the primitive Indians would need a secretary.

Unfortunately the truce was not observed for long, as the Indians failed to show up on the date set for the final treaty signing, and the war continued. The Indians had now been completely deserted by the French, as Frontenac had his hands full at home. The Indians were thus wandering aimlessly around, shooting scattered farmers and robbing and burning their houses.

Moxus was a well-known Norridgewock chieftain, who also went by the name of Egerement, and it was at this point that he came south to carry on the war against the English. Leading 200 Indians, Moxus attacked the garrison at York, where he was held at bay by Captain Converse. The Indians left, raided neighboring hamlets, and boarded a vessel in the harbor near Cape Neddick, killing the crew. Then they scattered, hiding in the woods. A captive later reported what Madockawando said when he heard about the unsuccessful attempt on York: "Moxus miss it this time — next year I'll have the dog Converse out of his den."

The settlers in York may not have taken this threat seriously enough. Several houses were well fortified and the residents kept a close watch, but it was relaxed in the dead of winter. This was unfortunate, as the clever Indians learned this and decided to attack just then. Early morning was chosen, and on February 5, 1692 three hundred Indians, led by several Frenchmen, attacked the town at several different points.

The surprise was complete and proved fatal. In one half hour more than 150 residents were killed, wounded or taken prisoner. There was no quarter given, and the scene of carnage was dreadful. One of those killed was the Reverend Dummer, who had been minister at York for almost 20 years.

The 100 captives were taken on the long march up the Kennebec River, probably to Teconnet, possibly

Garrison house at York, Maine, built about 1645. Reprinted with permission from Griffiths' Pictorial History of the State of Maine, *1970.*

some to Norridgewock. Their hardships must have been severe because of the winter weather and lack of food. Rev. Dummer's wife, one of the captives, was so heartbroken and exhausted that she soon died on the trail.

Surprisingly, an instance of Indian gratitude occurred at this time. To repay the English for setting free several Indian squaws and their children at Pejepscot, the Indians released some old women and several children between the ages of 3 and 7 years, returning them safely to the garrison house. By coincidence, one of the children released was a five-year-old boy named Jeremiah Moulton, who many years later would lead the expedition to destroy Norridgewock.

The massacre and burning of York was a staggering blow to the settlers, so serious that the remaining inhabitants considered leaving, at least for the duration of the war. However, Massachusetts sent provisions and promises of protection, which encouraged them to stay. The courage of these early settlers of Maine staggers the imagination, when we realize that they had seen friends, neighbors, and family members butchered or dragged away as captives.

An army of 500 French and Indians converged on Wells in June of the same year, 1692. Among the Indians were familiar names: Madockawando, Moxus, Warumbee and Egeremet. With their hideous war whoops the Indians attacked the garrison, continuing the assault all day with no success. The bravery of Captain Converse and his men, enduring a siege that lasted 48 hours, was not surpassed during the war.

At this time Sir William Phips, an illustrious native of Woolwich who had earlier led an expedition to Nova Scotia, was appointed the royal governor. He made one of his first objectives to step up the prosecution of the war with more vigor and in a more effective manner. In pursuance of this Phips commissioned Major Benjamin Church as commander of the forces in Maine. He also ordered a fort built at Pemaquid, and went to select the site himself.

The plot selected for the fort was twenty rods from high-water mark, on the east side of Johns Bay, a league above Pemaquid Point. It was to be quadrangular, 747 feet around the outside wall, with the inner square, including the citadel, to be 108 feet across. The walls were of stone, reportedly 2,000 cart loads of them, cemented in lime mortar. The garrison was finished in four months and cost 20,000 pounds. Fourteen to 18 guns were mounted, including six 18-pounders. Manned with 60 men, it was named Fort William Henry and was ready for service in the latter part of 1692.

The Norridgewock Indians had been actively engaged in all the events of the war so far, including attempts to make peace. One of the most famous of the Norridgewocks was about to play an important part in the Indian wars. This was Bomazeen, whose name is sometimes spelled Bomaseen, Bombazine or Bombazee, and whose name is still preserved on the Kennebec at Bombazine Rips between Madison and

Norridgewock. Bomazeen was a fierce man, one of his tribe's best warriors. He was also a persuasive orator, and represented the Norridgewocks at many war and peace councils. The story of the fascinating Bomazeen runs like a thread through the history of the Indian wars, and finally ends with his heroic death while trying to warn his people of the advance of the enemy.

Bomazeen, along with Madockawando and Toxus, another famous Norridgewock, led several raids during the year 1693. However, there are no recorded instances of barbarisms committed by this sagamore, nor of any abuses of captives, in spite of his reputation as a valiant fighter. Bomazeen was one of a group of thirteen sagamores who went to Pemaquid on the 11th of August, 1693, with an offer of submission of their tribes to the English. This effort to make peace was unsuccessful and Bomazeen was chosen to try again a short time later.

In November of 1693, Bomazeen traveled down the Kennebec and on to Pemaquid with two companions. They disembarked from their canoe and advanced toward Fort William Henry, with Bomazeen in the lead, holding a flag of truce aloft. He and the two Indians were quickly seized, while Bomazeen protested his innocence and argued that his seizure was an act of perfidy. All to no avail, as they were taken to Boston to join five other Indian hostages in a foul prison, where pestilence and famine were to be their lot for the winter.

There were serious repercussions to this incident,

and many people both then and later have called it illegal and unfortunate. The accounts given by the two sides are as usual entirely different. The English said that the Indians were spies, pretending to be voyagers just arrived from Canada who were ignorant of the recent raids and massacres. Bomazeen on the other hand maintained that they were there to try to come to an agreement for a new treaty. The fact that Bomazeen had a flag of truce in his hands made no difference; the English at this point did not trust the Indians at all.

Since Bomazeen had at times given the English information about the movements of the French, it is hard to understand why his flag of truce was disregarded. The injustice of his treatment resulted in a continuation of the war with added fury. His followers turned back to the French alliance, and the Norridgewocks held their war dances and took to the warpath. In 1695 they joined the French in capturing the hated Fort William Henry, the very spot where Bomazeen was captured.

The French formally ended the war with the treaty of Ryswick in 1697. The Indians paid no attention. They were still smarting at old insults and, with their chief Bomazeen still in a Boston prison, fought on for two more years. At last the Norridgewocks signed a treaty of peace at Brunswick, called the Mare Point Truce, on January 7, 1699. By the terms of this truce all English captives were returned and Bomazeen, sagamore of the Norridgewocks, was free at last.

The tally of losses at the end of the second Indian

war shows what a severe setback it was to the English settlement of Maine, as well as to the living standards of the Indians. The Kennebecs lost many of their numbers through the war directly, and also through famine and disease. They were destitute; with the men on the warpath the women and children had had to forage for food. They were able to sell scalps and plunder to the French to secure ammunition and some provisions.

As mentioned earlier, the original thirteen settlements in Maine had been reduced to four battered towns: Wells, York, Kittery and the Isles of Shoals. Four hundred fifty people had been killed and 250 taken captive, with some of those dead of disease or exposure. Assacombuit, one of the most savage of the Saco warriors, bragged that he alone had killed or taken captive 150 English men, women and children. In addition to the human losses, thousands of domestic animals had been butchered, and the dwelling houses and log forts still left standing were in wretched condition.

The peace that followed the treaty of Mare Point was to last less than five years. Queen Anne, the Protestant daughter of the exiled James II, gained the throne of England in 1702 and immediately declared war on France, asserting English sovereignty over Acadia to the St. Croix River. Naturally the French lost no time in alerting their Indian allies on the Kennebec.

The rumblings and war dances that followed Queen Anne's declaration reached the ears of Governor Dudley in Boston. He decided to try to conciliate the Maine Indians and sent invitations to the leading sagamores to attend a great meeting at Falmouth to renew the treaty of Mare Point. The assembly was held June 20th, 1703.

Governor Dudley went to a great deal of trouble and expense to impress his guests. He brought a large company with him and also brought a huge tent which was set up near the shore. On one of Maine's most brilliant June days the sagamores made their dramatic entrance upon the scene, handily outdoing the regal pomp of the governor and his entourage. There were eleven sagamores from five tribes.

Two hundred and fifty painted and plumed dark-skinned warriors paddled sixty-five sleek birchbark canoes in silent and perfect unison over the sparkling waters of Casco Bay. The eleven sagamores, robed in the richest of fringed and bright colored clothing, were, as befitted their high stations, delivered in high style before the tent of the awed governor. A large delegation of Kennebecs and Norridgewocks were present, including the sagamores Bomazeen, Moxus, and a new chieftain named Captain Sam. According to some reports, Father Rasle secretly accompanied the Norridgewocks but stayed in the background.

When everyone was assembled, Governor Dudley rose to speak. He said: "I have come to you commissioned by the great and good queen of England. I would esteem you all as brothers and friends. It is my wish to reconcile every difficulty that has happened since the last treaty."

Queen Anne's War

The sagamores replied in turn. First was Simmo of the Penobscots, who spoke with great dignity: "We thank you, brother, for coming to talk with us. It is a great favor. The clouds gather and darken the sky, but we still love the songs of peace. Believe my words. So far as the sun is above the earth, so far are our thoughts from war, or from the least desire of a rupture between us."

Next Bomazeen spoke: "Although several missionaries have come to us, sent by the French to break the peace between the English and us, yet their words have made no impression on us. We are as firm as the mountains and will so continue as long as the sun and moon shall endure."

There were professions of friendship, followed by feasting, dancing and singing. A state of peace seemed assured, which was happy news to the settlers, some of whom had prepared to leave for safer areas in Massachusetts, but now changed their minds.

The French were not pleased with this peace treaty, nor did they honor it. The Indians as usual succumbed to their wishes, and the raids on the English for booty and scalps started anew. The fort at Casco was attacked and destroyed by Abenakis in August of 1703. The English retaliated by sending a colonel named Hilton with 270 men to the Norridgewock Indian village.

Hilton and his men went in the winter of 1705 when the snow lay four feet deep and the country looked like a frozen lake. They stealthily approached the bend in the river on their snowshoes but soon realized that the quarry had gone; not a soul remained in the village. They burned the large chapel that Father Rasle had built, and departed. This foray was later described by Father Rasle, who wrote that the affair was a sudden attack made by the English when the Indians were absent from the village. He returned to mourn over the loss of his treasured chapel.

The war went on with many savage raids conducted by both sides, with the French and English sometimes adopting the guerrilla tactics of their Indian allies. The English enlisted the help of the Mohawks, who would fight especially fiercely against their old enemies the Abenakis; the French continued their alliance with the Abenakis, of which the Norridgewocks were most important.

One of the fiercest of the warriors was Assacombuit, sometimes called Nescambiouit. He was originally a Saco Indian, but had moved north to Canada in 1700 to join the St. Francis tribe, and he was closely allied with the Norridgewocks. From the first he was a great friend of the French, and he was present when the French captured Fort St. Johns from the English. Assacombuit was part of the group that attacked the fort at Casco in August 1703. Joined by fifty Abenakis and assisted by Montigney, he destroyed the fort and committed many atrocities.

About 1706 Assacombuit sailed for France, where he received an elegant sword from the king and was knighted with a pension of eight livres a day. On this important occasion he said to the king: "This hand has slain a hundred and forty of your majesty's enemies in New England." Assacombuit returned to New England the following year, and christened his new sword in blood during the 1708 attack on Haverhill. However, his French honors went to his head, which alienated his Indian friends, leaving him very much alone. He took to carrying a huge club with him wherever he went. It had ninety-eight notches, each representing someone he had killed. He was one of the cruelest of the Sacos.

An important Norridgewock in Queen Anne's War was Arruhawikwabemt. In 1710 the campfires of an English army caused some Indians to come too close and they were captured. Arruhawikwabemt was one of them. When the English interrogated him he did not reply, and when they threatened him with death, he laughed with contempt. At that they delivered him up to their allies the Mohawks, who soon became his executioners. He was reputed to have been one of the Norridgewocks' most fearless and valiant warriors.

Among the many examples of cruelty shown by both sides in Queen Anne's War, it is pleasant to be able to tell of the kindness of the legendary Bomazeen. It is true that, after his release from prison in Boston, he took part in a number of raids in Massachusetts and New Hampshire; but he went out of his way to rescue a young girl named Rebecca Taylor.

Rebecca had been taken captive by a huge warrior who was taking her to Canada by the overland trail. She became completely exhausted, which enraged her burly captor. He whipped off his girdle and, tying it around her neck, hung her to a tree. Her weight broke the cord, and he was in the act of again suspending the terrified girl when Bomazeen came upon the scene. He leaped on the Indian and rescued Rebecca, taking her back to her family. She herself told and retold the story of her deliverance.

Queen Anne's War lasted ten long and bitter years, until France and England signed the treaty of Utrecht, March 30, 1713. It was agreed that Acadia and its ancient boundaries, including Nova Scotia and Maine, would be resigned and turned over to the crown of Great Britain forever. The Indians and the English in Maine wanted peace, both having suffered cruelly during the war. As soon as news of the treaty signing reached the Indian villages, envoys were sent to the English to plead for an end to the fighting.

The victorious English drew up an agreement with humiliating demands. The Indians must confess their crimes and take the oath of allegiance to the British crown. They must sign whatever terms the council might dictate, and turn over hostages to insure the faithful performance of these harsh terms. To add insult to injury, the Indians were required to pay for the food and lodging of the hostages.

For the ratification ceremony, the council was to meet at Portsmouth on the 11th of July, 1713. Eight sagamores gathered from the St. John, Penobscot, and Kennebec rivers to meet the provincial governor and his councillors. Indians from the Merrimack, Saco and Androscoggin were not present, having moved to St. Francis to mingle with the Indians there. The delegates, however, declared that they were included in the agreement.

The eight sagamores, after the terms were explained to them, cast themselves upon Queen Anne's mercy, prayed for her pardon and favor, and proceeded to solemnly affix their marks upon the document. The marks, or totems, were usually birds, fish or animals adopted as the insignia of the Indian families. That of Wederanquin was a tadpole, of Joseph a fish, of Kirebenuit a raven. The distinguished Bomazeen departed from the usual and signed with a delicate drawing of a little girl's head with a feather in her hair. Remembering his rescue of little Rebecca Taylor, we can understand a side of his nature that was not often evident.

Again the Indian and English residents of Maine had the difficult job of picking up the pieces. The Indians had lost at least one-third of their warriors and as many of their women and children. Starvation, exposure and disease were dread specters of the Indian villages. Several tribes were so decimated as to have lost their identity. The terms of the treaty of Portsmouth were so hard that the Indians would never have accepted them unless compelled to do so to save what shreds of self-respect they had left.

The English were no better off. One-fourth of the inhabitants of Maine had been killed or captured. Many families had been wiped out, and nearly all mourned killed or captured relatives. The log houses were falling down and the fields, uncultivated, were

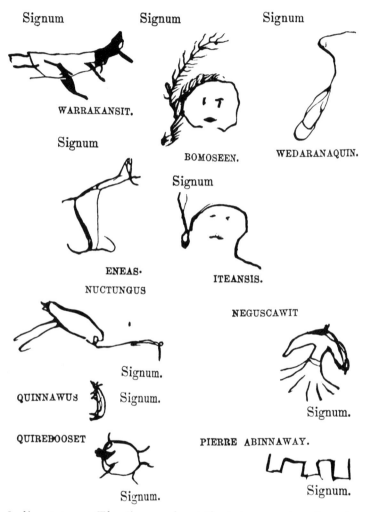

Signum

Signum

Signum

WARRAKANSIT.

Signum

BOMOSEEN.

WEDARANAQUIN.

Signum

Signum

ENEAS·

NUCTUNGUS

ITEANSIS.

NEGUSCAWIT

Signum.

QUINNAWUS

Signum.

QUIREBOOSET

PIERRE ABINNAWAY.

Signum.

Signum.

Signum.

Indian totems. The five marks at the top were signed to the treaty of July 13, 1713, at Portsmouth, New Hampshire. The bottom totems were signed at Portsmouth the following year, July 28, 1714. Reprinted from Collections *of the Maine Historical Society,* Vol. VI, 1859.

161

full of weeds and brush. The fur trade, lumbering and fishing were gone. In short, the country was poverty stricken and in ruins.

As in the other wars, the stories of the captives are heartbreaking. Children and their parents, husbands and wives were separated in the wilds of Canada or in some primitive Indian village. It was a year before a ship could be sent to Canada to retrieve the captured, and it took four months to round them up. Some of the children, taken very young, had become accustomed to their new lives and refused to return from Indian wigwams or from French homes. Their parents had a special cross to bear, especially John Wheelwright, whose daughter Esther never returned home in spite of his lifelong efforts to persuade her.

The mouth of the Kennebec, left utterly desolate by the war, began to attract settlers again, and by 1715 there were twenty-six dwellings on Arrowsic Island. The residents petitioned for incorporation in 1716, which petition was granted with the new town being named Georgetown. This was a more remote frontier than any other attempted resettlement, and it was hoped it might serve as a barrier in the event of any new wars. Thus the governor sent a guard of 20 soldiers to protect the settlers for a term of six months.

The settlement at Georgetown encouraged the proprietors of the Kennebec patent to start selling land on the Kennebec River as far north as Cushnoc. This was followed by the building of a stone fort at Cushnoc for the purpose of trade and protection from the Indians. The settlers' cabins and the English forts were getting nearer and nearer to the ancient lands of the Norridgewock Indians, who were becoming more and more restive and nervous. To add to the unrest, there were rumors of a new war between England and France. Things were becoming very tense on the Kennebec.

The English thought they might remedy the Indian unrest by using the tactics of the French. They determined to instruct the older Indians in the Protestant religion, run a school for the children and send young ministers to learn the Abenaki language, after which they would go out to preach. As usual, the English remedy was too little and too late. The Indians of the Kennebec had had Father Rasle with them for over twenty-five years, and they were well indoctrinated in the Catholic religion.

It certainly cannot be said that Governor Shute didn't try. He called a great parley at Arrowsic, inviting many Indians with their sagamores. The Kennebecs, believing themselves to be the most aggrieved, took the lead in the meeting. They told the Governor that they were very uneasy about the forts on the Kennebec and at Pemaquid, where Fort William Henry was being rebuilt. They considered these and the settlements as encroachments on their hunting grounds.

Governor Shute then presented them with an English-Indian Bible and told them that it contained the true religion, which Reverend Baxter would explain to them. The Indian spokesman returned the

Bible to the Governor, saying: "All people love their own ministers. Your Bible we do not care to keep: God has given us teaching, and should we go from that, we should offend God."

The council then turned to matters of land ownership. The Indians said they thought no land east of the Kennebec had been sold to the English, and they considered it their own. The governor replied curtly that the English would never part with an inch of their lands in that quarter. This broke up the meeting and the Indians left, paddling to their headquarters on the next island to confer with their advisor. They returned to the meeting later in the day with a letter from Father Rasle, which stated that the French king had never, by any treaty, conceded to the English any of the lands of the Indians, and that he would protect them against any encroachment. This angered the governor, who definitely had not invited the priest to the meeting and wanted no advice from him.

Again the meeting seemed on the point of breaking up. However, the Indians were in no way ready for another war and they returned yet another time, ready to make concessions. They dismissed Wiwurna, the speaker of the previous day, and appointed a more moderate orator. This time the Kennebecs agreed that the English could settle where their fathers had and that they wished to trade with them. They made it clear, however, that they feared and disliked having any new forts built on the Kennebec. The treaty of Portsmouth was then renewed and the sagamores accepted gifts from the governor, in turn presenting him with a wampum belt, magnificent beaver skins and a toast to his good health. Thus in August of 1717 the English and Indians seemed closer to settling their many differences.

Important events were shaping up in Norridgewock following the death of Toxus. Two factions had arisen, a peace and a war party. An election was held and to Father Rasle's surprise, and some said to his dismay, the leader of the peace movement was elected grand sagamore. A great feast was held and afterward a conference, at which it was decided that the new chief, Ouikouiroumet, would make peaceful overtures to the English. He would present them with 200 beaver skins and also offer four hostages, to insure the future good conduct of certain young braves who had caused some damage in the settlements. He was moreover to arrange for ample restitution for the losses they had caused.

Another meeting attended by the Norridgewocks was at Padeshal's Island, near Arrowsic, in August of 1721. Father Rasle accompanied the Kennebec Indians to this meeting and the young Castine came with the Penobscots. A rumor was started that the Indians had sent a letter saying that if the English did not remove themselves from the region within three weeks, their houses would be burned and their cattle killed along with the settlers.

It does not seem probable that any such letter was sent by the particular sachems attending the meeting. All the tribes represented were very anxious for peace, they had had enough of war, their numbers were decimated and their living conditions miserable. The Kennebecs had just sent a letter imploring a cessation of hostilities along with valuable gifts and hostages. It was well known that young Castine, who had wide influence among the Penobscots, was constantly advocating peace, and even more telling was the fact that three weeks had passed with not the slightest hostile move on the part of the Indians.

The English, however, still intensely wished to get rid of Father Rasle. Williamson wrote that "the people of the province, for good reasons, ranked him among the most infamous of villains, and would have given more for his head than for a hundred scalps of the natives." Thus by the year 1721 Rasle was regarded as an outlaw by the authorities of Massachusetts. After all, in addition to his other alleged crimes against the English, he did all in his power to prevent the Indians from selling land. He told them that God had given them the land to hold in trust for their children, and that they could not part with it lawfully, even though the English should offer their greatest treasures.

On the 23rd of August 1721, a special meeting of the general court was held, at which the decision was made to punish the Indians for the crime of "rebellion against the English government." Three hundred soldiers were to prosecute the war, for war it was.

A proclamation was duly issued, with the demand that the Indians should deliver up to the English Father Rasle and all other French missionaries. They were required to make restitution for all past injuries. If these demands were not met, the soldiers were ordered to seize all Indians wherever found and send them as captives to Boston.

These stern measures were strongly opposed by many good citizens, who said that the English had never fulfilled their part of the bargain made at Arrowsic; that the Indians had been grievously wronged; and that they had not been guilty of anything which warranted such severe measures. Both in and out of the legislature, men of honor doubted whether a war aginst the natives was justified. They said, in effect: We have been derelict in our duties both moral and civil. The strong drink dealt out to the Indians against the counsel of their own chiefs is a scandal to our religion and a reproach to our country. But, as in a Greek tragedy, nothing seemed able to stop the impending doom.

In December 1721, as described by Father Rasle, young Castine was improperly seized by the English and sent to Boston for several months. In this instance, as in the earlier attempt to provoke him, he showed great restraint. When he was examined by the court he said he had always been friendly with the English and had great respect for them, that he had recently returned from France to prevent his tribe from doing any mischief, and that he would do everything in his power to keep them from the warpath. He was released immediately after his deposition, but his tribesmen did not forget or forgive as quickly as he did, and it was war again.

Lovewell's War

The fourth Indian war, Lovewell's War, resembled the first one in that no foreign power was involved; it was entirely between the Indians and the English. Canada did not take part openly, but it was believed that they secretly aided the Indians.

The General Court sent Colonel Westbrook on an expedition to Norridgewock in January of 1722 with the express purpose of seizing Father Rasle. Two Indian hunters saw the British soldiers and ran swiftly back to the village, where they gave the alarm. As he later wrote, Father Rasle had barely time to swallow a consecrated wafer, stuff the sacred vessels into a small box and run into the woods where he crouched behind a tree. The English fanned out and beat through the underbrush, coming within a few feet of the Jesuit's hiding place. They didn't find him.

The results of the attack were serious for Rasle. He had hurried away without food, and when he got back to the village it had been cleaned out, not only of food but his precious possessions. The English took his strongbox with incriminating letters from Governor Vaudreuil, letters in which he urged Rasle to encourage the Norridgewocks to fight against the English. Also, Rasle's dictionary was gone, a monumental labor in which he had translated the Indian language into French, the first to do so.

It was war again, with blows being struck by both sides. However, the Indians were feeble and their numbers much reduced as a result of the three previous wars. They could not travel far. An Androscoggin and a Kennebec tribe seized nine families near Merrymeeting Bay; all were treated humanely and soon released, with the exception of four men who were kept as hostages.

Later, Captain John Harmon went up the Kennebec in pursuit of Indians. He had thirty-five armed men with him. Catching a glimpse of a campfire, the English landed, crept through the woods, aimed at the dark forms asleep on the ground, and with one volley killed all fifteen of the sleeping braves.

Next, four hundred soldiers were sent to ravage the coast between the Kennebec and the Penobscot with the objective of destroying every vestige of the Indian villages. Abbott says, in his history of Maine, "We blush to add that a bounty of fifteen pounds was offered for the scalp of every Indian boy of twelve years of age and over, and eight pounds for every captive woman or child." Skirmishes at Georgetown and then at Fort Richmond ended with Georgetown burned and the Indians retreating back up the Kennebec to Norridgewock.

The provincial government still had the death of Father Rasle as a prime objective. In February 1723 Captain Harmon made an attempt to surprise the Norridgewock Indian village. His soldiers went up the Androscoggin River to a curve near the source of the Sandy River, intending to go down the Sandy to its confluence with the Kennebec just opposite the village at Old Point. However, due to a January thaw, the land was flooded and the river full of broken ice, making travel very difficult. They retreated back down the Androscoggin without seeing an Indian or a wigwam.

Another raid on Norridgewock ended in failure when Captain Jeremiah Moulton led a party to Norridgewock in the dead of winter 1723. The wily Indians and Father Rasle had escaped and all the raiders found was an absolutely empty village. They did secure, however, a letter to Rasle from the governor of Canada, exhorting him to push the Indians into making raids against the English with all zeal.

Although the Indians did not undertake a winter campaign in 1723, skirmishes were commenced in the spring. The English were not doing well, as they could not stop the sniping Norridgewocks from killing and taking captives. It is quite clear that at this point the English were losing more men than the Indians. Georgetown and Brunswick had been burned barely six years after they were resettled following the first wars. A strong offensive campaign was called for, and as Rasle and the militant Abenakis lived there, Norridgewock was marked for destruction.

1724 saw the fourth Indian war increase in virulence. The Indians were on the warpath continuously. On the 17th of April they attacked Scarborough, killed William Mitchell and carried his two boys captive to Norridgewock. These two boys and one other prisoner would be rescued by Moulton later in the same year when the village of Norridgewock was attacked.

At this point the Indians decided to take the war to

the seacoast, and succeeded in capturing twenty-two vessels of various types, one being a large schooner armed with two swivels. In this new undertaking, they killed 22 men and captured 23. Some of the captured, being officers or captains, were forced to sail the boats for the marauding Indians, whose experience with canoes had not fitted them for sailing larger boats. However, they caught on fast enough to become a menace to the English along the coast of Maine. By the time the English realized that they were facing an Indian fleet, and got around to sending three large ships north from Boston, the wily Indians had tired of their navy and had taken to the woods in all directions. No doubt they watched with glee from the high coastal cliffs while the English in their well outfitted vessels searched vainly in the islands and coves for a non-existent Abenaki Navy.

Time was running out for the Indians, though. The English had tried a number of times to surprise them at Norridgewock in the winter; now they decided to try their luck in late summer. August 19th in the year 1724 saw a party of two hundred and eight men, under the command of Captain John Harmon and Captain Jeremiah Moulton, leave Fort Richmond opposite Swan Island to carry out an attack on Norridgewock.

Seventeen whaleboats bore the troops up the river. The 20th of August the party reached Teconnet, scene of the peace conference nearly fifty years before, where they landed. Here they left forty men as guards, and on the 21st the remainder marched off toward

The Destruction of Norridgewock

Norridgewock, a distance of about 30 miles. It is thought they headed directly across country toward the village, skirting the big bend of the Kennebec at Skowhegan and thus saving many miles.

Toward evening of the same day, according to some accounts, the soldiers came upon the famous Bomazeen, who was accompanied by his squaw and young daughter. Emma Folsom Clark tells the story in her *History of Madison:*

"Before night the advance surprised a solitary family of three persons living in fancied security near the site of the present village of South Norridgewock. There was a crash of musketry in the thicket and an Indian maiden fell writhing in death agonies on the reddened moss. The frantic mother fell an easy captive by the side of her dying child. The father, lithe and fleet-footed, started to carry warning to the distant village; the soldiers pursued him desperately, for the success of the expedition now depended on his fall. He finally rushed into the river at a fording place to cross to the other side, a league below Nanrantsouak; he had reached an island-ledge in the channel, when in the twilight the keen-eyed marksmen on the shore behind him riddled his panting body through and through with bullets. So died Bomazeen, the noted chief, while trying to escape to his village with the tidings that would have saved it. . . . The place where he was killed now bears the name of Bomazeen Rips. The widowed squaw, terrorized by her captors, told them of the condition of Nanrantsouak, and of a route by which the village could be reached by the utmost secrecy."

Moulton's men arrived in the vicinity of the village around noon of the 22nd of August. They separated into three groups so as to encircle the village and cut off all escape routes. The undergrowth around the village was so thick that the soldiers were hidden until they leaped out in a surprise attack with a volley of bullets bursting in the ears of the startled Indians. With loud shouts Moulton and his men rushed toward their terrified victims. Most of the braves were out hunting, leaving the older men, the priest, women and children in their wigwams or in the cornfields.

The scene of carnage that ensued was dreadful; the 40 or 50 men still there tried to save the old people, women and children. Father Rasle ran out in front of the chapel trying to draw attention from the flight of the squaws and children toward the river. Bullets rained upon him and he fell dead. For the others escape by crossing the river was their only chance. The mass of screaming women and children were forced into the water, which was low but still about six feet deep in the main channel. Moulton's men followed, firing a storm of bullets upon the crowded mass of Indians. Many drowned, many others were pierced with bullets and swept down over the rapids to their watery graves. The Kennebec ran red with the blood of the proud Norridgewocks.

The whole number killed and drowned at Norridgewock that day was eighty. This included the noted warriors and chieftains Bomazeen, Mogg, and

The Destruction of Norridgewock

Carabassett, for whom the Carrabassett River was later named. Most accounts say that Bomazeen was shot before the massacre, as he was crossing the river to try to alert the Norridgewocks of the attack. Some others have said that he did get back to Norridgewock and was shot during the battle; this is the version of events used by Whittier in "Mogg Megone."

The title character of the poem, Mogg, was an old man by this time. He would not retreat as the English stormed through the village, but continued to shoot until he wounded a Mohawk. The Mohawk closed in and shot Mogg. His squaw and children were then slain by the soldiers.

The massacre was soon over. Captains Moulton and Harmon and their soldiers, who had had not a single casualty, marched off through the woods after burning the chapel and wigwams. They took with them two English boy captives and twenty-eight scalps, including that of Father Rasle. These were to bring a handsome bounty when they were delivered to the authorities in Boston, especially that of the priest.

One by one the Indians who had managed to escape with their lives crept back to the smoldering village. Even the stoic Indians were overcome as they gazed at the gory bodies of their relatives strewed along the path. The body of their beloved priest, who had been their daily companion for thirty-four years, was carefully washed and laid to rest with lamentations and the prayers which he had taught them. His grave was beneath the spot where the altar had been and was marked with a crude wooden cross.

That day marked the end of the Norridgewocks as a tribe. Most of the survivors struggled up the rough Indian trail to Canada where they were welcomed by the St. Francis Indians. A few succeeded in crossing the Kennebec in safety and settled along the Sandy River. After settlers started arriving. in the area around 1770 they and their descendants drifted away, leaving only the old chief Peerpole and his family. Eventually he too loaded his family into his canoe and left for Canada.

Others traveled to the headwaters of the Kennebec and settled around Moosehead Lake. They had gone there every winter for hunting and were well acquainted with the area. When the first white settlers arrived at the foot of the lake, they found large encampments of Abenakis where the town of Greenville now is, and at Kineo.

A few years after the massacre, an attempt was made by some of the survivors to rebuild the Norridgewock village under the leadership of Father James de Sirenne. The king of France sympathized with the sad plight of the Norridgewock Indians, and ordered Father de la Chasse of St. Francis to "cover the body of Father Rasle." This meant, in Indian lore, to console them on their loss. Thus a group of Norridgewocks returned to the ruins of their former home by 1730, a few perhaps as early as 1726. The French monarch sent a generous gift of vestments and furnishings for a new chapel in 1738. Shortly thereafter, however, the Canadian government, fearful of a general exodus of Abenakis who were valuable fighting men, put a stop to further emigration and recalled Father de Sirenne. Old Point was again deserted.

The fifth Indian war, precipitated in the New World by yet another conflict between England and France, started in 1745. This and the last war did not have as much effect on the Kennebec region as did the first four wars, since most of the Indians had been cleared from the area.

It was during this fifth war that New England colonists boldly captured the French fortress of Louisbourg on June 17, 1745. The scattered Indians in the Kennebec valley took little part in the war, although the well-worn trail down the river was used by raiding parties from St. Francis, who on the way back were as usual accompanied by a sad group of straggling captives. The Maine Abenakis were of course blamed for the misdeeds of the St. Francis Indians and were labeled enemies. The government offered prizes for their scalps which were much higher than before and proved a real incentive to the colonists to embark on Indian hunting parties. The bounties ranged from one hundred to four hundred pounds, much higher than those offered for their French leaders, only thirty-eight pounds.

The peace treaty of Aix-la-Chapelle was signed October 7, 1748, but it was a year later, October 16, 1749, that eight Kennebec sagamores traveled to Falmouth to renew their humble apologies and submission to the governor. Joining the Kennebecs were eleven other sagamores and sachems from the Anasa-gunticook, Wawenock, St. Francis, and Penobscot tribes.

The treaty included the following terms: that all hostilities on the part of the Indians should cease and not be renewed; that all their captives should be immediately restored without ransom; that the English should enjoy all their possessions and places of settlement in the eastern parts unmolested. Further-more, that the trade between them and the Indians should be under the direction of the Massachusetts government; that all personal wrongs should be re-dressed by due course of law and justice, without any act of personal revenge; and that they, as the king's faithful subjects, would render obedience to his ordi-nances. The sagamores reserved to the Indians all lands and properties not conveyed by them, nor pos-sessed by the English; and all privileges of hunting, fishing and fowling, as in times past. Thus the fifth Indian war was brought to a close.

After the war there was as before the difficult job of recovering the English captives who had been carried to Canada. Sir William Phips, taking over for Gover-nor Shirley, inserted notices in the newspapers ask-ing for the names of all relatives and friends who had been taken. Then he sent two colonels, Chandler and Heath, to Canada on the errand of mercy. Ransoms had to be paid for the captives who had been sold to the French by the Indians, as they of course were not bound by the treaty and wished to recover the money they had spent.

The Fifth Indian War

The climate after the fifth war was very troubled. Warlike Indians from St. Francis and Becancourt, who had not signed the treaty, went on the warpath, using the Kennebec River as their thoroughfare. They had old scores to settle and had no intention of forgiving and forgetting. On December 2, 1749 a group of them went to Wiscasset where they quarreled with some settlers, and during the melee an Indian was killed and two badly wounded. This event was later called the Wiscasset tragedy, as it was to have serious consequences. The three settlers involved in the killing were arrested, tried and acquitted, which infuriated the Indians even more. Unfortunately, this all happened barely six weeks after the treaty of Falmouth and before peace had become settled.

Revenge was not slow in coming. Wild reports circulated among the pioneers of the lower Kennebec and the coast. Eighty well-armed warriors were said to be descending the river from Canada to be joined by 150 Penobscots in full war paint and regalia. It was rumored that a French ship of 64 guns, three or four brigs, and twenty transports full of troops, provisions and warlike stores had been seen wending their way toward the mouth of the Kennebec. The garrison at Richmond had been told by an Indian to expect an attack within forty-eight hours. Most of the rumors were false. However, the one about a party of warriors coming down from Canada to raid Fort Richmond was all too true.

Only fourteen men were in the garrison at Fort

Richmond when the raiding party swooped in on it from the woods and, had the Indians pushed their advantage at that point, they no doubt could have taken the fort. Instead, they wasted time butchering some cattle and lurking in the background until night, when reinforcements arrived under the command of Captain Samuel Goodwin.

The Indians then scattered to make small stealthy raids on both sides of the Kennebec. Some crossed the river to scout around the plantation of Frankfort (now Dresden). Their first victim was a Mr. Pomeroy, shot at sunrise as he was returning to his house from milking his cows. Mr. Davis, who lived in the same house, tried to bolt the door against the intruders, one of whom put his gun in the door to prevent its closing. Davis and the women of the family managed to grab the gun from the Indian and get the door closed, but not before the frustrated Indians seized one of the Davis children and took it away as a captive. Two other men were captured and one wounded in this encounter.

Another party of Indians was over on Swan Island burning houses and killing cattle. When they left the ravaged farms they took with them fourteen people as captives. Other Indians laid waste to Wiscasset and Sheepscot, Georgetown, and Parker's Island before gathering their forces and starting the march to Canada. They were accompanied by between 25 and 30 captives, one of whom was with the Indians for five years and learned both the Abenaki and French languages. This was Joseph Taylor, who was seized in

New Gloucester on the trail to St. Francis. Interestingly enough, when he was freed in 1755 he became an instructor of Indian students at Dartmouth College. Dartmouth then and later gave free tuition to any young Indian man who wished to further his education.

During the thirty years that had passed since the destruction of Norridgewock, the fort at Richmond had been the outpost of the English frontier on the Kennebec. The Plymouth Company decided it was time to claim the lands north of that point. The Norridgewocks who had protested so loudly a generation before were now crushed, with only a few survivors living in the Kennebec valley. The Plymouth Company feared them so little that they began dividing the land into homestead plots without informing the Indians.

The English however had misjudged the remaining Abenakis, as they still had a strong desire to keep the Kennebec valley for themselves. In February of 1754 sixty braves visited Fort Richmond to deliver a stern warning to the English. They were surly, and when they faced Captain Lithgow their speaker said: "Better for Englishmen to leave these rivers, else our French brothers, clad like Indians, will soon as the ice is out, help us drive you all away from here. Yes, and the Hurons will come also."

Governor Shirley, realizing that war could not be averted, raised a force of six companies to be ready for immediate action. He directed that they be ready to march up the river and see if the Indians were mass-ing at Norridgewock again. If they appeared ready for the warpath, the soldiers were to break up the village and kill or capture all to be found. Shortly afterward the governor himself headed an expedition to Teconnet and Norridgewock to find out whether any forts had been erected by the French or Indians in those places. There were none. Had there been any doubt, the governor now knew for certain that Norridgewock had been completely destroyed, and the survivors had moved elsewhere.

The decision was made to go ahead with building a fort on the upper Kennebec. The site selected was both strategic and beautiful, on the east bank just north of the confluence of the Sebasticook and Kennebec rivers, about 3/4 mile below Teconnet Falls. The building was of hewn pine timber 100 feet long and 40 feet wide, with flankers and blockhouses of the same material. It could accommodate 400 men and was fortified with cannon. It was completed September 3, 1754 and named Fort Halifax in honor of the Earl of Halifax. One of the blockhouses is still standing today.

Encouraged by this project, the Kennebec proprietors decided to build two similar fortresses on the east side of the river, one at the head of navigation at Cushnoc and the other in the plantation of Frankfort (now Dresden) about a mile north of Swan Island. The fort at Cushnoc (now Augusta), 100 by 32 feet, was built of hewn timber and had two blockhouses placed at strategic points, one at the southwest corner and the other at the northeast. Each blockhouse had

FORT HALIFAX, 1755.
(*Restoration.*)

This engraving shows Fort Halifax as it would have looked soon after its completion by William Lithgow. The blockhouse nearest the river, still standing, is thought to be the oldest block-house in the United States. It may be visited today in Winslow, Maine. Reprinted from Justin Winsor's Narrative and Critical History of America, *Vol. V, 1887.*

182

slits for muskets and portholes for cannons. A palisade between the buildings enclosed a parade ground of 160 by 62 feet. On its completion in 1754 the fort was put under the command of James Howard and named Fort Western.

The third fort was the most southerly of the three, named Fort Shirley in honor of the governor but sometimes called Fort Frankfort for the plantation in which it was situated. The parade ground was 200 feet square enclosed by pickets, with the west side close to the riverbank. Inside were two blockhouses with projecting second stories 24 feet square. The walls were ten inches thick, built of pine and hemlock timbers. Two blockhouses with watch boxes for sentinels and barracks for the men completed the fort. It was put in command of Samuel Goodwin, whose family lived with him in his quarters.

Along with the forts, Governor Shirley ordered a road built between Fort Halifax and Fort Western, to be adequate for carriages to pass. This was said to be the first military road constructed in Maine.

The Abenakis, most of them now at St. Francis, showed what they thought of all the fort building by raiding Fort Halifax almost as soon as it was finished. They killed and scalped a soldier, and captured four others. The government countered by offering a reward of 110 pounds for every captive St. Francis Indian, or 10 pounds for his scalp. They also sent reinforcements of men and cannon to Captain Lithgow. Fort Western was put on guard but was not attacked.

This was the beginning of the sixth Indian war in Maine. It became a part of the greater conflict between France and England, which only ended with the fall of Quebec and the supremacy of the English in North America. It was during this war that the Acadians were expelled from Nova Scotia, the event that inspired Longfellow's beautiful poem *Evangeline*.

Those who were left of the Kennebec Indians, although dispersed and decimated, still had much of their fighting spirit. They made sporadic raids with the help of their St. Francis allies, they took captives when they could find a few people off guard, they killed two men at Teconnet, a Mr. Preble and his wife near Bath, and took the three Preble children captive, killing the baby as it hindered them on the march. To all these people this war was just as fierce and cruel as the others, even though the number of victims was much smaller.

In the early part of 1757 some soldiers left Fort Halifax on a hunting trip. When five men failed to return, it was suspected that a party of Indians seen lurking in the neighborhood had captured them. Captain Lithgow sent a boat with ten men down river at once to warn the settlements. On their way back, eight miles above Fort Western, they were fired upon by a group of seventeen Indians, who wounded two soldiers. The volley was returned, killing one Indian and wounding another. The last the soldiers saw of the natives, they were carrying their fallen comrade across a field for burial.

This was the last encounter between Indians and soldiers on the Kennebec River, and as far as this region was concerned it was the end of the war. By an odd quirk of fate it took place at almost the exact spot where Captain Gilbert was entertained by Chief Sebenoa and his tribe 150 years before.

The war in Maine was over, but the war went on between the ancient antagonists, England and France. Events in North America were building toward a climax, and a heroic figure emerged, one with the goal of wresting Canada from the French and presenting it to England. James Wolfe was commissioned in the Royal Marines in late 1741, served in several campaigns with distinction and, having caught the eye of William Pitt, was sent to Nova Scotia with Lord Amherst to attack Louisbourg. The attack was successful and Louisbourg fell July 26, 1758, making Wolfe famous overnight. In spite of his youth, he was promoted to Major General and selected to command the proposed attack on Quebec.

The Plains of Abraham was the setting for the brilliant attack by General Wolfe. The French were surprised and ultimately routed, but the budding military career of James Wolfe was ended when he was mortally wounded during the battle. September 13, 1759 was the day of his greatest victory and the day of his death at the age of thirty-two.

The Indian wars, all six of them, were finally over. The people of the Kennebec Valley, both red man and white, had to start building a new life from the ashes of the past.

Excerpts from
"Mogg Megone"

by John Greenleaf Whittier

Hark! what sudden sound is heard
   In the wood and in the sky,
Shriller than the scream of bird,
   Than the trumpet's clang more high!
Every wolf-cave of the hills,
   Forest arch and mountain gorge,
   Rock and dell, and river verge,
With an answering echo thrills.
Well does the Jesuit know that cry,
Which summons the Norridgewock to die,
And tells that the foe of his flock is nigh.
He listens, and hears the rangers come,
With loud hurrah, and jar of drum,
And hurrying feet (for the chase is hot),
And the short, sharp sound of rifle shot,
And taunt and menace, — answered well
By the Indians' mocking cry and yell, —
The bark of dogs, — the squaw's mad scream,
The dash of paddles along the stream,
The whistle of shot as it cuts the leaves
Of the maples around the church's eaves,
And the gride of hatchets fiercely thrown
On wigwam-log and tree and stone.

"Mogg Megone"

Black with the grime of paint and dust,
  Spotted and streaked with human gore,
A grim and naked head is thrust
  Within the chapel-door.
"Ha — Bomazeen! In God's name say,
What mean these sounds of bloody fray?"
Silent, the Indian points his hand
  To where across the echoing glen
Sweep Harmon's dreaded ranger-band,
  And Moulton with his men.
"Where are thy warriors, Bomazeen?
Where are De Rouville and Castine,
And where the braves of Sawga's queen?"
"Let my father find the winter snow
Which the sun drank up long moons ago!
Under the falls of Tacconock,
The wolves are eating the Norridgewock;
Castine with his wives lies closely hid
Like a fox in the woods of Pemaquid!
On Sawga's banks the man of war
Sits in his wigwam like a squaw;
Squando has fled, and Mogg Megone,
  Struck by the knife of Sagamore John,
Lies stiff and stark and cold as a stone."

Fearfully over the Jesuit's face,
Of a thousand thoughts, trace after trace,
Like swift cloud-shadows, each other chase.
One instant, his fingers grasp his knife,
For a last vain struggle for cherished life, —
The next, he hurls the blade away,
And kneels at his altar's foot to pray;
Over his beads his fingers stray,
And he kisses the cross, and calls aloud
On the Virgin and her Son;
For terrible thoughts his memory crowd
  Of evil seen and done,
Of scalps brought home by his savage flock
From Casco and Sawga and Sagadahock
  In the Church's service won.

"Mogg Megone"

No shrift the gloomy savage brooks,
As scowling on the priest he looks:
"Cowesass — cowesass — tawhich wessa seen?
Let my father look upon Bomazeen, —
My father's heart is the heart of a squaw,
But mine is so hard that it does not thaw;
Let my father ask his God to make
   A dance and a feast for a great sagamore,
When he paddles across the western lake,
   With his dogs and his squaws to the spirit's shore.
Cowesass — cowesass — tawhich wessa seen?
Let my father die like Bomazeen!"

Through the chapel's narrow doors,
   And through each window in the walls,
Round the priest and warrior pours
   The deadly shower of English balls.
Low on his cross the Jesuit falls;
While at his side the Norridgewock,
With failing breath, essays to mock
And menace yet the hated foe,
Shakes his scalp-trophies to and fro
   Exultingly before their eyes,
Till, cleft and torn by shot and blow,
   Defiant still, he dies.

"So fare all eaters of the frog!
Death to the Babylonish dog!
   Down with the beast of Rome!"
With shouts like these, around the dead,
Unconscious on his bloody bed,
   The rangers crowding come.
Brave men! the dead priest cannot hear
The unfeeling taunt, — the brutal jeer;
Spurn — for he sees ye not — in wrath,
The symbol of your Saviour's death;
   Tear from his death-grasp, in your zeal,
And trample, as a thing accursed,
The cross he cherished in the dust:
   The dead man cannot feel!

"Mogg Megone"

Brutal alike in deed and word,
  With callous heart and hand of strife,
How like a fiend may man be made,
Plying the foul and monstrous trade
  Whose harvest-field is human life,
Whose sickle is the reeking sword!

*   *   *   *   *

'T is springtime on the eastern hills!
Like torrents gush the summer rills;
Through winter's moss and dry dead leaves
The bladed grass revives and lives,
Pushes the mouldering waste away,
For glimpses to the April day.
In kindly shower and sunshine bud
The branches of the dull gray wood;
Out from its sunned and sheltered nooks
The blue eye of the violet looks;
  The southwest wind is warmly blowing,
And odors from the springing grass,
The pine-tree and the sassafras,
  Are with it on its errands going.

A band is marching through the wood
Where rolls the Kennebec his flood;
The warriors of the wilderness,
Painted, and in their battle dress;
And with them one whose bearded cheek,
And white and wrinkled brow, bespeak
  A wanderer from the shores of France.
A few long locks of scattering snow
Beneath a battered morion flow,
And from the rivets of the vest
Which girds in steel his ample breast,
  The slanted sunbeams glance.
In the harsh outlines of his face
Passion and sin have left their trace;
Yet, save worn brow and thin gray hair,
No signs of weary age are there.

"Mogg Megone"

His step is firm, his eye is keen,
Nor years in broil and battle spent,
Nor toil, nor wounds, nor pain have bent
    The lordly frame of old Castine.

No purpose now of strife and blood
    Urges the hoary veteran on:
The fire of conquest and the mood
    Of chivalry have gone.
A mournful task is his, — to lay
    Within the earth the bones of those
Who perished in that fearful day,
When Norridgewock became the prey
    Of all unsparing foes.

*   *   *   *   *

Hark! from the foremost of the band
    Suddenly bursts the Indian yell;
For now on the very spot they stand
    Where the Norridgewocks fighting fell.
No wigwam smoke is curling there;
The very earth is scorched and bare:
And they pause and listen to catch a sound
    Of breathing life, — but there comes not one,
Save the fox's bark and the rabbit's bound;
But here and there, on the blackened ground,
    White bones are glistening in the sun.
And where the house of prayer arose,
And the holy hymn, at daylight's close,
And the aged priest stood up to bless
The children of the wilderness,
There is naught save ashes sodden and dank;
    And the birchen boats of the Norridgewock,
    Tethered to tree and stump and rock
Rotting along the river bank!

The Captives

A vale of blood and tears for the
English prisoners of the Indians.

D URING THE INDIAN WARS, as in most
wars, the object was not only to kill
the enemy but to take prisoners. Bounties were
offered by both the English and the French governments for enemy scalps and captives. Most of the New
England captives, including those from Maine, were
taken to Canada to be sold to the French. Father
Maurault in his *Histoire des Abenakis* credits the
Indians for helping to import new blood into Canada
at a time when they needed settlers. He wrote: "The
Abenaki Indians rendered a great service to New
France by bearing arms and also by augmenting the
population with the numerous English captives
which they brought to Canada."

Hundreds of the captured were never heard from,
and many, if taken while very young, chose to stay
with their captors, especially if all their relatives had
been killed and they had no one to return to. The Gill
family was used as an example by Maurault. Two

white captives, taken when children, chose to remain with the Indians of St. Francis. They married and had a large family. Their numerous descendants included a famous Superior Court judge of Canada, professors and other distinguished persons. The story of the Gill family will be told more fully later.

The Kennebec Indians were in the forefront of the fighting during these wars and took many captives. Most of the captives traveled through the Kennebec wilderness, some staying at least for a time with the Sebasticooks or the Norridgewocks, some going straight through to Canada. It was said that the first settler on the Sandy River, James Waugh, was told of the region's beauties and fertile soil by a man who had been taken to Norridgewock as a captive in his youth.

The stories of New England captives of the Indian wars are as varied as the captives themselves. Men, women, boys, girls, and even infants in arms were among the thousands of English pioneers who were marched through the wilderness to the Indian villages of Maine and Canada. For almost a century, a virtual slave trade went on among the prisoners of war of the Indians. The captives were bought and sold back and forth between the French and Indians and in most cases finally ransomed by their families. They were taken one by one, two by two, and in a few cases by the hundred: 128 from Deerfield, 39 from Wells, 19 from Swan Island, etc.; over one hundred from York alone in February 1692.

The story of Hannah Swarton is told in Cotton

Hannah Swarton

Mather's *Magnalia Christi Americana,* in an episode entitled "A narrative of Hannah Swarton, containing wonderful passages relating to her captivity and deliverance." Hannah was deeply religious and her story is interlaced with biblical quotations and verses that she found consoling.

Her narrative begins: "I was taken by the Indians when Casco Fort was taken in May 1690. My husband was slain and four children were captured with me. The eldest of my sons they killed about two months after I was taken, and the rest they scattered from me."

After her capture by the Norridgewocks Hannah was given Indian clothing, consisting of a dress made of animal skins, a thin blanket, no stockings and thin Indian moccasins. She was taken up and down the Kennebec valley on the Indians' constant voyages to hunt and fish. From time to time she saw her children, but they were not allowed to talk or console each other on the threat of death. About this sorrow she quoted from Ezekiel: "We durst not mourn or weep in the sight of our enemies, lest we lose our own lives."

During the first few days of her captivity the Indians feasted on the provisions taken in the raid on Casco, some from Mrs. Swarton's own kitchen. She was so grieved and worried that she could not eat, and when the English food was gone they had to subsist on what they could forage from the forest. By now it was winter and the only meat they found was one bear. Their food consisted of groundnuts, acorns, hogweed, and roots; when they were desperate a dog was killed. Occasionally they would meet another group of Indians who had had better luck at hunting than they, and Hannah mentions being given part of a moose liver, a turtle and some fish.

This woman, unused to the wilderness, suffered from the cold, frostbitten feet and exhaustion from the continual days on the trail carrying a heavy pack. In February she thought she had come to the end of her endurance and wrote: "I thought I could go no further, but must lie down, and if they would kill me, then let em kill me. The Lord renewed my strength and I went on as my master would have me."

She briefly met other prisoners on the Kennebec trip but said that at Norridgewock there were seldom other captives. There was one man named John York who stayed for a time but could not keep up with the Indians on their hunting expeditions, as he was weak from lack of food and exposure. They killed him and threatened Mrs. Swarton with the same fate.

At times she was left alone with her master's squaw while the men went on hunting trips or raids. On one occasion they were left for a week with no food except a small piece of moose meat from which they made a broth. Moose meat is not nourishing as it has little or no fat, so they were near starvation when on the last day Mrs. Swarton's mistress sent her to an island to try to get help. She made smoke signals as directed and succeeded in attracting the attention of some squaws in a canoe. They gave her a roasted eel which she pronounced to be the most savory meal she had ever had.

Hannah Swarton

Mrs. Swarton's strong religious faith gave her the strength to withstand the hardships and sorrows she underwent during her captivity. When they told her that her eldest son had been killed by the Indians, she thought of these lines from Jeremiah: "I will cleanse them from all their iniquities whereby they have sinned against me, and I will pardon all their iniquities."

The bitter cold and snows of February saw the captive following her master over rugged Height of Land between Maine and Canada and through the trackless swamps around the foot of Lake Megantic. Burdened with a heavy pack, she lost heart many times but always found the strength to go on. Besides fearing that she could not survive the trip, she dreaded going to Canada for another reason. She had heard that the zealous Jesuit missionaries would try to convert all the English captives to Catholicism. This she was prepared to resist at any cost.

By the time Hannah, her master and mistress made camp on the outskirts of Quebec she could hardly stagger along and left bloody tracks in the snow after her. Her master sent her to a French house to beg for food, and she returned with beef, pork and bread. She asked for permission to go back to spend the night in the Frenchman's house, and this was granted. On her return there the Frenchwoman made a bed for her near the fire and she slept comfortably for the first time since leaving her home.

In the morning an Englishman arrived, also a captive. He greeted her with "I am glad to see you, countrywoman!" They were the first English words Hannah had heard for a long time. He asked her to go to Quebec with him, but she replied that her Indian master would surely kill her if she did. The French-woman then urged her to go, and said they would arrange to have her ransomed if her Indian master and mistress followed her into the city.

Mrs. Swarton was taken to the house of the Lord Intendant, a man named Le Tonant who was also the chief judge, second only to the governor. To her amazement she was hospitably received by Madame le Tonant, who gave her fresh clothing, food and lodging. The next day they took her to the hospital where she was "physicked" and "blooded" and "very courteously provided for." It is difficult for us to understand how the doctors of that day cured any-body with their harsh measures of bloodletting and strong physic. However, it is obvious that Hannah Swarton was a woman of very strong constitution, and also of very strong mind.

After Hannah had been in Quebec for a time and was settled in her job as a house servant in the Le Tonant home, she was, as she had feared, pressured to convert to Catholicism by her mistress, the nuns and the friars. She went to Mass a few times, but when her mistress realized how strongly she was attached to her own church she allowed her to have an English Bible. After that Hannah and Margaret Stilson, another English captive living in the house, would read together. This was a great comfort to them both.

During all this time letters had been passing back

and forth between the governments of New England and Canada. At last one arrived with orders for the release of Hannah Swarton and her youngest son. A ship was sent for the freed prisoners and they landed safely in Boston in November of 1695, five years and six months after their capture at Casco.

As the mother and son sailed away from the dock at Quebec, their joy at being free was clouded by the knowledge that they were leaving behind in Canada two more of Hannah's children: a daughter of twenty, somewhere in Montreal, and a son whom Mrs. Swarton had not seen since the morning of their capture.

The devout mother could still write in her memoirs: "I desire to praise the Lord for his goodness, and for his wonderful works to me. Yet I still have left behind two children and I earnestly desire the prayers of all my Christian friends that the Lord will deliver them." The reader is left in suspense, as the memoir ends without telling whether the Swarton son and daughter ever returned.

Another story told in Cotton Mather's *Magnalia* concerns Hannah Dustin and her nurse Mary Neff, in a chapter entitled "A Notable Exploit: Dux Faemina Facti." The Latin phrase may be roughly translated as "A woman who was the leader in the deed."

The story opens with a raid on Haverhill, Massachusetts during King William's War in 1697. A raiding party of Indian warriors broke into the Dustin house where Hannah Dustin lay in bed with a newborn infant. Her nurse, Mary Neff, grabbed the child and tried to escape with it, following Mr. Dustin who had shepherded his seven other children into the fort. She was too late and was quickly overtaken. After the band of Indians grabbed all the household goods they could carry and set the house on fire, they ran for the shelter of the woods, carrying with them Hannah Dustin, Mary Neff, the infant, and about a dozen other captives from the town.

Before they had gone far the Indians decided the baby was a hindrance and killed the child before the eyes of its mother. Other captives who could not stand the pace of their Indian captors were also dispatched from time to time along the forest trail. Hannah and Mary surprisingly were able to satisfy their masters with their speed and endurance, and covered twelve miles the first day before camping for the night, and another one hundred and fifty miles in the days that followed. The two women were depressed and silent as the trip wore on. Their masters noticed it and said to them, "What need you trouble yourself? If your God will have you delivered, you shall be so!"

The captors consisted of a family group of twelve people: two men, three women, and seven children of varying ages. The Indian family was traveling toward a village where there was to be a large pow-wow. These Indian gatherings were usually celebrations of some kind, or a rally for the start of a war, or an exhibition to show off captives and scalps after a successful raid. The three remaining captives, Hannah, Mary and a young boy captured in Worcester a year and a half before, were regaled with stories of powwows and told what they might expect. After being stripped and scourged, they would have to run the gauntlet through the whole army of Indians, this being the custom when captives first entered the town. The squaws laughed and ridiculed the Englishmen who had fainted under the torments of the fearsome Indian gauntlet.

Hannah Dustin, more and more angered at what had been planned for them as well as at the murder of her baby, decided to take the law into her own hands. She asked Mary Neff and the young boy to help her, and they armed themselves with hatchets while all their captors were sound asleep. With Hannah in the lead they fell upon the Indians and killed all of them with the exception of one squaw who got away, though severely wounded, and one boy whom they intended to take back as a captive (however, he ran away and escaped in the woods). The incensed women didn't stop there but took the scalps of ten Indians.

The astounded General Assembly of the province paid the women fifty pounds bounty for the scalps, and when the governor of Maryland heard of their exploit he sent them a generous gift of money.

Returning to the Kennebec River, we find a strange story concerning the Noble and Whidden families during the last Indian war. The events that led to so much bloodshed and heartache for these families were a sad commentary on the state of relations between the English settlers and the Kennebec Indi-

The Wiscasset Tragedy

ans. The train of events was precipitated by the so-called Wiscasset tragedy.

The tragedy took place on a cold December night in 1749, when a band of Abenakis made camp in the forest about a mile from Wiscasset Point. The recent peace treaty of Falmouth, bringing the fifth Indian war to an end, had given both the Indians and the settlers a feeling of security, and the Indians had resumed hunting, fishing and trading near the villages. Peace was in the air — or was it?

Around midnight of that winter night, a group of sailors from a boat lying in Pemaquid Harbor decided to engage in the sport of driving off Indians. They stealthily approached the sleeping families and opened fire. The squaws and children scattered into the woods, followed by the men. When they dared to stop, they found two of their number critically wounded, and their chief, Saccary Harry of the Wawenocks, was lying dead by the campfire. The murderers, perhaps thinking they could hide the evidence, dragged the dead chief to a nearby stream and pushed him beneath the ice before leaving.

The squaws reported the crime three days later to Magistrate Denny of Georgetown, and the word spread, causing worry about the consequences. Officials decided to do everything possible to ease the situation. They sent surgeons to treat the severely wounded Indians, Captain Job of the Norridgewock tribe and Andrew of the Androscoggins. The dead chieftain was taken up the Kennebec River to Old Point for burial.

The Wiscasset Tragedy

In spite of the conscientious efforts of Denny, Captain McCobb, and Governor Phips, time passed and the Indian tribes became more and more outraged that the guilty parties had not been arrested. On the other extreme, the people of Wiscasset rioted to try to prevent the arrest of the three accused men. Once the men were arrested, there was delay before their trial, since only one session of the Superior Court was held every year in York County.

Loran, the grand chief of the Penobscots, sent a letter to the authorities asking the reason for the delays and postponements of the trial. He made an appeal for justice that was distinguished by its moderate tone, although he hinted at serious repercussions if justice was not done. In fact, Loran wrote that if the injured men and the family of the dead chieftain were not satisfied with the way the white man administered justice, there might be ill consequences.

Finally the Superior Court of Massachusetts sat in York County for its annual session on June 12, 1750. One of the first cases heard was that of Obadiah Albee Jr., seaman, who was arraigned for the murder of Saccary Harry, alias Hegan. After the trial the jury, led by their foreman Job Banks, brought in a verdict of "not guilty," and Albee was a free man. On June 15 Parson Smith of Falmouth entered the result in his diary: "Albee was acquitted, to the great surprise of the court. This unhappy affair gives the county an ill name, and it is feared it will bring on war."

Loud protests arose from the vicinity of the Kennebec. A message was sent to the governor by Asserimo, alias Sawwaramet, who had replaced Saccary Harry as chief of the Wawenocks. Asserimo pointed out details of the agreement that had been recently made at Falmouth, to which he said the Indians had faithfully adhered. Now, he went on, the white men had broken their word and killed his brother Wawenock, as well as grievously wounding a Norridgewock and an Androscoggin. The Indians had waited a long time for justice, and were out of patience. He, as chief, and the young braves of his tribe demanded that the murderers be put to death within a month "to cover the blood that still lay on the ground," or there would be dire consequences.

The trial already accomplished, Governor Phips tried to placate the Indians with a gesture of friendship. He invited all the Indians involved in the incident to come to Boston where they were entertained and given sympathy and presents. Thirteen Indians attended, all men; they were shown the sights of Boston, then a thriving city of eighteen thousand inhabitants. One can imagine their wonder at seeing the busy waterfront, the streets with throngs of people, shops, houses, churches, ships with cannon, uniformed soldiers, even the elegant mansions on Beacon and Tremont streets. Presents were handed out to each one before they left on the sloop for Maine: such things as blankets, shirts, stockings, and English hats, which all Indians loved and wore constantly if they could get them. Fine gifts were sent to the murdered man's widow, a blanket, a dress, stockings and a handsome brass kettle. The children also received presents of clothing and money. Everyone was provided with a supply of food and rum to take back on the ship.

Some of the Indians may have been satisfied that restitution had been made, but in the wigwams along the river small groups of young braves became more and more warlike. They did not consider that the blood of their brother had been covered by the English, and were not going to be silenced with a few presents of food and clothing. They were eager to follow the warpath once more. The settlers on the Kennebec were filled with foreboding; they kept their guns handy and bolted their doors.

The warpath this time led the Indians straight to Swan Island in the Kennebec. This is a fertile island lying just south of Richmond. Rolling hills and beautiful green fields made it a garden spot, attractive to settlers, and it was often called "Garden Island." In earlier days it had been the home of the famous and powerful Bashaba of all the tribes of the area. In the 1750s it was home to the Whidden and Noble families, whose farm was about three miles south of the head of the island.

The elderly Captain James Whidden and his wife lived there on Indian Point overlooking the eastern channel of the Kennebec River. The Whiddens' daughter had married Lazarus Noble of Portsmouth, and they lived with her parents. They were joined every year or two by a new baby until there were seven young Nobles; in addition, the two youngest sons of the Whiddens still lived with their parents. With the hired man and hired girl, there were fifteen people in all living on the farm.

The marauding Abenakis swooped down on these unsuspecting farmers on September 8, 1755. As usual they came in the pre-dawn hours, even before the men had gone out to start the chores. Mr. Noble and the hired man shot at the invaders from the top of the stairs, wounding one Indian, but were outnumbered and overcome. Thirteen captives were taken to the water's edge and tied up, then the Indians began the work of looting and destroying. The barn was burned, feather beds were cut open and the feathers scattered to the winds. Tables and chairs were smashed, silver and other objects were gathered up and slung over shoulders along with food for the trip ahead.

But the Indians seem to have forgotten something; not one of them had thought to put the torch to the farmhouse. A tradition has come down to us that the raiding party did not forget to burn the Whiddens' house, but suspected that the old couple were hiding in the cellar, and didn't want to harm a man with whom they had traded and who had always treated them well. Whatever the explanation, the fact remains that Captain and Mrs. Whidden were hiding in the cellar and were the only ones who escaped being taken to Canada.

The Noble family and the other prisoners were to be separated from each other as soon as they reached Canada; even the infant and mother were torn apart. Eventually, after negotiations had been carried on with the French government for some time, a party of captives were sent to Crown Point to be returned to their homes. Lazarus Noble, his wife Abigail, and four of their children (Mary, John, Mathew and Benjamin) were in this group. Their two employees, Jabez Chubb and Hannah Holmes, also returned at this time.

The homecoming was marred by the absence of three of the children: Abigail, two months old, Frances, thirteen months, and Joseph, who was eight years old. The parents and grandparents could not have known but obviously feared what eventually proved to be true, that two of the three would never return. Also mourned were the two Whidden sons, Solomon and Timothy, and for some time no word came from them.

Timothy Whidden, on arriving in Canada, had been sold to a resident of Three Rivers. He was ransomed by Captain Phineas Stevens, one of the agents sent to recover captives, and arrived in Boston shortly after his sister's family. Later that year, in September 1751, Timothy and Hannah Holmes were married. Many years later Hannah told about her adventures in captivity, remarking that when the Indian served muskrat, a dish they relished, she was forced to fast as she could not learn to like it.

Solomon Whidden, showing a great deal of courage, managed to escape from his captor and went to Quebec. The governor there refused to return him to the Indians and declared that he was free to live and work as he pleased, but told him to stay away from the Indians. Tragically, he died from disease before he could be found and ransomed. One Philip Jenkins, a young man captured at Richmond, also died only a month or two later.

In June 1752 Phineas Stevens and Nathaniel Wheelwright were appointed to go to Canada to search for captives and to ransom them if possible. They succeeded in freeing eight people but reported news of thirteen others whose release they failed to obtain. Among these were Joseph Noble, Daniel Mitchell and John Foster, who had been adopted by the Abenakis of St. Francis. Not only did the Indians refuse to release them, but the boys themselves wanted to stay with their Indian masters and refused all offers of redemption.

When the commission returned without a single Noble child, the family was deeply disappointed. Mr. Noble decided to go to Canada himself, accompanied by Mr. Mitchell whose two boys were still in Canada. Armed with a passport provided by Governor Phips, and money from the General Court, the two men set out for Canada by way of Albany and Crown Point on Lake Champlain. Due to an unfortunate misunderstanding and official red tape, the two fathers were forced to leave Canada without regaining their children, although Mr. Noble caught a fleeting glimpse of his daughter Fanny.

Years went by and hope grew dimmer in the Noble home. Joseph, captured at the age of eight, was adopted by an Abenaki family in St. Francis. He became thoroughly Indian and loved his new life and

A portion of Thomas Johnston's Plan of Kennebek & Sagada-hok Rivers *of 1754, showing some of the settlements. At this time the northern frontier for the English was Fort Halifax, near "Takonnik Falls." Reprinted with permission from Griffiths'* Pictorial History of the State of Maine, *1970.*

207

relatives. His brothers traveled to Canada at least once to try to find him and persuade him to return home, but with no success. Abigail, a tiny infant when captured, was also adopted by an Indian squaw and had not even been seen by her parents since the day they arrived in Canada. Later the family received news of her death. But what happened to the remaining daughter, Frances or Fanny, captured at the age of little more than a year?

No stories remain to tell of Fanny's journey to Canada up the Kennebec and over the wild and rugged Height of Land into Canada. The first account of the child appeared when her Indian master took her to the home of a Monsieur St. Ange in Montreal for sale. He asked 300 livres for the child, a higher price than any of the Noble family had brought. The sale was made by the pathetic little girl herself. She had been taken to the kitchen door and put on the floor, where she immediately started crawling around picking up crumbs and eating them ravenously. However, when the mistress of the house came in, Fanny, recognizing a motherly face, grabbed her long skirt and burst into tears. Madame St. Ange, whose own little girl had died, was won over immediately by the ragged little waif, and gladly paid the high price asked by the wily Indians. Soon Fanny was the pet of the family, treated like a daughter, baptized and given the new name of Eleanor.

When Mrs. Noble was ransomed she learned where Fanny lived and went to see her. The child did not recognize the strange lady and ran to her French mother for protection. Mrs. Noble left saddened, but with the satisfaction of knowing that her little girl was in loving hands.

According to Fanny's account many years later, she was enticed away from her French parents by Mr. Wheelwright, who had been sent to Canada to recover captives. They stopped in Three Rivers where he was to pick up more prisoners, but before they left for Boston an old squaw came by in a sleigh and stole Fanny. She was secreted in St. Francis for about two weeks but cried and carried on about being separated from her French parents. Her mistress tried to comfort her by drawing pictures on her dress and painting her face Indian fashion, but she cried all the louder; she was about five years old at that time.

Fanny remembered running away to the finest house in the village, which belonged to the priest. He talked to her kindly and asked many questions but returned her to her mistress. While in St. Francis her brother Joseph visited her, but she felt a greater aversion to him than she had to her mother. After all, she could not remember this boy who said he was her brother. He was dressed like an Indian and he spoke like an Indian, and she refused to have anything to do with him.

The Indians soon afterward took her back to her home in Montreal and Monsieur St. Ange rewarded them generously, which was no doubt the reason why she had been stolen in Three Rivers.

Fanny was watched closely, as her owners knew that her family were trying to find and recover her.

Fanny Noble

She related in her memoirs that one day she was sent to the attic where the servants were supposed to watch her while her parents were gone. She didn't like being confined, and ran downstairs to get a drink of water. While there she saw a man looking in the window, stretching out his arms toward her and speaking in a strange language. She was alarmed, of course, and ran to her room. She didn't recognize her own father, but it was he. He had recognized her but was not permitted to enter the house or visit his daughter before he was forced to leave Montreal. Three members of her family had seen Fanny by now, but she did not remember any of them.

At a convent school in Montreal Fanny was taught music, needlework of all kinds, geography, and painting. There were several other young New England captives in the same school, including two of Susannah Johnson's daughters and two daughters of the beautiful Mrs. Howe, who had been captured with her seven children in Hinsdale, Massachusetts in 1755. Fanny always remembered the sad scene when Mrs. Howe came to school to take her children with her to return to their home in Hinsdale. The girls were grief-stricken to leave their friends and school to return to a home and relatives they couldn't remember.

Joseph Noble came to Montreal to see his sister again, bringing their little sister Ellen, as she was then called; she was about seven years old. They were both still living with the St. Francis Indians. Again Joseph was repulsed until he was persuaded to wash the red paint off his face and take off some of the gaudy Indian clothing he wore. The visit was not a great success, and Joseph and his little sister returned to St. Francis the next day. However, Fanny's French father had seen Joseph and decided to buy him away from the Indians. When he did, Joseph wore French clothing, went to school, and became much attached to Monsieur St. Ange. Some years later, when Fanny left to return home, her brother told her not to tell where he was, as he had no intention of leaving his friends in Canada to return to Swan Island.

When Fanny was about eleven she was sent to Quebec to attend the school of the Ursuline nuns there. The discipline was much more strict than in Montreal and the girls were kept secluded in the convent buildings and gardens, even being locked in at night. This restricted atmosphere did not suit Fanny and she was allowed to return to Montreal after one year in Quebec. She happily returned to her old familiar school and continued her studies.

One day Fanny was alarmed at a commotion when a strange man entered the nunnery and demanded that she be delivered to him as a redeemed captive. It was a Mr. Arnold, whom Fanny's father had hired in desperation after being unable to pry her away from her French family himself. Mr. Arnold was skilled at his job. He was secretive, subtle, resolute and, most important of all, persevering. He had found out where Fanny went to school, he had secured the necessary orders from the governor, and when he went to the strongly walled convent he was accompanied by a sergeant of the police and a number of armed men.

At the gate the nuns refused to let him enter and asked what right he had. He convinced them that he had orders from the governor and that they must obey the directive. They tried to stall for time so they could send for the girl's French father, but Arnold would not be kept waiting. He demanded that they bring Fanny Noble to him in the name of the governor of the province of Quebec. They obeyed, and brought Fanny weeping and trembling to the door, where they turned her over to this strange man she had never seen in her life. When she caught sight of the soldiers, she collapsed on the ground, heartbroken at leaving her school and the weeping nuns, and frightened at the idea of being a prisoner of Arnold and the soldiers.

Fanny Noble, by her own description, did not suffer silently; she wept, she pleaded, she protested every step of the way. At one point she dropped to the ground and wailed that she could not and would not go one step further as a prisoner of those frightful soldiers. People gathered around, among them an English officer in uniform. He talked to her and reasoned with her, offering to walk the rest of the way by her side, saying that the guard would be dismissed if she would only go quietly.

Another crisis developed when they passed the door of the St. Ange home on their way to the inn. Here Fanny again refused to proceed. The guard, which had merely fallen back a short distance, returned to make sure a rescue would not be attempted, and the English officer assured her that she would be allowed to visit her French parents the next day to say good-bye. They finally reached the inn where they were to spend the night. She visited the St. Anges the next day as promised and found them in tears. Her foster father blessed her and gave her a sum of money and rushed from the room, unable to control his emotions. His wife presented her with clothing and other gifts and their parting was a difficult and emotional one. Fanny would live to an advanced age, but would never be able to talk of this parting without deep emotion and tears.

The day after saying farewell to her French parents she was taken to Quebec, where she sailed for Boston on Captain Wilson's ship. The ship arrived in Boston in July of 1761, one month before Fanny's fourteenth birthday. She recalled that she was joyfully received by her family and friends. Her father did not live long after her return, and after his death she went to Boston to live in the home of Captain Wilson. Like many of the young returned captives, she had a language problem, having never spoken English at all. She lived with the Wilsons until she was proficient in what would have been her native language.

One guesses that Fanny Noble had trouble adjusting to life in rural New England, so different from the French town of Montreal, and she never went back to Swan Island after her father died. She lived with a relative of her father's in Newbury for a while and recalled that she found peace and a loving atmosphere there. She became a successful teacher in Hampton and there married a Mr. Shute, and died in September 1819 at the age of nearly seventy.

Next we turn to the story of the Mitchell brothers, Joseph Chandler, and the boy who didn't want to come home.

Richmond was attacked by the Abenakis September 11, 1750, but foresight and reinforcements prevented its capture. The residents of the area were alarmed and took steps to guard their crops and their lives from the roving bands of Kennebec and St. Francis Indians. They bought ammunition and set up patrols with the scouts covering the territory from the Saco to the St. George River. This included the lower Kennebec and the garrisons there. However, daring bands of Indians evaded the patrols from time to time.

On the morning of May 25, 1751 a group of Indians watched Benjamin Mitchell and Joseph Chandler and their boys at work in the fields, on the bank of the Royal River in North Yarmouth. No one dreamed the Indians were near, and the two men sent the boys to round up the cows and drive them to the barn. The boys started out but never reached home, and fathers and sons were to be separated for many years.

The three boys were Solomon Mitchell, eleven, his brother Daniel, seven, and Joseph Chandler, twelve. As they walked toward home they discovered some Indians hiding in the grass beside the road, waiting to attack the men on their way home from work. Once discovered, the Indians didn't dare let the boys go to alert the village and the fort, so they dragged them off into the woods, even though they had expected to get more in the way of loot from the raid than from three young boys. However, the fathers were prominent citizens of North Yarmouth and could be counted on for good stiff ransom payments.

The Indians took time only to stop in a nearby pasture to kill two oxen and cut off the meat for provisions on the long trip to Canada. Then they took their young captives along the Indian trail up the Kennebec and no doubt stopped at Old Point, which by then was only a ghost village of ruins and memories. One wonders whether the Mitchell boys had ever heard of two other Mitchell brothers, captured by Indians in 1723 and rescued by Captain Moulton's men when they reduced Norridgewock village to ashes.

After leaving the Kennebec River the trail became more difficult, and although the two older boys were able to keep up with the Indians fairly well, little Daniel fell behind. The Indians took turns carrying the child on their backs until he was rested enough to march along with the rest. When the party arrived at St. Francis the boys were separated. Joseph Chandler was sold to a Frenchman who in turn sold him to Colonel Schuyler of Albany for twenty-five pounds. His father ransomed him in a few months and he returned home about six months after being captured, the first of the boys to be redeemed. Solomon was also sold to a Frenchman, a resident of Montreal named De Pins.

Daniel Mitchell

Mr. Mitchell, in the meantime, was making every effort to redeem his two boys. Envoys were sent to Canada, letters were sent, petitions were drawn up, and finally Mr. Mitchell and Mr. Noble of Swan Island started out for Montreal in search of their children. They were armed with passports and an interpreter named Anthony Van Schaick. They made slight progress, able only to locate Solomon Mitchell and one of Mr. Noble's children in French homes.

Before they could negotiate for their release, they were ordered to leave Canada at once. The excuse given by the governor was that their interpreter had been insolent and abusive. The very disappointed fathers left Canada and returned home with the news that they had accomplished nothing. Letters were exchanged again with the governor saying that Solomon Mitchell was devoted to his French master and was unwilling to leave him. Later, during the winter of 1754, Solomon Mitchell was released and returned to his parents in North Yarmouth, after two and a half years of captivity.

Daniel Mitchell had been adopted by the St. Francis tribe and they would not let him go. His master trained him to go on hunting trips with the braves of the village, and he showed great aptitude in the use the bow and arrow and the ways of the woods. In fact he became so fond of Indian ways and life that he seemed like one, which is perhaps why Susannah Johnson never mentioned him in her memoirs of captivity at St. Francis; she probably never noticed him. He had forgotten his first years and his parents,

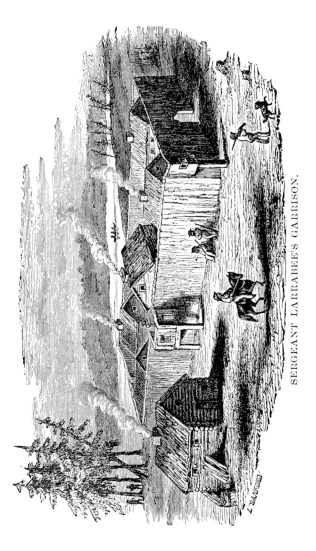

SERGEANT LARRABEE'S GARRISON.

Plate V: This fort at Wells, Maine, large enough to enclose five houses, was built by Stephen Larrabee around 1723 to protect against Indian attacks. This measure was taken too late for the Wheelwright family, who had lost their daughter Esther to Indians twenty years before. This engraving is reprinted from Edward E. Bourne's History of Wells and Kennebunk, *1875.*

*Plate VI: This painting depicts Esther Wheelwright during her
long life as Sister Esther Marie Joseph de l'Enfant Jesus at the
Ursuline convent in Quebec. It can still be seen there. The
Maine-born English girl, captured by Indians at Wells in 1703,
was raised as a Frenchwoman and later became Mother Superior
at the convent. See pages 219-230.*

Plate VII: This portrait of Esther Wheelwright's mother Mary was brought to Esther at her Quebec convent by her nephew in 1754. After her capture at the age of seven, Esther never again saw her real parents. In this painting, robes and a veil have been added by the Ursuline sisters to the lady's Puritan garb, so that she resembles the Virgin Mary; but the face is that of Mary Wheelwright.

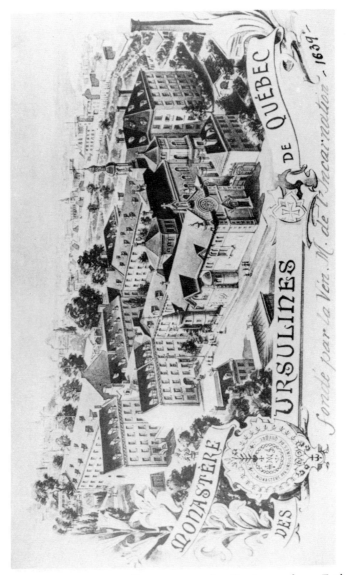

Plate VIII: The Ursuline convent in Quebec, where Esther Wheelwright lived from 1712 until her death in 1780.

(Plates VI, VII, and VIII have been provided through the great kindness of Soeur Marcelle Boucher, archiviste *at the convent.)*

brothers and sisters. All this had been blotted out by his new and exciting life as an Indian boy. Daniel's adopted father taught him how to steal up on animals in the woods without making a sound, how to paddle a canoe, how to march for hours along a forest trail, how to fish. In short he could do all the things required of a growing Indian boy, and surely looked forward to spending his life with his new Indian family.

His real parents, with one son back home, could not rest until Daniel came back to them. They sent an urgent plea to the authorities to make every effort to redeem Daniel in 1756 after the sixth Indian war had begun, when the boy had been absent for more than five years. His parents knew that the longer he stayed away, the more difficult it would be for him to adjust to life at home. They had heard reports that he was happy with his new life and was not anxious to leave, and that he had almost forgotten how to speak his native English.

More years passed and finally the last Indian war was over. Captain Samuel Harnden of Woolwich, a man well acquainted with the Abenakis, set out over the old Indian trail up the Kennebec during the summer of 1761, with the object of ransoming captives, particularly Daniel Mitchell. The boy, now seventeen years old, was swarthy from his life in the woods. Captain Harnden succeeded in ransoming Daniel and started back over the woodland trail with his unwilling companion. The boy tried to escape several times, and once did return to his Indian family, who having received ransom for him had made up their minds to let him go. They persuaded him to return to Captain Harnden and to go home with him. Daniel had apparently forgotten his home and family after ten years and ten months' absence, but when his mother took him in her arms he exclaimed, "I know you my mother, I know you!"

Daniel Mitchell was slow to adjust to the tame life of his home village, and his family and friends were very careful not to upset him as they feared that he would leave to go back to his Indian family for good. As time went on he became more settled and his watchful parents were able to relax. Daniel always retained some of the characteristics of the Indians, and he felt the call of the wild from time to time for the rest of his life. He was an expert woodsman and loved to spend time in the wilderness.

He graduated from Harvard College in 1773 and married Mary Lewis, the daughter of a prominent judge. Daniel himself became a judge and had a distinguished career. He wanted a more adventurous life, however, so he enlisted in his country's service. His first appointment was as commander of the sloop *Fortune* on the ill-fated Penobscot Expedition in 1779. He was also an officer during the War of 1812, being captain of a company from North Yarmouth. After the war Captain Daniel Mitchell became post-master of North Yarmouth, serving from 1816 to 1834.

The former boy captive had successfully adjusted to two major upheavals in his life, the first at age seven when he was snatched from his secure life with his loving parents in North Yarmouth, and the second ten years later when he was forced to leave the Indian parents he had grown to love and a way of life to which he had become much attached. We cannot know which was the more difficult.

A very famous English captive, as mentioned earlier, was Esther Wheelwright of Wells. Her story begins nearly half a century before that of Daniel Mitchell, at the beginning of Queen Anne's War.

The settlers of Maine pinned high hopes for peace on the treaty of Casco, signed June 20, 1703 with much ceremony and oratory. Unfortunately, the noble speeches of the orators were soon forgotten, along with the totems they had so solemnly marked on the documents. Within two months seven bands of warriors were on the warpath, ready to fall on the scattered settlements and farms in southern Maine. Wells, Cape Porpoise (Kennebunkport), Winter Harbor (Biddeford), Saco, Scarborough, Casco (Portland), Spurwink (in Falmouth), and Falmouth itself, were all attacked. At Hampton, New Hampshire the Indians killed five people including the Widow Mussey, a remarkable Quaker who was deeply mourned by the sect. At Haverhill, Massachusetts Joseph Bradley's garrison house was raided just as his wife was boiling soap on the fire. She threw the kettle at the invaders, scalding one of them to death. They took her captive for the second time and she was taken to Canada. Her husband and Ensign Shelton went to Canada the next year and redeemed forty-four captives, among whom were Mrs. Bradley and James Adams of Wells.

The tragedy at Wells began on the morning of August 10, 1703 and resulted in the death or capture of thirty-nine people. The Wheelwright home was among the first to be attacked and Esther Wheelwright, seven years old, was taken. Mary Storer, age eighteen, was another captive. No word came from these two girls for a long time.

The survivors in Wells could think of nothing but their missing children, mothers and fathers. The winter passed slowly, they planted their crops, summer passed without a word from the captives in Canada. A second harvest was gathered before the people of Wells learned the fate of some of the captives. To the joy of the whole town a letter arrived, dated October 4, 1704, written by Samuel Hill, with assurances that his family and the family of his brother Ebenezer were safe.

In the meantime Deerfield had been sacked with over a hundred more captives joining the scattered Wells prisoners. Some of them got together to exchange news, but others were kept with the Indians and news of them was difficult to obtain. Bits and pieces of information leaked out of Canada. James Adams of Wells sent the following: "I pray give my kind regards to Landlord Sheldon and I am sorry for his loss . . . God was kind in carrying your daughters Hannah and Mary through so great a journey though they were very lame. The rest of your children are with the Indians. Remembrance lives near Quebec and Hannah lives with the French." Ebenezer Hill wrote that his cousin Pendelton Fletcher of Saco, Mary Sayer, Mary Storer, he and his wife and child were all well. He ended the letter with the request that they pray that God might keep and in due time deliver them from captivity.

Happiness reigned in many homes in Wells on the receipt of the letters. The Storers were able to sleep and to make plans for the return of their daughter Mary. But where was little Esther Wheelwright? She had not been mentioned in any of the letters. She seemed to have completely disappeared from sight. Her father mourned for her constantly.

The truth, as related in a previous chapter, is that Esther was captured by an Abenaki from Norridgewock who decided to adopt her into his family; she was well hidden in the Indian village where she lived with her master and his squaw. Days, weeks, months and years passed, before she was discovered by a white man. Father Vincent Bigot, on one of his visits to Norridgewock, saw the little girl in rags and tatters, and realized that she was not Indian. He called to her but she did not answer; she had forgotten how to speak English. Her pale face and shy withdrawn manner touched his heart and he resolved to find out more about her. He called her master and learned that she was Mr. Wheelwright's child and had been taken at Wells. He spoke to the Indian sternly and said, "The English rose is drooping; forest life is too hard for her and she should be taken to Canada where the nuns can nurse her back to health." Her master refused, saying: "Let her grow up among the pine trees, to deck by and by the wigwam of some young brave."

So Esther stayed. Her master and his squaw tried to be kind to her as they feared the French governor might order her to Canada. The priest taught her the catechism and the credo in French and Abenaki. She was a very intelligent child and learned readily. Probably through Father Bigot, whose headquarters were in Canada, the French governor and Esther's parents in Wells finally learned that she was alive and where she was.

Even though Esther's parents knew she was alive they could not reach her, hidden in the Indian village by her master. She was not happy and mourned for her parents and brothers and sisters. When she asked when her father would come for her, her master was angry and the priest frowned. Father Bigot was more sympathetic than he dared show and worried about her state of health. Finally he persuaded the Abenaki sachem to give up the little English rose, and he took her up the old Indian trail to Montreal in the autumn of 1708. Esther had been with the Indians living their primitive life for five years and two months.

The priest took Esther to the home of the governor of Quebec where she was warmly welcomed by Monsieur de Vaudreuil and his wife. The parting between Esther and Father Bigot must have been painful for them both. For five years this kind man had been her teacher and protector, trying to help her overcome the shock of being torn from her family and familiar surroundings.

Now she must make another adjustment, from a primitive Indian wigwam to the luxury of the Château Saint Louis. She was now twelve years old and on the threshold of womanhood. Was she dazzled by her new surroundings, or did she still remember her old home and long to see her parents again? We cannot know, as Esther left no impressions of her move to Montreal. We do know that no effort was made by the governor to return her to her father and mother, in spite of pleas sent through Governor Dudley of Massachusetts.

The next change in Esther's circumstances shaped the course of her life. Madame de Vaudreuil received a coveted appointment as assistant governess to the royal children of the French court, so she entered her daughter Louise and Esther in the boarding school at the Ursuline convent in Quebec. Due to her studies with Father Bigot in the Indian village, Esther was able to pass the examination and take her first communion shortly after entering the school.

The young girl was happy in the school, beloved by the nuns, and she expressed the desire to become a nun. The governor would not give his consent to this, as Esther, whether she realized it or not, was an important political prisoner. Up to this time, Governor de Vaudreuil had given no indication that he would release the Wheelwrights' daughter, in spite of the prominence of her father. However, negotiations between the two governments had been stepped up and pressing demands had been made by Colonel

John Wheelwright that his daughter be returned immediately. In June 1712 the French governor proposed an exchange of prisoners and Lieutenant Samuel Williams, twenty-three years old and a redeemed Deerfield captive, started out from Deerfield with the French prisoners and returned to Boston from Montreal with nine New England captives, but Esther was not among them.

In the meantime Esther was living in the Château again, apparently considered a daughter in the family. At this time also she acted as godmother for the infant daughter of Abigail Stebbins de Noyon, a Deerfield captive who married and remained in Canada. Esther missed the nuns and convent life and begged Governor de Vaudreuil to let her go back; since his wife was still in France he gave in and took her to the Ursuline convent. Her mind was made up and she began her novitiate as a nun October 2, 1712, taking the white veil January 3, 1713.

Her benefactor, Father Bigot, was overjoyed to see his protégée and pupil wearing the white veil as the bride of Christ. He paid all the expenses of the ceremony, and preached a long and emotional sermon in which he mentioned her sad state when he had first seen her in rags as a captive at Norridgewock.

In April, following the treaty of Utrecht that ended Queen Anne's War in 1713, more envoys arrived in Canada pressing for the return of all captives taken during the war. Special demands were made for the return of Eunice Williams of Deerfield and Esther Wheelwright of Wells. The first letters to reach

Esther from her parents arrived at this time with entreaties for her to return home. The teenage girl must have been torn by doubts, even though she had chosen her profession. The entire length of Queen Anne's War had been spent away from her family, five years as an Indian captive at Norridgewock and another five in Canada. She had learned to speak Abenaki and then French and no doubt had forgotten much of her native English through disuse.

The authorities of the convent, knowing the mental strain the young novice must be experiencing, decided on a drastic measure never done before: it was decided to shorten the term of probation, with the approval of Esther herself. Historians do not know what Governor de Vaudreuil thought of this plan to remove the novice from the temptation of loving and admonishing letters from home. Even if he did not approve, the church won out over the state this time. On April 12, 1714, Esther Wheelwright was invested with the black robe and veil of the Ursulines, at the age of eighteen, in a ceremony attended by the Marquis de Vaudreuil, the Bishop of Quebec and many people from fashionable society. With this ceremony Esther turned away forever from her father, mother, brothers and sisters, and her former home in Wells. She took the name Esther Marie Joseph of the Infant Jesus.

For many years there was no further word of Esther, but back in Wells her parents had not forgotten their child. They grew old, and Captain Wheelwright wrote his will. After providing for his wife and children, he wrote, "I give and bequeath to my daughter Esther Wheelwright, if living in Canada, whom I have not heard of for this many years, and hath been absent more than 30 years, if it should please God that she return to this country and settle here, then it is my will that my four sons, each of them pay her twenty-five pounds, being on the whole one hundred pounds, within six months after her return."

Esther's mother survived her husband ten years and she in turn made provision for her absent daughter if she should return home. According to the Ursuline annalist, Esther wrote to her parents from captivity and they were notified when she became a nun; but apparently the Wheelwrights did not understand that this meant a final parting.

In 1754 a young Bostonian presented himself at the grilled door which separated the nuns from the outside world and asked for an interview with his Aunt Esther. The bishop was consulted and gave his consent, so aunt and nephew met for the first time. There is no record of their conversation or even of what language was spoken. We do know that Major Wheelwright left some gifts for his aunt, including a miniature painting of her mother and also several beautiful silver pieces for the entire Ursuline community.

The last Indian war was still dragging on in 1759, but it was entering its final stages. The siege of Quebec started on July 12, 1759 with the roar of the cannons audible even inside the thick stone walls of the Ursuline convent. It was no longer safe for the nuns to remain and the order was given to vacate the buildings. Eight were chosen to stay, Esther Wheelwright among them. She was by that time sixty-three years old, and as strong and fearless as were her Maine pioneer ancestors. Weeks went by as she cared for the wounded and dying, only resting when the church bells called her to her prayers. It was a bloody and noisy siege, with cannons roaring, crashes as buildings collapsed in fiery heaps, and, worse, the moans and screams of the wounded soldiers.

Sixty days the awful siege had lasted when the battle came that tipped the scales. The English redcoats had marched up the hill to the Plains of Abraham and faced the French army across the field of battle. In that battle the English won Canada, at the price of losing their gallant commander, James Wolfe, on the field of battle. The French lost New France and also their beloved General Montcalm, who was mortally wounded and died the morning after the battle, September 14, 1759.

The French nuns were heartsick. Their whole future was in question with the English in charge. However, there were more immediate worries. They came out from the basement of the convent where they had stayed during the siege and were horrified to see the damage that had been done to the city of Quebec.

Of first importance was the burial of Montcalm. They could not find a carpenter to construct a coffin, so the old man employed by the Ursulines put

Louis Joseph, Marquis de Montcalm de Saint-Véran. Engraving reprinted from Justin Winsor's Narrative and Critical History of America, *Vol. V, 1887.*

together a rough box from boards found in the ruins of nearby buildings. At nine o'clock in the evening after the fall of Quebec the famous and brave Marquis de Montcalm was buried; no pomp, no ceremony attended the burial. A few people fell in line after the cortege which led from the house of the surgeon Arnoux to the Chapel of the Ursulines where no bells tolled. Three priests chanted the Mass; the nuns sang the responses, their voices breaking as they suppressed their sobs. To them the last hopes of New France were being buried with their general.

The Ursuline convent was repaired by the English, who needed it to house their wounded soldiers. Esther Wheelwright and other nuns nursed the soldiers and worked to restore their quarters. A Scottish regiment was among those assigned to the temporary hospital, and the kindhearted sisters immediately started knitting knee-high socks to cover their bare legs!

When the final peace treaty was signed in September of 1760, it assured the Canadians of religious freedom, and the Catholic orders retained all their former privileges. By a strange coincidence, as the English came into power in Canada, the first Englishwoman to be elected Mother Superior of the Ursulines took office. It was none other than the beloved former Indian captive, Esther Wheelwright. Mother Esther had a distinguished career as superior of the Ursulines, and on the 12th of April 1764 she celebrated the golden anniversary of her final vows as a nun. Again the Bishop of Quebec and a throng of people crowded the church to take part in the ceremonies.

Esther's spirit and energy did not diminish as she approached the age of seventy. The convent owed large sums for taxes and even their habits were becoming frayed, so Mother Esther taught the nuns to embroider on birch bark and to do other fine embroideries which were much in demand by wealthy Englishmen. In this way they made ends meet and were able even to buy black bombazine for new veils.

As her eyesight began to fail Esther was forced to give up the exacting work of fine embroidery and did the mending and ordinary sewing instead. Always busy, always devout, she had spent almost seventy years in the convent. She was a very successful teacher; she had a sweet disposition and a fine mind that commanded the respect and love of her pupils.

Mother Esther Marie Joseph, formerly Esther Wheelwright of Wells, Maine, died on the 28th of October, 1780 at the age of eighty-four years and eight months. The Ursuline annalist wrote of her: "She died as she had lived in continual aspiration toward Heaven, repeating unceasingly verses of the Psalms . . . Her ancestors were noble, but her heart was nobler still, and the memory of her virtues will be forever dear to this house . . . From 1712 to 1780 she was one of its finest ornaments and firmest supports."

One of the most amazing stories of Indian captivity during the Indian wars is that of the Johnson family of Charlestown, New Hampshire. Although this story takes place outside the Kennebec valley, I have included it because it is one of the best accounts we have of an Abenaki village and the experiences of a New England captive there. Susannah Johnson wrote her experiences many years later in a book, long since out of print and very rare, entitled *A Narrative of the Captivity of Mrs. Johnson, Containing an Account of Her Sufferings, During Four Years, with the Indians and French.*

At the beginning of Mrs. Johnson's story she was living with her husband and three children in Charlestown, New Hampshire. She was momentarily expecting her fourth child, and had her fourteen-year-old sister living with her to help with the household chores.

At daybreak on the morning of August 30, 1754, there was a knock on the door of the Johnson house, presumably the hired man ready to begin the day's work. Mr. Johnson quickly put on some clothes and opened the door, only to be met by a frightening scene. What seemed to him to be a horde of Indians, in full war regalia, their faces painted red and toma-hawks and hatchets in their hands, pushed past him uttering the most frightful cries. Mrs. Johnson afterward said that the first warning she heard was the cry "Indians — Indians."

The sack of the farmhouse and the abduction of the family and the hired man didn't take long. Mrs. Johnson's description of the scene is graphic: "I screamed and begged for quarter but by this time the savages were all over the house, some hauling my little sister out of bed; another had hold of me and another was approaching Mr. Johnson to bind him up. I was led to the door fainting and trembling and to complete the shocking scene, my three small children were driven naked to the place where I stood. On viewing myself I found that I too was naked. An Indian who had plundered three of my gowns, on seeing my situation, returned them to me. I begged for a petticoat but that was refused: We then heard the dread order to march."

The attack on the Johnson home was made by seventeen St. Francis Indians; six remained to do further mischief and eleven led the captives away through the woods. Each captive was considered to be the property of the Indian who had first laid hands on him or her. The captives were James Johnson; Susannah Willard Johnson, his wife; their three children, Sylvanus, age six, Susannah, four, and Polly, two; Miriam Willard, Susannah's sister, fourteen; a Mr. Farnsworth, and a Mr. Larrabee. Mrs. Johnson's heart went out to the latter in particular as he had left a wife and four young children behind.

Susannah Johnson had other more pressing worries, however. Her children were being forced to march through the forest with only thin shifts to wear, they were crying, which annoyed their masters, and she herself had lost a shoe, which made walking painful. They were able to rest awhile when they stopped for a breakfast which the Indians shared with them — a loaf of bread, apples and raisins taken from the house. Here a neighbor's horse wandered by, one they all knew, named Scoggins. Before the Indians could shoot the animal Mr. Johnson pointed to his wife and the Indians nodded, saying "Squaw ride." Mr. Larrabee gave her a pair of stockings for her swollen and bleeding feet, the Indians gave her a pair of moccasins, and she was helped to mount Scoggins.

After a river crossing on homemade rafts and another eight miles on the wilderness trail, the Indians motioned that they would camp for the night. Fresh humiliations were the lot of the prisoners, as the Indians had no intention of losing their prizes during the night. The three men were secured by having their legs put in splints, somewhat like leg stocks, which were tied to the limbs of trees too high to be reached. Miriam, much to her mortification, was forced to lie between two Indians with a cord placed over her with the ends under each of her captors. Apparently they decided that Susannah could not go far in her condition, and she was not tied up. She and the children were given blankets, and, exhausted by the long day, they slept.

They were roused before sunrise. The Indians made a fire, hung up the kettles stolen from Susannah's kitchen and made what she called water gruel. After this scanty meal she again climbed on the horse with help from her husband, who then walked along by her side to hold her on. After about an hour it became evident that she could no longer continue; the birth of her child was imminent.

Her Indian master took charge of the situation,

leading them to a brook where he and the other Indians built a rude hut for her use. They then took the three children off with them, leaving Mr. Johnson and Miriam to attend the mother. Mrs. Johnson was far from home, on a cold rainy day, without any conveniences, listening to her little girls crying in the distance, when she gave birth to a daughter at 10 o'clock in the forenoon of her second day of captivity. The child was named Captive.

The Indians returned, bringing baby clothes which they had brought from the house. Mrs. Johnson's master looked into the shelter and clapped his hands for joy, crying, "Two monies for me, two monies for me!" This meant that he now had two captives and would receive bounties from the French accordingly. Susannah was permitted to rest for the remainder of the day while the Indians made a litter for her use on the next stage of the trip. They also brought a needle, some pins, strips of birch bark to tie on the child's clothing, and a wooden spoon to feed it with. They gave these things to Mrs. Johnson's sister, who was caring for her. This was a responsible job for a fourteen-year-old girl, but in those circumstances young girls became women overnight, and Miriam Willard showed great maturity through all the long years of her captivity. Their supper that night was more substantial with porridge, johnny cakes and herb tea all brought in birchbark dishes.

The next day the party started out again. Mrs. Johnson with her infant in her arms was carried on the litter by Mr. Johnson, Mr. Larrabee and Mr.

Farnsworth in turn. Miriam and Sylvanus rode Scoggin and the two little girls were carried on their
masters' backs. Many privations and difficulties
arose, with the men becoming so feeble they could
hardly lift the litter with the mother and child on it.
She again tried to ride Scoggin, fearing that if she was
unable to proceed she would be abandoned in the
wilderness to die of starvation. They took her off the
horse every hour and laid her on the ground to rest.
This, she said, preserved her life during the third day.

The fourth and fifth days were remembered as
periods of almost complete exhaustion, with the
Indians sending out hunting parties with no luck.
The flour was gone and starvation was a threat. The
horse must be shot. The meat was thrown into kettles
of boiling water and when done it was divided
between Indians and captives alike: in fact, Mrs.
Johnson said the tenderest pieces were given to the
captives. The children were so hungry that they ate
too fast and too much and were not well for the next
few days. Mrs. Johnson and the infant were given
broth seasoned with roots. Because of the scanty
rations she was not able to nurse the baby and Mr.
Larrabee undertook the job of carrying the child and
feeding her soft foods, thus saving her life.

On the sixth day another crisis arose. The faithful
Scoggins was no more, which meant that Mrs. Johnson would have to march with the rest, when the
Indian war whoop sounded to signal the beginning
of the day's journey. Her master came over to her and
tied up her skirts with some bark and then ordered

her to "Munch." "Munch" she did with her little boy and three Indians somewhat in the rear of the main party, until all of a sudden her strength failed and she fell to the ground. As she fell she saw an Indian raise his hatchet over her head while her son screamed, "Mama do go on, for they will kill you." As she revived she saw her master angrily berating the Indian who had threatened her life and his hopes of a good price for two captives.

They went on in this manner day after day, fording cold and swift streams, in one of which the baby was dropped but miraculously recovered, suffering through a severe thunderstorm with torrential rains and going without food after the horsemeat was gone. The captives were in a pitiable state, and looked more like ghosts than anything else. Sylvanus had marched the whole time barefoot, as had most of the others, and every foot was lacerated and bleeding. Mr. Farnsworth and Mr. Johnson took turns carrying Mrs. Johnson although they themselves were exhausted and almost at the end of their strength.

On the ninth day the Indians made signs indicating that they would arrive at Lake Champlain before night. This gave everyone new life; it meant that they would at last travel by boat and would arrive at a French settlement where they could get help. Mrs. Johnson wrote that the hour she spent on the shore of the huge lake looking out over it toward the other side was one of the happiest she had ever experienced.

The stormy night passage across the lake proved to be almost as bad as marching through the woods.

Mrs. Johnson was told to lie flat on the bottom of the boat, and when stiffness and pain forced her to move she was hit with the paddle. At daybreak the group reached a large rock on the west side of the lake where they landed and built a fire. Some of the Indians went to a French house nearby and brought back meat, bread and green corn.

At this place the captives were initiated into a custom of the Indians which they had not anticipated. Who would have thought that these New England villagers would be taught to dance by their Indian masters? The war dance they were to learn would be used to celebrate their arrival in home territory. Every prisoner who could move must take part and learn the dance steps; in addition he must also sing the accompaniment.

Their imminent arrival at the Indian village was the time the captives most feared as it was then, in most tribes, that prisoners were tortured and forced to run the gauntlet. However, these captives were fortunate to have been taken by Abenakis, who did not torment their prisoners. Indian scholars have said that there are no recorded instances of women or girls being molested in any way by any of the Abenaki tribesmen, and Mrs. Johnson's story bears out this fact. The hardships they endured on the trail were only those which the Indians went through themselves.

The war dance began with Sylvanus, who was taught a song and dance that had to be done around the campfire. Mrs. Johnson had to perform also with a song which she remembered many years later as "Danna Witchee nathchepung." During the whole thing the Indians carried on an infernal yelling and screeching that was very hard on the captives' nerves. Some other Indians joined the group and the war dance started all over again for the benefit of the new arrivals.

The war dances, which were frightening and painful for the captives, were finally over and the party embarked again in their frail crafts. The prisoners did not realize it, but they were about to taste the comforts of civilization for the first time since leaving Charlestown. They arrived around noon at Crown Point on the shores of Lake Champlain, where there was a fort and a French settlement of around 1,500. There they were handed over to the French very formally, as the Indians were very fond of ceremony. Each captive was taken by the hand and led by his master to be presented to the commandant and his wife.

One can easily imagine the scene: the pitiful parade of the prisoners, formerly residents of a civilized community, living in comfortable well-furnished homes, well dressed and well fed. Now they were emaciated, dirty, with their clothes in tatters and rags, being taken by their savage masters to meet elegant foreigners who no doubt could not speak a word of English. The captives would not be able to communicate with the French any better than they had with the Indians.

First in line was Mrs. Johnson's master, who not

only seemed to be the leader of the group but had the added prestige of owning two captives, even though one was only a week old. He was leading Mrs. Johnson with her baby girl in her arms. The little girls followed with their respective masters. Miriam, Sylvanus, Mr. Johnson, Mr. Farnsworth and Mr. Larrabee completed the slow procession through the grounds and up to the residence of the French commandant.

After they were paraded before the officer and answered questions, the captives were taken to his private apartments, away from their Indian captors. The language barrier proved no barrier at all to the hospitality and sympathy lavished upon the prisoners by the family of the commander. They were served brandy and a good dinner, given milk for the infant and clean clothing. They could not believe their good fortune, but more was to come. Mrs. Johnson was provided with a nurse, who restored her exhausted strength by feeding her nourishing broths and keeping her in bed. The commander's wife found clothing for all the older children, and as for the baby, she took it while Mrs. Johnson was napping on the first day and returned it so beautifully dressed that Susannah simply could not believe that it was her baby.

On the fourth day of their stay at Crown Point, much to their disappointment, the captives were delivered back to their Indian masters and boarded a boat for the trip to the St. Francis Indian village. A little while after they embarked another boat drew up beside them. In it was a white woman on her way to Albany. Mr. Johnson begged her to take a letter to the authorities there, to inform their relatives and friends that they were prisoners of the Indians, on their way to Canada.

The voyage continued with several stops until they reached a plateau of land a few miles from St. Francis. They landed and preparations were begun for the triumphal entry into the home village of the Indians. For this the captives were forced to submit to being painted with vermilion mixed with bear grease, which was applied in stripes on their cheeks, foreheads and chins. Then two Indians went ahead to the village to announce the imminent arrival of the band of warriors with their spoils and captives. As soon as the news spread pandemonium broke loose, and the victory celebration was on. Yells, shrieks and screams resounded from every side and were returned by the approaching Indians. As soon as the group landed a horde of Indians rushed to the shore and formed themselves into two lines, men, women and children. The captives knew that they must march through the dreaded gauntlet and feared, at the very least, to be badly beaten. Much to their surprise, each Indian merely gave them a tap on the shoulder.

When they had run the gauntlet each captive was led to the wigwam of his master. When Mrs. Johnson entered the wigwam, her captor's brother greeted her with a wampum belt and her master gave her another; the two belts were placed over her shoulders. The wigwam had no floor, an open fire in the center, and little furniture. There were only a few birchbark dishes for cooking, and wooden bowls for eating.

This night was a very depressing one for Mrs. Johnson; she had her baby with her but she did not know how her husband and other children were faring. She worried about Polly — two years of age, hardly more than a baby — and Sylvanus, a sensitive little boy. She herself was in a primitive dwelling with several warriors and their squaws, not knowing how long she must live there.

One of the squaws cooked hasty pudding and put the whole mess into a large wooden bowl. Mrs. Johnson was given a wooden spoon, as were all the others, and motioned to draw up to the dish. There were no chairs, as the Indians were accustomed to squatting on their heels. This the captive found impossible to accomplish, even though the squaws showed her how they first fell upon their knees and then effortlessly sat back upon their heels. She realized that they were making funny remarks about her awkwardness, and all in all it was not a comfortable night. The sleeping arrangements were as informal as everything else. She was given a small raised platform covered with a blanket for her bed and the Indians just threw themselves down anywhere they found a space in the wigwam.

The next afternoon Mrs. Johnson and her infant were taken to the main square of the village to attend the grand parade. A large crowd was there; when everyone was assembled and quiet an aged chief walked forward and began to talk. His oration was delivered in a solemn manner with expressive motions, the audience giving close attention. Mrs. Johnson was much impressed with his sincerity and oratory even though she could not understand a word he said.

When the speech was over she was startled to see her little boy brought forward and a pile of blankets put by his side. It appeared that his master and Mrs. Johnson's wished to exchange prisoners. Her master was a hunter who preferred to have a boy who could be taught to hunt. So the deal was made; Sylvanus plus the blankets were exchanged for Mrs. Johnson, her baby and the two wampum belts.

It was a fortunate exchange for Susannah Johnson, for when she was taken to the home of her new owner she found he was the son-in-law of the grand sachem; he was rich and lived in a comfortable house instead of a wigwam. Soon after she arrived an interpreter came to inform her that she had been adopted into the family and would be considered one of them. It is thought that this interpreter was old Samuel Gill, her master's father. He himself had been brought to the village as a captive when very young and had decided to stay there, even though his father made a trip from New Hampshire to take him back home. He later married a young girl captive, taken from Kennebunk, Maine, and they raised a large family, becoming life-long residents of St. Francis. Their son, Joseph-Louis Gill, was the man who had just purchased Mrs. Johnson; thus her master was a white man. He told her later that he had an English heart but his wife was

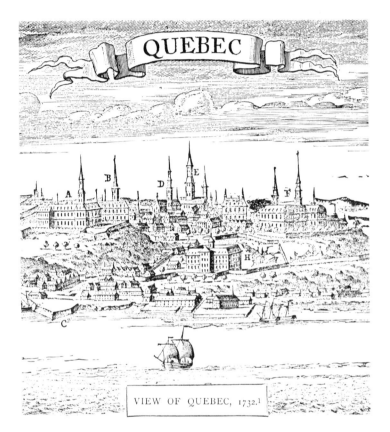

VIEW OF QUEBEC, 1732.[1]

Visible in this engraving of Quebec are buildings which would become very familiar to captives from New England. According to the legend, A marks the Fort; B the Recollets; C the Platform; D the Jesuits; E the Cathedral; F the Seminary; and H the Bishop's House. The Ursuline convent would be located between spires B and D and some distance behind them. In the foreground is the St. Lawrence River. Reprinted from Justin Winsor's Narrative and Critical History of America, *Vol. V, 1887.*

of pure Indian blood.

Mrs. Johnson was introduced to the family and told to call them brothers and sisters. She replied that she was grateful to have been brought to a house of such high rank, and if they would be patient she would try to learn the customs of the village.

They were interrupted by the announcement of another grand parade. This was to be a celebration of the return of some warriors from raiding parties in New England. Much to our captives' horror the spoils of war on this trip turned out to be a collection of scalps, carried on long poles so all could see them. Mrs. Johnson wrote, "This is savage butchery on my murdered countrymen. The sight was horrid!" She escaped as soon as possible and returned to her new home, with the savage yells that accompanied the war dance ringing in her ears.

The captives tried to adjust to their new and primitive environment but it was difficult. Mrs. Johnson was treated with kindness by her new sisters and brothers, but she had trouble learning to work with bark in making canoes and baskets, or to make a tumpline, a strap to be slung across the chest or forehead to support a heavy load carried on the back. However, she was an expert seamstress, and made shirts and jackets for her brothers. She was also allowed to milk the cows, often accompanied by her master's youngest son, a boy of seven or eight named Sabbatis who had taken a great liking to her baby, Captive.

The Johnson family visited each other during the

day and talked over their fears. The men might at any time be taken to the deep woods on long hunting trips, or, worse, be forced to accompany the warriors on raids to New England. Trying to escape from the wily Indians was futile and those who had tried it were dealt with very harshly, the penalty being death.

The Indians, in most cases, were anxious for a monetary return for their captives, so within a few days of their arrival in St. Francis Mr. Johnson was taken to Montreal to be sold, followed by Mr. Larrabee, Miriam Willard, and little Susannah and Polly Johnson. Mr. Farnsworth was taken on a hunting trip by his master but apparently was a poor hunter, so he too was sold in Montreal. The adults were sold to wealthy French families for use as house or garden workers, and the children were probably bought for reasons of humanity to rescue them from the Indians.

Some of the Indians would not sell their child captives. In the first place they loved children, and if they were boys they hoped to make good hunters and warriors of them. This is what happened to Sylvanus Johnson; he never was sold to the French but would live with the Indians for six years, until his parents finally ransomed him after the last French and Indian War.

Mrs. Johnson saw her family leave St. Francis one by one until only she, Captive, and Sylvanus were left. One morning a fresh disaster struck. Her little boy came running to her sobbing hysterically, saying that his master was going to take him to the northern wilderness on a long hunting trip. His Indian master followed and started to drag him away while the boy begged his mother to keep him with her. She could not, as the Indian unclenched his arms from around her waist and carried him off. As they went she heard him cry, "Mama, Mama, I shall never see you again." She shouted after him, "Farewell, Sylvanus, God will preserve you." She could not know whether he heard her or not and she burst into tears.

It was now the 15th of October, forty-five days since her capture, and Mrs. Johnson was sinking into a deep melancholy. She was allowed to visit a French family who lived three miles away and to go fishing with a group of squaws. She had become so weak that she often stopped to rest, causing the Indian women to think she was lazy. They showed no resentment but some called her a "no good squaw," which, she said, was the only reproach her sisters ever gave her.

At the time of Mrs. Johnson's stay there, the village of St. Francis contained about thirty wigwams which were scattered about in a disorderly manner. There was a church in which Mass was said every night and morning, and on Sunday the parishioners were called by the ringing of a bell. A French Jesuit priest was in charge of the parish and he lived on the edge of the village. He was a person of great authority and was almost on a par with the Grand Sachem, who was the leader in all non-religious affairs.

The Grand Sachem in 1754 was the father-in-law of Joseph-Louis Gill, who was Mrs. Johnson's master. Joseph-Louis Gill himself became Grand Sachem on the death of his father-in-law and held the post for over fifty years; he was a remarkable man and had the complete respect of the Abenakis of St. Francis, in spite of the fact that he was of pure English blood. The sisters whom Mrs. Johnson mentions were his sisters, Josephte and Marie-Appoline, who as unmarried women lived with their brother. Even though they were white women they had both been born in St. Francis and raised as Indians, and Mrs. Johnson referred to them as squaws.

The village priest was concerned about the young captive's depression and held many conversations with her, trying to convert her to Catholicism, thinking that the solace of religion would improve her mental condition. This she could not bring herself to do as her Protestant background was too strong.

In early November she received a letter from her husband, who had been busy in Montreal trying to make arrangements for the remaining three members of his family to come there with him. She showed the letter to Mr. Gill, who agreed to take her to Montreal to be sold. They set out in a little canoe on the four-day trip to Montreal with Mr. Gill, one of his sisters, Mrs. Johnson and her baby. Unhappily, Sylvanus had gone up north with his master on an all-winter hunting trip; there was no way of reaching him even if his owner would have allowed him to leave.

When they arrived in Montreal she was met by her husband, sister, children and friends. They had all been purchased by Frenchmen of means and were being well treated. A Monsieur DuQuesne had bought Miriam Willard and she was acting as the family seamstress. The eldest daughter Susannah had been taken by three wealthy sisters, Mesdemoiselles Jaisson; and two-year-old Polly was owned by the mayor of the city, whose wife had fallen in love with her.

Mr. Johnson had obtained a parole of two months in order to return to New England to raise funds for the ransom of his family and employees. He left the day after Mrs. Johnson's arrival. This devoted husband and father never ceased working for the release of his family for the six long years of their captivity, in spite of the fact that he was himself a prisoner, part of the time behind bars. It is a great loss to history that most of the voluminous correspondence which he carried on with both the French and English authorities seems to have disappeared.

Mrs. Johnson was still an Indian prisoner and negotiations must be completed before they would let her go. Her master demanded one thousand livres for the mother and child, but M. DuQuesne had decided on seven hundred as his top offer. When the Indians threatened to take the captives back to St. Francis, he gave in and the deal was completed. Mrs. Johnson's joy on being delivered from Indian captivity was unbounded, with the only flaw the absence of her six-year-old boy. She was received kindly by the DuQuesne family and worked as a housemaid during her stay there. She built her hopes on the success of her husband's trip to Boston and looked forward to freedom on his return.

Susannah Johnson

At this time Susannah Johnson reflected on her life with the Indians, and although it was a very painful period for her she wrote the following tribute to them:

"In justice to the Indians, I ought to remark that they never treated me with cruelty to a wanton degree; few people have survived a situation like mine, and few have fallen into the hands of savages disposed to more leniency and patience. Modesty has always been a characteristic of every savage tribe; a truth which my entire family will corroborate. They are aptly called the children of nature, and those who have profited by education and improved themselves should receive our esteem.

"Can it be said of civilized conquerors that they are willing to share with their prisoners the last ration of food when famine stares them in the face? Do they ever adopt an enemy and salute him by the tender name of brother or sister?"

Thus ended Mrs. Johnson's captivity by the Abenakis and her stay in St. Francis. However, it was by no means the end of the Johnson family's adventures. The worst was yet to come.

Back in Boston Mr. Johnson appealed to the General Assembly of Massachusetts for money to redeem the prisoners. He was granted only 10 pounds to help defray his expenses. He then went to New Hampshire where the General Assembly gave him 150 pounds sterling in the form of a letter of credit to Col. Cornelius Schuyler of Albany. But before he could leave for Canada, he was ordered by Governor Shirley of Massachusetts to return to Boston, as the increased fighting made it impossible to cross the Canadian border. Mr. Johnson was now in a dilemma: his leave was good for only two months, his Indian guides were waiting at Albany to escort him back to Montreal, but he was denied a passport or permission to leave by Gov. Shirley.

He was detained the remainder of the winter and into the spring, while the situation of Mrs. Johnson and her family in Montreal was becoming critical. M. DuQuesne made every provision for them for two months; but when Mr. Johnson failed to return as agreed, Mrs. Johnson and her sister took a small room and made a living by sewing.

When Mr. Johnson finally made his way back to Montreal the French and Indian War had accelerated to the point of halting all prisoner redemptions. The $438.00 which he brought for that purpose somehow disappeared in the hands of corrupt officials. Mr. Johnson was thrown into jail for overstaying his leave, while Mrs. Johnson and her sister continued as seamstresses to earn a living.

While in Montreal Mrs. Johnson visited her little girl Polly, who had been bought by the wife of the mayor of the city with the apparent intention of keeping her for life. Polly's cries when her mother left the visit were very upsetting, and the mother was forbidden to visit her again. Mrs. Johnson at once called upon an interpreter to take her to the mayor's lady, who received her with coolness and informed her that Polly was hers and that she had no intention of giving her up. Mrs. Johnson left with a heavy heart; but in a day or so the mayor's wife had a change of heart, and Mrs. Johnson received a message that she might have her child. She joyfully went to pick up Polly, along with a large amount of clothing given by the mayor's wife to the little girl as a parting present.

On July 22 Mr. Johnson was released from jail and he and his wife and two youngest children were put on board a vessel for Quebec. To leave their friends and relatives in Montreal was difficult. Ransom had been paid for Miriam Willard, Mrs. Johnson's sister, but she was not permitted to go with them. Larrabee and Farnsworth had paid the full price of their redemption but also were not allowed to go home. Not a word had been received from Sylvanus, who was still with the Indians.

Upon arrival in Quebec, the Johnsons, children and all, were taken to the criminal jail, even though they were political prisoners. Mrs. Johnson gave a graphic description of the place:

"We now, to our indescribable pain, found the fallacy of the governor's promises for our welfare! The jail was too shocking for description. In one corner sat a poor man sick with the smallpox; in another were some lousy blankets and straw; in the center stood a few dirty dishes, and the whole presented a scene miserable to view. The terrors of starvation and the fear of suffocating in filth were overpowered by the more alarming evil of smallpox, which none of us had had."

Susannah Johnson

On the fifteenth day Mrs. Johnson's fears were realized and she was moved to the hospital with the dread disease, leaving her husband and two small children in the prison. Mr. Johnson found a woman to take the infant to the Lord Intendant with a plea that she be taken care of until their release. The commander took the baby in his arms, said that it was a pretty little English devil and it would be a pity for it to die. He furnished money for its care and the woman took it home with her.

Mr. Johnson, little Polly, and even the baby came down with smallpox in turn. It is amazing that all of them recovered, as little was known about the treatment of smallpox in 1754. Mrs. Johnson rejoined her family after the worst was past. Winter approached, adding to the suffering of the Johnson family. They had in their cell only two chairs, two dirty blankets, a heap of straw, and a small cooking kettle. Six slow months passed in the criminal jail.

Finally an appeal reached the ears of the Lord Intendant and he went to see them; he professed himself shocked at their living conditions and said he would write a letter to the governor. In answer Governor Vaudreuil gave the order for the Johnsons to be moved to the new jail, called the civil prison, where conditions were much better. They had a decent bed, candles, fuel, and other necessities allowed prisoners of war. Mr. Johnson was allowed fifteen pence per day, because of his lieutenant's commission which he held under King George II. Mrs. Johnson was permitted to go to town to buy supplies once a week.

This was in such contrast to their former living conditions that they were in much better spirits and health. Mrs. Johnson even remarked that they imagined themselves the favorites of fortune, and in high life! Other prisoners joined them from time to time in the civil prison: a Captain Milton and his crew who were captured at sea; Captain McNeil and his brother from Boston; and Colonel Schuyler, taken during the capture of Oswego by the French in August 1756.

In December of that year Mrs. Johnson bore a son, who lived only a few hours. They buried the infant boy under the cathedral church. To add to Mrs. Johnson's sorrow she received a letter from her sister Miriam with sad tidings from home. Their father Moses Willard had been killed by Indians on his own farm at the age of 53. At the same time her brother was wounded, escaping to the fort with a spear sticking in his thigh. All this grief weakened her to the point of collapse; she was carried to the hospital where she remained for a month before starting a slow recovery.

In May of 1756 a petition to the governor was granted and Miriam Willard was sent from Montreal to be with her sister's family. The teenage girl had supported herself as a seamstress until then. The two sisters had not seen each other for two years.

James Johnson was a man of determination and continued his attempts to be released. An appointment was finally obtained and he and his wife were conducted to the home of the Lord Intendant of Quebec to make their appeal. They stated that they had been prisoners for more than three years, had suffered everything but death and feared that that too would be their fate unless they were freed. His lordship listened with sympathy and promised to take action. In seven days they received a permit to leave the prison. Mrs. Johnson wrote: "It is not easy to describe the effect of such news; only those who have felt the horrors of confinement can imagine the happiness we enjoyed when we breathed, once more, the air of liberty."

The family found lodgings in town, and in early June heard of a ship which would sail to England with prisoners of war for an exchange. Mr. Johnson wrote another letter begging that his entire family be included and that his daughter Susannah be sent from Montreal and his son from St. Francis so the family could leave the country together.

Unfortunately, conditions in Canada during the French and Indian War were so chaotic that one official did not know what the other was doing. Orders were given and countermanded right and left. First the Johnsons were told that their two eldest children would be sent to Quebec to join them. The ship arrived without Susannah or Sylvanus but with a letter saying that Mr. Johnson was to stay as a prisoner of war and that only Mrs. Johnson and her two youngest children could sail. At the last minute her sister Miriam was allowed to go also.

This young mother, still in her twenties, who had gone through so much, was now offered the chance to sail to a foreign land with no money, no friends, with only part of her family, leaving the remainder in the hands of the enemy. She could not get Sylvanus off her mind; how had he fared on the long winter hunting trip? She knew, too, that a trip to Europe was a lengthy and dangerous journey, and after she got there she must somehow find a way to get back to America. All this with a teenage sister and two small children.

Her decision was a hard one to make, so hard that she called in their captive friends to help them decide. With Col. Schuyler as chairman the committee urged Mrs. Johnson to take her youngest children and leave. Mr. Johnson would continue his efforts to redeem Susannah and Sylvanus and follow when he could. Mrs. Johnson's story continues:

"I had so long been accustomed to danger and distress, in the most menacing forms they could assume, that I was now almost insensible to their threats; and the decision to go was based on desperation . . . But then to leave a tender husband, who had so long, at the hazard of his own life, preserved my own; to part forever from two children, put all my resolution to the test, and shook my boasted firmness.

"Col. Schuyler, whom we had ever found our benevolent friend, promised to use his influence for Mr. Johnson's release, and for the redemption of our children.

"On the 20th of July we went on board the vessel accompanied by Mr. Johnson, who went with us to take leave. We were introduced to the captain, who was a gentleman; he showed us to the best cabin, and after promising my husband that the voyage should be made as agreeable for me as possible, he gave the order to weigh anchor.

"The time was now come that we must part — Mr. Johnson took me by the hand — our tears imposed silence — I saw him step into the barge; but my two little children, my sister and I were bound for Europe.

"We fell down the St. Lawrence River only a small distance that night. The next morning the captain with a cheerful countenance came to our cabin and invited us to rise and take our leave of Quebec; none but myself complied, and I gazed, as long as sight would permit, at the place where I had left my dearest husband."

The trip was uneventful and a landing was made at Plymouth, England on the 19th of August. After unraveling much red tape, and with help from John T. Mason of New Hampshire, Susannah Johnson, her sister Miriam Willard, and her little girls Polly and Captive finally set sail for America on the warship *Orange*. On the tenth of December, after a passage of seven weeks, the ship dropped anchor at Sandy Hook, New Jersey, and Susannah Johnson had the supreme satisfaction of setting foot on her native soil, after an absence of three years, three months and eleven days.

In New York the family were given lodgings, ordered by the mayor of the city, and Mrs. Johnson was overjoyed to meet Col. Schuyler, who had been released and gave her news of her loved ones in Canada. Mr. Johnson had been released and was on his way home via Halifax; he had redeemed Sylvanus from the Indians for the sum of five hundred livres. Larrabee had made his escape from the French and was on his way home.

The little group traveled to New Haven by water, from there to Springfield and then to Hartford. At Hartford they met some men bound for Charlestown, who offered to take Miriam along with them; she accepted, as she was anxious to get home to her widowed mother and other relatives.

In the meantime Mr. Johnson had left Boston and started out for Charlestown when he met a man who had heard that the family were in Springfield. The news was received late at night, but he pushed on, and as Mrs. Johnson wrote, "At two o'clock in the morning of the first of January 1758, I again embraced my dearest friend — I would describe my emotions of joy, could words only paint them sufficiently forcible; but the pen shrinks from the task."

Mr. Johnson settled his family safely in Lancaster, New Hampshire, since Charlestown was still a frontier town periodically raided by the Indians. Then he set out for New York to settle his Canadian accounts, which were in a tangle. On the trip he met Governor Pownal, who persuaded him to take a captain's commission and join some forces bound for Fort Ticonderoga.

Susannah Johnson received the sad news that her husband had been killed in battle on the eighth of July, and wrote in her memoirs: "Humanity will weep with me. The cup of sorrow was now replete with bitter drops. All my former miseries were lost in the affliction of widowhood.

"In October 1758 I was informed that my son Sylvanus had reached Northampton, and was sick of a scald. I hastened to the place and found him in a deplorable condition; he had been brought there by Major Putnam, with Mrs. Howe and her family on their return from captivity. The town of Northampton had taken charge of him. When I found him he had no recollection of me, or of his father. It was four years since I had seen him being dragged away to hunt with his Indian master; he was now eleven years old. During his absence he had forgotten the English language, spoke a little broken French, but was perfect in Abenaki. He had been a captive with the savages for three years followed by one year with the French. His habits were Indian; he had suffered numerous hardships on hunting expeditions; he could brandish a tomahawk or bend a bow. I carried him home to Lancaster."

Mrs. Johnson became homesick for her old home and returned to Charlestown in 1759, five years after being dragged half naked from her house with all her family. She remarked that the return to her former residence gave her a strange mixture of joy and grief, while the desolations of war, and the loss of a number of dear and valuable friends and relatives, including her own father, combined to give the place an air of melancholy.

Soon after the Johnson family returned to Charlestown, Major Robert Rogers marched through with his Rangers on their way back from the village of St. Francis, which they had destroyed, killing most of the inhabitants in their early morning raid. In addition to the Indians killed, they had taken many captives, including the wife and children of Joseph-Louis Gill, Susannah's former master. Mrs. Gill, her mistress, had been killed, but her two sons were finally able to make their way back to St. Francis.

One of these boys was with Rogers' Rangers now. When they stopped at Mrs. Johnson's house, the Indian boy cried out, "My God, my God, here is my sister." It was little Sabbatis who used to go with Mrs. Johnson to milk the cows and who loved little Captive. He was overjoyed to see her, and declared that he was still her brother. Mrs. Johnson wrote: "Poor fellow, the fortunes of war had left him without a single relative, and in the hands of his country's enemies; in me he had found someone who could feel his miseries; I felt the purest pleasure in administering to his comfort."

Sabbatis went from Charlestown to Crown Point with Major Rogers. At Otter Creek he met Sylvanus, who had gone into the army with his uncle Col. Willard. When Sabbatis recognized him, he clasped him in his arms in a demonstration rare for an Indian, and said, "My God, the fortunes of war!" Mrs. Johnson always remembered this young boy with affection, the son of a white father and an Abenaki mother. She said he had a high sense of honor and good behavior, was affable and good natured.

There was still a sad empty spot in the Johnson

home. Daughter Susannah was still in Canada, and while she was treated with love and kindness by Mlles. Jaissons, she missed her mother, brother and sisters and was extremely grieved over her father's death. But the moment had not arrived for her to return, and there were still some troubles ahead for the Johnson family.

The Indians still had revenge in their hearts and Charlestown was again their target. In the summer of 1760 Mrs. Johnson's brother-in-law, Mr. Joseph Willard, was taken from his home in Charlestown with his wife and five children. They went over the same route the Johnsons had. For fourteen days they endured the hardships of the trail and two of their children died of exposure in the wilderness. They arrived in Montreal a few days before the French finally surrendered to the English, and after four months' absence, they returned home bringing young Susannah Johnson with them.

Mother and daughter embraced after more than five years of separation. Susannah did not recognize her mother, as she had not seen her since the age of four. She spoke nothing but French. Mrs. Johnson remarked that her family was now a mixture of nations; Susannah spoke nothing but French and Sylvanus spoke Abenaki and a little French. With the arrival of Susannah, the family was complete, with the exception of James Johnson, the father who had died on the field of battle.

Our nation was forged by people like these, who suffered a great deal during its stormy birth.

The Abenakis:
Aborigines of Maine

A final farewell to the Kennebec Indians.

Hereditary Chief of the Abenaki Indians is the title held by Stephen Laurent of Intervale, New Hampshire. He was born on the St. Francis reservation in the province of Quebec; he is a graduate of Nicolet Academy and College, Nicolet, P.Q. His father, Chief Joseph Laurent, was a student of Indian culture and language and wrote the authoritative Abenakis and English Dialogues, *which contains, among other things, an etymology of Abenaki names. The foreword of the book is signed with his true Indian name, Sozap Lolo, followed by "alias Joseph Laurent."*

It was Joseph Laurent's desire to return to the land from which his forefathers had come, and Stephen has lived in Intervale since his teens. There he and his wife Margery now run an Indian shop and conduct research on the language and history of the Abenakis. The shop carries Indian-made moccasins, dolls, and other souvenirs, as well as books and magazines pertaining to Indian life and culture. Along with the purchases, the interested customer receives lively conversation about the history of the shop and how Indian baskets were made by Stephen's mother. Samples of her beautiful handiwork are exhibited along with the original molds she used in fashioning them. There is also a replica of a birchbark wigwam nearby. The Laurents make regular visits to Odanak, formerly St. Francis, where Stephen's sister still lives. They buy most of their Indian goods on these trips to Canada.

Stephen Laurent. Photograph by the author.

The Abenakis: Aborigines of Maine

Stephen Laurent has followed his father in trying to keep alive the culture and language of the Abenakis. He has translated Father Rasle's French-Abenaki dictionary into English, and is now working on another French-Indian dictionary. He has made recordings for the Maine State Museum of the Lord's Prayer and stories in Abenaki, to demonstrate and preserve the sound of the language. He is also a popular lecturer on the Indians.

The following chapter is a lecture given by Stephen Laurent to the Vermont Historical Society some years ago. It has been published in Vermont History *magazine under the title "The Abenakis: Aborigines of Vermont," but his comments apply equally well to the Abenakis of the Kennebec valley. Mr. Laurent kindly gave me permission to use this material.*

PAAKUINOGWZIAN, NIDOBAK! In other words, How do you do, my friends! Although the word *paakuinogwzian* really means "you look new to me," it is the nearest approach to the English greeting, "How do·you do?"

Since my topic is the Abenaki Indian tribe, it would seem that the first step would be to define the terms and see how the Abenakis relate to other groups ethnically, and then to consider our group under the aspects of language, religion and medicine.

The Abenakis were a subdivision of the Algonquin nation. According to ethnologists, there were two great native confederacies at the time of Cartier and Champlain: the Algonquins and the Iroquois. The Algonquins stretched from Newfoundland to the Rockies and from Hudson's Bay to the Carolinas. Like an island in the midst of these Algonquins were the Iroquois, or Five Nations, with New York state as their main habitat. Generally speaking, the Algonquins were divided as follows: the northern division, north of the St. Lawrence and the Great Lakes; the northeastern division, comprising the Maritimes, eastern Quebec, and Maine, New Hampshire, and Vermont; the central division, in the mid-western states; and the western division, as far as the Rocky Mountains. The Abenakis belonged to the northeastern division.

The Abenaki Indians were only one of many New England tribes and were themselves subdivided into smaller groups, like the Sokokis, the Penobscots, the Coosucks, the Missisquoi, and others, according to the names of the regions, rivers or lakes near which they lived. The difficulty that specialists today have in making strict tribal distinctions is due to the fact that these names are geographical rather than racial. Once an anthropologist from the University of Pennsylvania, Dr. Speck, said to my father, "Well, Chief Laurent, I have studied your language and culture from an ethnic standpoint, and my conclusion is that you belong to that group of Abenaki Indians known as the Kanibessinoaks." A few years later he came back to visit my father and said, "I'll have to take that back, about your being a Kanibessinoak. Further research leads me to believe that you belong rather to the Penawobsket sub-tribe." My father just smiled and said: "Well, Dr. Speck, I hope that I'll live long enough to find out before I die just what kind of an Indian I am!"

The Abenaki Indians, as I said, belonged to the northeastern division of the Algic family. The term

The Abenakis: Aborigines of Maine

Wobanaki means Eastlander, "from the land of the rising sun."

Delving into the past history of the Indians of northern New England is made difficult because of their nomadic habits, the many epidemics that decimated them after the white man arrived, and their habit of taking everything with them as they moved from one stream to another. Even the burial-ground evidence is scarce because of the Indian practice of disinterring their dead and taking their ancestors' skeletal remains along with them when they moved on. This was commonly practiced when the encroachment of the white man's cornfields threatened profanation of their ancestors' relics. In Hemenway's writings mention is made of a group of Indians who went to an Indian graveyard in the vicinity of Nilhegan Pond and removed the bones of their ancestors lest they be desecrated by the white man's furrow.

Truly, therefore, most of what the historian has to go by must be found in the field of linguistics. It is for this reason that the study of place names is recognized as a significant field for research. Our friend, Dr. John C. Huden of the University of Vermont, has engaged in a serious study along those lines, and has done splendid work. Language study, by the way, in one instance saved the reputation of the Abenakis. The St. Francis Indians, who were the remnants of the Abenakis driven out of northern New England, go down in history as fiends; they have been painted in red for their many raids upon the English colonies.

265

The Abenakis: Aborigines of Maine

However, in one case the evidence of a chance word clears them of guilt. In Thompson's *History of Vermont* we read that in 1780 the Indians came down from Canada and destroyed Royalton. The casual reader might conclude that the raiders referred to here were the St. Francis Indians. It seems, however, that while the plundering was going on, one of the Indians suddenly espied a pair of silver buckles on some shoes. Immediately he cried out *"Wistaneron! Wistaneron!"* — "Silver! Silver!" Again our reader might think the word *wistaneron* is Abenaki for silver. But anyone familiar with both the Abenaki and the Iroquois dialects would know that *wistaneron* is an Iroquois word. Therefore the finding of this one word would be sufficient evidence for us to assert that the Iroquois Indians were the guilty ones in the destruction of Royalton.

Because of its importance as a tool of historical research, it might be appropriate to point out some facts about the Abenaki language and its characteristics.

Like all North American Indian languages, the Abenaki dialect belongs philologically to the group called "holophrastic," from a Greek compound meaning that a phrase or entire sentence or description is telescoped into a single word. The Indian mind delights in synthesis and compresses into one word both object and action, with all that modifies either object or action.

For instance, the word *awanoch*, meaning "white man," consists of *awani* and *uji*, or "who" and "from." We are told that when the Indians first beheld the white man, they exclaimed to one another: *"Awani uji? Awani uji?"* meaning, "WHO is this man and where does he come FROM?" but they considered it a waste of time and breath to say the whole sentence. To the Indians it was sufficient to say just: "Who from?" Ever since then the white man has been called *awanoch* (pronounced awanoots), and it comes from that memorable day when the red and the white race met for the first time. Since the word *awanoch* was on everybody's lips, lacking a name for the white man, the Indians figured they might as well call him *awanoch*.

Another interesting example descriptive of Indian synthesis may be found in the remarkable word *skenekwati,* Iroquois for "the left side." Actually it means, "the side from which the blood flows." That is worthy of notice since it would seem to indicate that the Indians had discovered the circulation of blood even before the celebrated scientist Harvey propounded the theory. *Skenekwati* is broken down as follows: *nekw,* flowing blood; *ati,* the side from; while the initial syllable *ske* shows return to the point of origin. In Abenaki the word for "moon" is *nahnibossat,* "the one that travels by night"; for "northern lights" we have *abasandogonal,* "lights in the shape of trees."

The coming of the Europeans demanded an expansion of the Indian vocabulary, which they met by Indianizing strange terms or coining their own names for new objects. Strangely enough the St.

The Abenakis: Aborigines of Maine

Francis Indians, living amongst French-speaking people, Indianized the English word "pancakes," *pongoksak;* while the Penobscot Indians, surrounded by English communities, have instead Indianized the French word *des crêpes* (pancakes) into *tayklapsak.* Trousers are called *peljes* from "breeches," "vinegar" has been changed into *pinegal.* As examples of coined words, we have, for "umbrella," *abagawatahigan,* or "the thing that makes a shadow"; the word for "rum" is *akwbi,* "bitter water," while a Prince Albert coat (or tuxedo) was called *papsigagihlonk pitkozon,* meaning "the coat with a slit in the back." One of the most amusing and characteristic examples of word Indianization is the Abenaki word for "clock." Not realizing the usefulness of the clock, but noticing that it was a noisy contraption which made quite a racket during the night as well as in daylight, they promptly called it *papizokwassik,* "the thing that makes a lot of noise for nothing."

The main characteristic of the Abenaki tongue is its softness. Rowland E. Robinson poetically describes it as so soft and fluttery that it would not disturb the birds or jar with the rippling streams. It does not have the harsh sounds that one is liable to find in the Iroquois. Perhaps this harshness in the Iroquois language contributed to their ferociousness. The Abenaki dialect has no letter *r,* neither does it have the guttural *ch* sound so frequent in German. For the soft *ch* as in "chin," they would substitute a still softer *tz* or *dz.* An example is the Abenaki word for "king": *kinzames,* coming from "King James." The harsh *j* is here replaced by the softer *dz* sound. When first the Abenakis came in contact with the whites, they inquired what they called the chief in the country they came from. Since King James I was then reigning, the answer was "King James." Now the nearest the Indians could come to pronouncing "King James" was "Kinzames." It did not occur to them that it consisted of two words, the last of which was a proper name; they thought they had been taught to say "chief" in English. Therefore when other kings came to the throne, whether it was Charles, George, or Edward, they would refer to him as Kinzames Charles, Kinzames George, or Kinzames Edward. Even today the Indians use the same word *kinzames,* without suspecting that it really means "King James." The derivatives from this word may seem to slight the dignity of the royal family, but at any rate we have to give credit to the Indians for coining enough words so no one could possibly feel left out. They lined them up as follows: the king was *kinzames;* the queen, *kinzamesqua,* or the king's squaw; a prince, *kinzamessis,* meaning a small king; while *kinzamesquassis* meant a small queen or princess. Finally, the Indians housed them all comfortably in a *kinzamesigamigw,* palace (or "king's wigwam").

The etymology of Indian place-names is of great importance to all students of Americana. Unfortunately, that is an exceedingly difficult branch of philology because of the fact that these Indian words have been so corrupted by the English. Sometimes the Indians themselves were at fault through either mispronunciation, faulty diction, or inadequate articulation, as a result of which there arose frequent misunderstandings and false conclusions. In his *Etymology of Missisquoi* Dr. MacAleer gives an amusing example illustrating how some white men would jump to erroneous deductions as regards the meaning of Indian words. He writes that there was a hunting lodge in the Adirondacks called *Nehasne,* and the owner told all and sundry that the meaning of this Iroquois word was "beaver on a log." Doubting the correctness of that etymology, someone got in touch with Iroquois-speaking persons and was told that it was a common enough expression meaning: "There it is! There it is!" They explained his delusion thus: probably the owner of this lodge had been out hunting beavers in the company of two Iroquois guides. They came to a beaver dam but found no beaver. Finally, one of the Iroquois espied a beaver squatting on the end of a log. Excitedly he cried out to his companion: *"Nehasne! Nehasne!"* and at the same time pointed to the beaver on the log. The white man, overhearing this, immediately concluded that it means "beaver on a log."

The Etymology of Missisquoi is itself proof of what a will-o'-the-wisp chase etymologizing on Indian names can be. At the conclusion of the book, after having consulted innumerable maps, read countless volumes, corresponded with numberless savants in the field of linguistics, Dr. MacAleer concludes: "This study was undertaken with an unbiased mind and it is ended without predilection." In other words, after all was said and done, the meaning of Missisquoi was still a mystery.

The New Hampshire State Development Commission likes to assert that "Winnipesaukee" means "the smile of the Great Spirit." Actually nothing in that word even remotely suggests either "smile" or "great" or "spirit." There is the word *nebes* or *nepes,* meaning "lake" or "region" or "territory." It is anybody's guess what the initial syllable means; therefore, no one can be dogmatic about the word and state as a fact that it means this or that. The best that any etymologist will do is to hazard a guess. I once asked Dr. Speck, Professor of Anthropology at the University of Pennsylvania, how far back he had traced that erroneous etymology for "Winnipesaukee." He replied that he had come across it in the writings of the Jesuit Father Vetromile, missionary to some Maine Indians in the 1860s. In fact, one old Penobscot Indian named Lobal told him the following story and vouched for its authenticity:

Once Father Vetromile was entertaining a visiting priest. Lobal and another Indian were paddling them lazily along the Penobscot River while the good Father was holding forth on the etymologies of this, that, and the other Indian name. When he came to the word "Winnipesaukee," he said, "Take the word 'Winnipesaukee,' for example. That means 'the smile of the Great Spirit.' " Then he turned around to Lobal for confirmation. "Isn't that right, Lobal?"

The Abenakis: Aborigines of Maine

Lobal, drowsing over his paddle, assented with a nod, saying, "Yes, Father." When they reached their destination, the priests and the Indians parted company. Suddenly Lobal's partner upbraided him for supporting the Father in his error as to the meaning of "Winnipesaukee." Said he, "You had a good chance there to put an end to that nonsense about 'Winnipesaukee' meaning 'smile of the Great Spirit.' " Lobal merely smiled and explained that it was such a beautiful afternoon, he was enjoying so the singing of the birds, the soughing of the wind in the trees, the skating of the insects over the water, that he just didn't want to spoil it all by starting an argument over something so inconsequential as the meaning of an Indian word. Lobal's viewpoint seemed to be: after all, if the white man liked to think that "Winnipesaukee" meant "the smile of the Great Spirit," what harm did it do? It wouldn't make or break the world whether "Winnipesaukee" meant that or something more prosaic like, let us say, pork and beans.

The linguistic difficulties of Father Vetromile with the Abenakis in Maine were paralleled by those of Father Aubery and other missionaries with the Abenakis of St. Francis. The Abenaki word for priest is *patlihoz*, from the French *patriarche*. Since the Abenakis always substitute the letter L for the letter R, they Indianized the French word *patriarche* into *patlihoz*. Well, there was nothing wrong in that. But sometime later the nuns put in an appearance. Since they were dressed in black like the priests, and led similar lives of prayer, meditation, and dedication to God, the Indians naturally assumed that these were wives of the priests. So they called the nuns *patlihozsqua,* or the "priest's wife." No insinuation was intended. They just figured that since it was normal for every man to have a wife, this time the priest had brought his wife with him; they were glad for him, knowing that he had heretofore led rather a lonely life, whereas now he would have someone to look after him. Needless to say, the priests were much exercised at first and went to no little trouble to explain that there was positively no relation whatsoever between the priests and the nuns. They even went a step further and forbade the use of the Indian word *patlihozsqua.* But to no avail; as with the white man, so with the Indian: pass a law against anything, and that thing becomes all the more popular. To this day, the Abenakis still use the word *patlihozsqua* when referring to a nun.

The missionaries did not make out so badly at that, when we consider the term wished upon the Trappist monks by the Iroquois on the Oka Reservation north of Montreal. Since the Indians live close to nature, they like to find names taken from plants or animals or birds with which they are familiar and apply them to new objects or persons they come across. In the case of the Trappists, the garb of that religious order brought to mind an analogy with a small animal, mostly black but with a white stripe lengthwise on his back. So the natural word for the Trappist, according to Indian deduction, was *Ratinitas,* which is Iroquois for "skunk." This story was told to me by a missionary attached to one of the Iroquois Reservations in Canada; he chuckled goodnaturedly as he explained the meaning of the word *Ratinitas,* knowing full well that the Indians had not the slightest intention of being malicious or even disrespectful.

On the Abenaki Reservation of St. Francis, the old Indians still relate how much trouble the nuns had with the mischievous little boys when they first attempted to teach them the dogmas of the Christian faith. The sisters were pretty much dependent on the Indians for the translation of French words into Abenaki. One day a nun asked a boy: "How do you say 'morning prayers' in Abenaki?" The boy paused for a moment, then replied: *"Segueskejakhigan."* (That's Abenaki for "fricassee.") The next question was a little more complicated: "Now, how should I say, 'To go to heaven you must say your prayers every morning'?" The Indian boy scratched his head for a moment, closed his eyes as in laborious concentration, as if contriving the correct answer in his mind, and came out with: *"Chaga kadi llosa spemkik, kdachowiba mitsi segueskejakhigan attassi kisgad."* (Real meaning: "In order to go to heaven, you must eat fricassee every day.") The unsuspecting nun committed the boy's answer to paper, and the next morning, at the opening of her classes, said in French: "Now we'll have to start the day right by first saying our morning prayers, because, you know, if you want to go to heaven you must say your prayers every morning." Then she went on, in her halting Abenaki, hoping to reach those who did not yet understand French: *"Chaga kadi llosa spemkik, kdachowiba mitsi segueskejakhigan attassi kisgad."* On seeing the little Abenaki boys and girls look at one another, giggling behind their books, she immediately (and correctly) suspected that she had been given a wrong "steer" by her translator.

At other times, the missionary would be led astray. It was necessary for him to obtain the Abenaki equivalents for those abstractions in which all religions abound. Unfortunately, the Indians had no use for the abstract: to them only the concrete was worth bothering with. Therefore, they had no words meaning "contrition," "mortification," "absolution," "Extreme Unction," and such. They had an abundance of words for the plants, for the animals, and for the birds; just for the moose, for example, they had no less than six different words according to whether it was a one-year-old male moose, or female moose, a two-year-old male moose, or female moose, etc. The same was true for many other animals. So that the Abenaki Indians did not encourage their missionaries too much in their questioning. To translate French terms into Abenaki meant too much strain on the Indian's lazy intellect. In most cases they would take the easiest way out and give the first word that in any way approximated the French idea. As an example, one Abenaki, on being called on to translate "Extreme Unction" in his dialect, answered, *"Awassoswipemi."* The good Father dutifully recorded the strange expression in his rudimentary lexicon, not at all suspecting that he was writing down the Abenaki equivalent of "bear grease." The Indians had observed that in giving the last rites the missionary would dip his finger in oil or grease (to an Indian the two being the same) and rub it on the body of the dying Indian. So they figured it must be bear grease. But imagine the missionary's surprise when next he visited a dying Abenaki and said to him, *"K'dachwaldam awassospemi?"* to have the moribund brighten up momentarily and say, *"Kaalatta, n'mitogwes!"* — "Sure, Father!" The priest had wanted to say, "Would you like to receive Extreme Unction?" What he actually had said was, "Wouldn't you like to have a little bear grease?" Now an Indian, even on his death-bed, is not going to refuse the gift of a bit of bear grease.

All his life the Indian used bear grease liberally: it made him handsome, he thought, by giving his skin a glistening appearance. He attributed the sickly appearance of the white man's skin to the fact that the white man did not use bear grease. We are told that it was not unusual for an Indian to walk up to a white man, observe him closely, especially the white skin with hair growing all over it, then turn away in disgust muttering, "How ugly you are!" And he meant it too. There is no doubt about it, the Indians seemed to say, *we* are the superior race, if for no other reason than that we have the best-looking skin. The mental superiority of the white man, which they readily conceded, left them indifferent: to the Indians, the appearance of the skin was of far greater

The wampum belt at top, now in the Chambre des Trésors in Chartres Cathedral in France, was made by devout Abenakis of the St. Lawrence valley around 1699. The wampum belt shown below was made by the Hurons. The Abenaki belt is approximately six feet long by five inches wide and the Huron one slightly smaller.

moment. As the eminent historian John Fiske well expressed it, "There never has existed, anywhere in the world, a people that did not take for granted its own pre-eminent superiority."

Apparently, the Abenaki Indians were no exception: like the rest of mankind, they considered their own race to be the cream of the crop. This belief was further strengthened by their theory of the creation of man. This is how it went: first, the Great Spirit made the white man and found him too white. Next, he decided to make a black man; so he made the colored race. Well, this time the man was too black. Finally, he thought he would try making a man neither wholly white nor completely black; so he made his masterpiece, the American Indian, correcting in this last creation the various imperfections which he had found in the two previous models.

Before leaving the subject of language I shall give you, as I promised, a sample of story-telling in Abenaki, so that you may have an idea of how it reads and sounds. It deals with an encounter between a party of Iroquois and a smaller group of Abenaki Indians from Missisquoi. As you undoubtedly know, there were, even as late as 1790, a cluster of about fifty Abenaki lodges at the place now called Swanton, Vermont. They had extensive cornfields near their huts, but it was also necessary to do a certain amount of hunting and fishing, and sometimes they had to go quite a distance. Once they were intercepted by a greater number of Iroquois somewhere in the vicinity of Saranac Lake. Although the Iroquois were in

The Abenakis: Aborigines of Maine

greater number, they did not quite dare to attack the Abenakis; so they just stayed on their guard, very much like two wildcats ready to spring at each other. Finally, the Abenakis got hungry and started eating the pith of a pine tree. This restored their energy and gave them new courage; so they said to one another: "Well, we might as well fight now!" So they sang the war song, executed the war dance, and uttered the war whoop. On seeing this, the Iroquois slyly retreated. When the Abenakis saw their enemies pulling out, they shouted after them: *"Maguak! Maguak!"* — "Cowards! Cowards!" And ever since then the Iroquois have been called *Maguak* by the Abenakis.

In return the Iroquois called the Abenakis *Adirondacks*, meaning "bark-eaters." They gave this name scornfully, as much as to say: "We Iroquois are man-eaters, but you soft Abenakis are mere bark-eaters!" (The word *Iroquois* does mean "man-eater": this name was given to them by the Algonquins on seeing how cruel and ferocious the Iroquois were.) But the old Indian who told me the story, far from being ashamed that his ancestors had been called bark-eaters, was actually proud of his forebears. He reasoned it this way: our ancestors were so hardy that if game was scarce, or if hard times came their way, they could always go off into the woods and live off the bark of trees, while awaiting the return of better times. His old eyes glinted as he boasted: "Nos ancêtres étaient des mangeurs d'écorce!"

In Abenaki the story goes thus:

Ni agua pasgueda wakaswak Wobanakiak wesko-

279

The Abenakis: Aborigines of Maine

kogonozsa Maguak, kwahliwi Salonnaki Nbesek.
(Once upon a time a few Abenakis were intercepted by the Iroquois, not far from Saranac Lake.) *Maguak paamalozhanik ondaki agmowo, ni mziwi Wobanakiak wmataoogwobanik chaga Maguak onda wzakpowlegwo.* (The Iroquois were more numerous than they, and all the Abenakis would have been killed if the Iroquois hadn't been afraid.) *Ninawa wibiwi wdaskooldino, taholawiba niswak pezoak ompchi kadawi awdidida.* (Therefore, they just waited, very much like two wildcats about ready to fight.)

Ni Wobanakiak kadopidid, azi pazgo w'mowon manhakwogana; ni sibiwi kistodid waji migakadit. (Finally, the Abenakis got hungry, and began to eat the pith of a pine tree, and then decided to fight.) *Nitta achi adoji moja nawadwadid, pmegodid, ta kwakwahomidid.* (Immediately they started their war song, performed the war dance, and shouted the war whoop.) *Ni kadonalgodijik kizi polwaadid, wmamhlawi Wobanakiak kogolwano: "Maguak! Maguak!"* (The enemy slyly withdrew, whereupon the Abenakis cried out: "Cowards! Cowards!") *Ni onka waji askwa liwihlomek Maguak.* (Since then they have been called Maguaks (Cowards).) *Ni ozidaiwi Maguak wdeliwihlono Wobanakiak "Adirondack" (Manhakwogana mowojik).* (In return the Iroquois called the Abenakis "Adirondacks" (Barkeaters).)

Like all other Indian peoples, the Abenakis had a conception of Divinity, but this conception was not much higher than might have been expected. Instead of yielding homage to one all-pervading and omnipotent Spirit, they would pray and make sacrifices to a multitude of greater and lesser gods. To the Indian mind it was a superiority to have many gods, and they made it clear at the outset to the missionaries that they were not going to be so foolish as to give up their thirty-seven gods for the white man's one god.

One great characteristic of the Indian religion was their worship of the Devil. In their mind it was far more important to pray to the Evil Spirit than to the Good. The latter could always be depended upon to do that which was right by them, but it was vastly different with the Devil: he had to be propitiated with offerings, prayers, and sacrifices. Of course, to the Indians the gods are not thought of as being morally good or evil, but rather as benevolent and malevolent forces. The Devil is not a tempter: he is the source of diseases, death, afflictions, and misfortunes. The Good Spirit, on the other hand, is the spirit which brings good fortune and ministers to the necessities and desires of mankind.

In addition to these good and evil spirits, the Indians had a veneration for certain animals. The bear, for instance, which by the way was the totem of the Abenakis, was held in especial esteem. They have been known to address a wounded bear with a harangue of apology. Some Indians, in fact, would apologize indiscriminately to all animals they were forced to kill. Never approving of taxidermy, they would often blow tobacco smoke at a stuffed moose, deer, or other animal: this was intended to be a propitiatory offering, since, in their opinion, the spirits of these animals must have been offended at the indignity shown to their remains.

Since the bear was the totem of the Abenakis, it was considered a good omen to have children born bow-legged. The parents would then say: "He'll turn out to be a good Abenaki: he'll go through life walking just like our totem, the Bear." A would-be wit, or nitwit, wanting to jest at the Indians' expense, once asked my father (who was very bow-legged): "Chief Laurent, are all the Indians bow-legged?" My father replied, very seriously: "No, only those who belong to the Bear clan." Not expecting to have his joke boomerang in that fashion, the inquirer went on: "Do you mean to say that those belonging to the Bear clan are invariably born bow-legged?" "Well, if they are not born that way they are made so by their parents. In my case, for instance, my mother took a small log and placed it between my knees when I was very, very young, then tied my ankles securely with *wattap* (fine roots of the red spruce). As I grew older, she used still bigger and bigger pieces of wood, until a time came when I was permanently bow-legged." "But," said the *awanoch* (white man), "where was the advantage in that?" "For the future hunter, and most of us would finally end up by becoming hunters, it was of considerable advantage to be bow-legged, if for no other reason than that we could straddle ever so much better on our snowshoes. Going to the opposite extreme, imagine a knock-kneed man trying to go on snowshoes!" Then my father explained that he could snowshoe and make only one furrow, whereas most white men snowshoe so much like knock-kneed men that they actually make two parallel furrows. In a way it means all the difference between having to look after the upkeep of a one-lane road as against a two-lane highway! When my father got home that night, he told the story to my mother, and they both had a good laugh at the white man's credulity. My father's comment was: "The white man will swallow everything, arrow, bow and quiver, just so long as it's an Indian that tells it!"

Since they had a belief in immortality, the Abenakis always showed great respect for their dead. It was customary to keep a fire burning over a fresh grave. Their conviction was that it took seven days for the souls of the departed to reach the happy hunting-grounds, and they must on no account be left in the dark, lest they lose their way. I remember, as a boy, that there were still a few at St. Francis who clung to this old pagan custom of keeping a light burning over the recently deceased. Since the custom was frowned upon by the missionaries, only a very few dared to go through with it. But I still recall vividly seeing some old Indian going towards the graveyard at dusk with a lantern in his hand; this he would plant on a pole over his relative's grave. The next morning he would go and fetch the lantern, then repeat the same performance in the evening, and this for the next five or six days.

In very ancient times, food also was left on the grave, the purpose being the same: namely, that the departed should have a little food for the journey, since they might have some difficulty at first finding the necessary victuals in their new surroundings. Since the woodchucks and the raccoons probably took care of all such delicacies left on the graves, the Indians would believe that the departed had made good use of the food left there the night before.

Indian superstition made a bridge between religion and medicine, as we see in the institution of shamanism. The shaman, or "medicine man," combined the functions of priest or soothsayer, and physician. As an example of the former of these functions we have the following story, which also explains the origin of a place-name:

It seems that once the Iroquois attacked an Abenaki village when all the warriors were absent, and, of course, killed most of the old Indians, women, and children. Upon their return to the village, the Abenaki warriors took stock of the situation, held a council, and decided to lay their case in the hands of a shaman and abide by his decision. After many incantations, adjurations, and magical songs, he said to those listening outside his magic tent: "I see our enemies: they are forty in number and are about ready to eat; they are on a small island. We will go after them immediately, and not one of them will escape."

Wdali payononi wlogwiwi, tadbogo menahanizek aoldidid Maguak. (They arrived in the evening, exactly at the little island occupied by the Iroquois.) *Niga agua niswak Wobanakiak, Tmakwa ta Moskwas, wbikagokamguinno li senojiwi menahanizek.*

The Abenakis: Aborigines of Maine

(And we are told that two Abenakis, Beaver and Muskrat, dived to the shore of the island.) *Wzokwassino ompchi maowi mitsoldowak Maguak.* (They remained submerged, while the Iroquois were in the process of eating.) *Ni sogmo adoji idak: "Tcha, nguilotahon Wobanaki."* (And the chief said: "Tcha, I am going to hit an Abenaki.") *Ni adoji mamhlawakad kchi wskan li senojiwi.* (And he hurled a big shin bone towards the shore.) *Nigaki na wawlitahon Moskwassa wdepek.* (And behold, it hit Muskrat right on the head.) *Nitta Tmakwa wgedobanon widoba waji onda waolwakw.* (Immediately, Beaver ducked his friend's head under the water so as not to attract attention.)

Ni kizi mziwi Maguak kaoldidid, ni agma adoji tedozek mziwi wiguaolal, ni sibiwi pedgi kamguid li widobaikok. (As soon as the Iroquois were all asleep, he punctured all their canoes, then dived back to his friends.) *Nitta Wobanakiak wgizojoldino, kanwa momanni wbikagono nanni achakwak.* (At once the Abenakis got ready, but they crossed very cautiously at dawn.) *Ni kizi wli wiwnikawodid Maguak, nitta w'moja migakomono: sibiwi mamhlawi kwakwahomidid ta wmattaowo mziwi Maguak.* (After they had surrounded the Iroquois, immediately they began to fight: they shouted the war-cry and killed all the Iroquois.) *Ni oji wnimakwhamno mziwi Magua'wdepal, ni yulil wiwnigobadono menahanizek.* (Then they stuck on poles all the heads of the Iroquois, and these they planted all around the little island.) *Ni onka enni menahanis waji liwitozik "Wdepsek."*

(And ever since this island has been called "Head's Island.")

This incident explains why one of the islands north of Grand Isle in Lake Champlain appears on the old maps as Head's Island, or, in French, Île aux Têtes.

The subject of illness and medicine should interest the layman as well as the medical profession. Since there is an estimated population of 20,000,000 Indians of pure or of mixed blood still living in North and South America, and since the Indian blood is continually becoming more widely diffused among the white people, we have a practical reason for inquiring into just what the Indian represents in illness and in health.

From an article entitled "Disease, Medicine, and Surgery among the American Aborigines" appearing in the *Journal of the American Medical Association*, November 12, 1932, we gather certain similarities and differences between the red and the white races. Under normal conditions, the American Indian had a markedly slower average pulse than that of the white and other races. Common opinion to the contrary, the Indian gives a lower record of muscular strength than does the white man. Furthermore, according to the medical profession, the Indian in general differs from the white man in the chemical properties of the blood. According to the anthropologist Coon in *The Story of Man*, the American Indians, barring a few exceptions, all belong to the recessive group O. These differences must needs have a bearing on his illnesses and the course they follow.

To a certain group of diseases the Indians were singularly immune, while to others they had a complete lack of immunity. Before the coming of Columbus, this country was apparently one of the most healthful continents. Ethnologists and curators of museums, who have access to the skeletal remains of Indians of undoubtedly pre-Columbian dates, tell us that these remains are remarkably free from disease. And as you know, much can be predicated as to the health record of a person from a study of that person's skeletal remains. There was no tuberculosis. Cancer was rare. There was no plague, cholera, typhus, smallpox, measles, or leprosy. There was a greater scarcity than among the whites of many diseases of the skin and of most mental disorders. On the other hand, the following illnesses were comparatively frequent: digestive disorders, pneumonia, arthritis, and a certain affliction of the eyes which is called, I believe, trachoma. Even on our reservation, I have noticed that many of our Indians, as they grow older, are very much subject to eye trouble. Many lose one eye; some become even totally blind.

Some four and a half centuries ago, the white man started bringing his diseases to this country. He brought in scourges to which the Indian lacked any immunity — to name only three, typhus, smallpox, and measles, which went through the native population like a wildfire. Syphilis and other venereal troubles brought from Europe also wrought great havoc. But the most insidious scourge of all was tuberculosis. At that time the contagious nature of the disease was unknown. Therefore, whole tribes became infected and great numbers perished. Of course, it must be admitted that many of the Indian customs are flagrantly unhygienic. As an example, take calumet-smoking on important occasions. They would take *one* calumet, which they would decorate with feathers, fur, porcupine quills and fine beadwork. In all treaty ceremonies, this calumet, called a ceremonial calumet, was passed around to everyone, even before the speeches were made and the problems discussed. The belief was that it made one think clearly and endowed the smoker with great wisdom. Perhaps it did. But it also was an important factor in spreading contagious diseases from mouth to mouth.

From the viewpoint of the white man, the discovery of America was one of the greatest events of the Middle Ages. From the viewpoint of the American Indian, it was the greatest calamity that ever befell a race, because, along with gunpowder, firewater, and other so-called benefits of civilization, the white man brought a multitude of infections against which the Indian was woefully helpless. For the diseases they knew they had various methods of treatment, but they had none for those unknown complaints brought in by the white man. Even as recently as 1925, one epidemic of measles killed off most of the Ona or Foot Indians at the southernmost tip of South America. It was apparently their first contact with the white man. What we call minor ailments or pesky nuisances, like the common cold and measles, turn out to be major affairs and fatal to primitive peoples. It has been said, and with considerable truth, that germs and bacilli did a much better job than the cannon and gunpowder when it came to ridding this continent of the American Indian.

Their treatment of diseases was partly natural and partly supernatural. Disorders of which they knew the cause were considered rationally and treated in the same manner. In every tribe the older men and women knew scores of herbs and various mechanical and other means, which they used exactly as did your country grandmothers and grandfathers, simply, rationally, and often with marked success. They knew poisons, emetics, cathartics, tonics, and narcotics. They had antidotes. They employed massage, pressure, cauterization, bandaging, enemas, cutting, scraping, suturing, and the sweat bath. The latter was probably one of their most rational forms of treatment. It was used before all ceremonial occasions — also, after a battle or when a person just felt tired out. It was almost always used in the treatment of arthritis and rheumatism. It was generally taken in what they called a sweat lodge — a small conical hut made of wickerwork and covered with skins, blankets, bark or some other fabric. Stones would be heated in the center of the lodge, then cold water poured on them, generating steam, which, in turn, would induce profuse sweating.

But whenever the cause of a complaint was obscure or when all known modes of treatment had failed, then their minds turned to the supernatural. The ailment was then conceived as an affliction caused by some offended or evil spirit or deity, as the vengeful act of an enemy, or as the magic of a sorcerer. And since the causes of the disease were supernatural, the cure could be effected only through supernatural means. And this is where the shaman, or medicine man, came in. There would be several such in each larger tribe. They had their specialties, and they had differing reputations. Some became thoroughly imbued with their function and power. They grew into venerable healers who exerted a great and generally beneficial influence in the tribe, aside from healing. They tended to become also the preservers and transmitters of the tribe's sacred traditions.

On the other hand, many of the medicine men were of lesser caliber. They ranged all the way from the well-meaning but not highly competent to mere and not seldom mischievous imposters.

There comes to mind one of these medicine men who achieved such success, not only on the St. Francis Reservation, but also in the outlying French communities, that he decided to expand his territory. In fact, he actually went to the bustling city of Montreal and opened an office on St. Denis Street. He had noticed that there were many professional men on that street — doctors, dentists, chiropractors — so he decided he would have his office right there. He hung out his shingle, which read thus: "Abenaki Indian Medicine, Inc." I called on him one day. In the course of our conversation, one of his patients, a middle-aged man, came. The shaman said to me, "Why don't you go into the other room? This will take only a short while." Through the partly open curtains I could see from where I sat what went on in the consultation room. After the usual preliminaries, the patient said to the doctor, "I have a feeling that I have high blood pressure." Without batting an eyelash, the shaman replied, "Is that so? Well, why don't I take your blood pressure right here and now?" So the white man sat on a straight-backed chair, and the Indian stood behind him, with his hands on the patient's shoulders. Then he instructed him to take a deep breath, exhale, and say "99." The white man complied repeatedly, and the Indian meanwhile pressed the patient's neck with his hand so as to give the impression that he could tell by the pressure on the neck just what the pressure was in the veins and arteries as the blood coursed up and down. After this had gone on for a few minutes, the shaman finally said, "Well, you do have a little high blood pressure, but it's nothing to worry about. I can give you some medicine that will correct that right away." The patient presently left, with an expression of satisfaction and relief, and — who knows? — it may be that the old spell of shamanism or the modern technique of suggestion had wrought a cure!

As I pointed out at the outset of my talk, it is sometimes difficult to get the Abenaki equivalent of our everyday expressions. In the case of "How do you do?" the Indians generally used *"Paakuinogwzian,"* meaning, "You look brand new to me." Likewise, for their parting words they had not the exact translation of the white man's "Farewell" or "good-bye"; but there was one expression which they invariably used whenever they had to separate to go off on their hunting expeditions, or when they had to bid their friends adieu. It was, *"Wli nanawalmezi,"* meaning, "May you have good health." I can think of no better expression than to wish each and every one of you *"Wli nanawalmezi!"* or "Good health to you all!"

The Lord's prayer in the Indian tongue, viz: the Indians of Norridgewock and Penobscot in New England, and Nova Scotia, as it was translated for their use by a French Jesuit, and attested to by four of the Indian hostages in the presence of an interpreter at Boston, Jan. 22, 1720.

> *Nemmetunx in naw   Spùmkeeg abean*
> Father ours   Heaven sitting
> *Sùngamawary moagvadtch   aveivisian*
> Made great or glorious   thy name
> *Amantenège   pàtchee   wàwittaw   wàgisaw*
> we wish and desire, or may it be
> *Kòewtepèrmoc   wāwungaunūka   ketūngwat*
> *koewtaraevtamanwungan   oownūmbbe   kikpatchey*
> *Kitùngwat   Mawmer'enee   Aramagesekog*
> give us   to-day and to come
> *Noewtoewtaskèskwaw   Awbùnnae   maenaw*
> bread
> *oowbawawtche   awnawerlaw   mawweāga*
> we desire   Forgiveness
> *Kagaungwe   whoorèegpawn*
> wherein we have made angry.
> *Neunawk   nageesee   awnawher   dawmawwaun*
> *nawshwauke*
> *Kagungweyaw   Keitbawneke*
> we forgive faults against us
> *Moosawk   awrawque   Setermekike*
> must not think or take revenge
> *Toung   moung   pawe   whootche*
> keep us from evil things
> *Sawàwgee   oownènamehènaw*
> nor persuaded to, or put upon wicked things
> *Mukka   wungguarrawtàwkesaw   kenusue*
> *Wungmenèher   meh   meuotche   keyk*
> Ill   things
> *Neawritch*
> So be it, or Amen

John Montresor's map,
later used by Benedict
Arnold to guide his
expedition to Quebec.
Original in the collection
of the Library of Congress.

294

The Surveyors

*Three British trailblazers who
explored the river valleys of Maine.*

AFTER THE INDIAN WARS, it seems likely
that the next white man to visit the
region was Lieutenant John Montresor of the British
army. In fact he made two trips, the first a scouting
party which he led in 1760. The party traveled from
Quebec on snowshoes, arriving in Topsham on February 20th almost dead from cold, hunger and
fatigue. Kenneth Roberts states in his *March to
Quebec* that Montresor and his men ate moccasins,
bullet pouches, leather breeches, belts and raw wood-
peckers to stay alive.

Montresor made a second exploratory trip on the
Kennebec in 1761, arriving from Quebec by way of
the Rivière du Loup, Penobscot Lake, Penobscot
Brook, and the West Branch of the Penobscot River.
He left an excellent journal describing the day to day
events on his journey. As we try to follow his travels
by means of the journal, difficulties appear due to the
fact that it was a military document with many

295

John Montresor

phrases containing distances and compass courses blanked out. It is like trying to figure out a mystery story, but with the help of veteran woodsmen, Lindon Collins and others, we have attempted to link the vivid descriptions with as many present-day locations as possible.

On this trip Montresor started on the 14th of June, perhaps having had enough of winter travel in the wilds of northern Maine. The small party of one white man and several Indian guides embarked on the Chaudiere River on the first lap of the trip, which was to take them on a circle tour of the upper Kennebec watershed.

The route was as follows: the Chaudiere, Rivière du Loup, Penobscot Lake and River, Moosehead Lake to the Kennebec, then down that river as far as Fort Halifax. At that point they started the return up the Kennebec to the Indian carrying place; they portaged across to the Dead River, crossed the Chain of Ponds, the Height of Land, Chaudiere Pond (now called Lake Megantic) and there entered its outlet, the Chaudiere River, and so back to their starting point.

Shortly after starting down the Chaudiere, Montresor had the misfortune of having his canoes burned in a forest fire despite the efforts of the Indians to rescue them. Fortunately, they were able to buy more from a roaming Indian tribe.

Following the trail was difficult. Montresor found that the Abenakis were jealous of the knowledge of their country and took great care to leave scanty vestiges of their trails. The Indians used blazes on the trees as their constant guides in the woods, but could follow with very few.

Entering what is now the state of Maine by crossing the Boundary Mountains, by way of a pass between Portage Lake and Penobscot Lake, the party camped, repaired the canoes, allowed the guides to rest and then searched for the Penobscot River as their waterway trail to Moosehead Lake.

At the end of the portage, which led them through a gap in the mountains, they found themselves on the banks of Penobscot Lake, which is about 4 miles in length and ½ mile wide. Montresor paddled the whole length of this lake on a southeasterly course. On this body of water he had his first sight of the mountain he called the Onegla, which we believe to be Boundary Bald Mountain. He thought it was one of the highest mountains in this part of North America.

From the southern end of this lake rises a brook which is one of the sources of the Penobscot River. The brook, said Montresor, is too inconsiderable to be of any service for canoes, so they were obliged to portage a little to the eastward of the brook. This portage is about a mile in length, the course southeasterly. It leads into another lake called Cheney Pond. Cheney Pond is divided into two large basins separated by a narrow passage about ¾ mile long and only two or three hundred yards wide, according to the journal. The above-mentioned brook enters Cheney Pond and leaves at the southern end. This stream, evidently, was not suitable for canoes either, as the party was forced to portage again, as before on the east side of Penobscot Brook. On the Penobscot River, the party found that opening beaver dams often released enough water to make traveling easier. The country improved as they came downriver. After the junction of the north and south branches of the Penobscot, they went along slowly, looking for the carry that would take them into the Kennebec River watershed.

[June] 30th. . . . The windings of the Penobscot, with the many islands that it forms, would afford a noble prospect. After having sailed about three leagues we found the river divided itself into two almost equal parts to form a large woody island. We kept close to the south shore, and began to see the end of the island, when we came to a large but deep brook, which empties itself into the river. This was the place so much sought for. We entered the brook and bade adieu to the Penobscot [near Seboomook]. We advanced . . . very slowly, clearing away the bushes which choked up the brook and at length came to a beaver dam, at least ten feet high. We lifted our canoes into the upper stream, and after having gone further, we came to a small lake. . . . At this time, thanks to the beavers, it was pretty full. . . . We had no sooner landed than our guides found out the carrying place. This lake . . . has a discharge by this brook into the Penobscot. We were now to cross over a small mountain, on the other side of which the streams run a contrary way, and empty themselves into the great lake Orignal [Moosehead Lake].

The carrying place is [three miles in length and the course southeast.] At the end of it we found ourselves on the banks of a small river [Carry Brook], into which we put our canoes. It was deep, but so narrow that the passage was often barred up by trees fallen across. After sailing half a mile, we entered the Orignal, and put on shore at a small rocky island near the mouth of the river.

The wooded island, the brook and the shallow pond were all flowed out when Seboomook Dam was built. Northwest Carry is still there but now only a mile long from Seboomook Lake to Moosehead.

Montresor calls the lake he entered "Orignal"; this is, of course, the present Moosehead Lake. The connection can be seen when we realize that the French word for "moose" is *orignal*.

He continues with his day to day diary and relates the scenes they saw while paddling down the lake. He mentions a ridge of high mountains on the opposite side, which were Big and Little Spencer. He also notes that the lake extended southerly, but that they were kept from a full view of it by points of land. They were, of course, still in North Bay and did not know the size or shape of the body of water they were on. Most of its forty-mile length was still hidden from them.

Paddling close to shore in a southerly direction, they found themselves opposite two islands, then a large arm of the lake that had been concealed from them by the shore. This was probably Northeast Cove. Montresor thought the breadth here to be about four miles. They paddled on and, leaving a small island on the left, the party encamped on a point of land covered with fine birch trees. Montresor remarks that the birch was highly valued and that this lake was particularly famous for them. The shores of Moosehead Lake are still abundantly wooded with beautiful birch trees, which in autumn frame the lake in gold.

On July 1 they left the birch-covered point of land and again paddled southward. After passing several islands, they came within view of Mount Kineo. The

John Montresor

journal states that this mountain resembles a moose in a stooping posture and it is from this that the lake received its name.

. . . As we passed along we had the pleasure of beholding at the same time the most considerable mountains in this part of the world: the Onegla, which I formerly mentioned; the Panavansot hill, higher, at the foot of which runs the Penobscot [Katahdin]; . . . [and] the Ongueachonta on the banks of the Kennebec [Squaw Mountain]. We saw many others, but these were most remarkable. We left the Usgha and having passed the large island [Farm Island], we altered our course to the [southwest], . . . endeavoring to gain the right-hand shore. Here the river Moose empties itself into the Orignal. . . .

We passed several islands, and after having sailed about seven miles, stopped at a spot well deserving notice. A very narrow point of land runs out about four hundred yards into the lake, after which it expands itself with the most graceful regularity. It forms a peninsula equally remarkable and beautiful [Kineo]. We had already passed one discharge of the lake [West Outlet]. This stream, after a winding course through the woods, joins the Arransoak [Kennebec, at Indian Pond], and is navigable in the spring only. Where we now were, the shores incline to each other so much, that the lake is not half a mile over; but they soon fall off, and the lake is ever after of a great breadth. Leaving this very remarkable spot, we sailed two miles, keeping close to the western shore. The opposite shore seemed to retire from us, till islands intervening, we lost it altogether. We saw three large points of land almost parallel, running out a great way into the lake, but which of these were islands, and which the main land, if any, was not in our power to know. [The points of land were Squaw Point, Deer Island and Sugar Island.]

Leaving a large bay on our right, we stood over the lake, steering southeasterly, and keeping betwixt the nearest of these great points of land and a cluster of islands on the outside of the bay. [This cluster of small islands includes Ledge, Green, Snake and Black.]

After having sailed about two miles, we perceived a motion

300

or gentle descent in the waters of the lake, which informed us of our approach to the Arransoak. This river is considerable from its first source. Its breadth is about 150 yards; its depth more than is required for canoes. Being used to suffer from the shallowness of the river, we rejoiced to see it so full of water, little expecting other difficulties we were to meet with. Having gone a little way with great velocity, all at once we found ourselves engaged in rapids. The river was narrow, deep and full of rocks. To go back or gain the shore was equally impossible. One of the canoes was overset; all the rest filled with water, but with much difficulty we gained the shore. Our provisions being all wet and in danger of being lost, we were obliged to encamp. We had not the consolation of a better prospect before us, for along the bank, as well as in the river, there was nothing to be seen but rocks; the woods filled with spruce, cedars, etc., certain marks of a country good for nothing. The descent everywhere so great, that the river runs with vast rapidity. [Montresor didn't think spruce trees were good for much.]

July 2nd. Having repaired our canoes we pursued our voyage. After going some miles with great swiftness without meeting with any disaster, by the great dexterity of the Indians, we entered the lakes of the Arransoak [Indian Pond] under the mountain Ongueachonta [Squaw Mountain]. . . .

The first lake is about a mile in length and from four hundred to six hundred yards in breadth. The second is not so broad, but is almost two miles in length. . . . These two lakes are separated by a fall, where the river contracts itself to fifteen yards in breadth. We were obliged here to make a short carrying place. [This is, of course, a description of Indian Pond before the flowage from the dam made the two ponds one.]

We halted about an hour on a small island nigh the end of the two lakes. The island and country all around make a most desolate appearance, and a great part of the woods bear the marks of having been burnt. Those who enter this lake from the river Arransoak will see two high mountains close together and much resembling one another in figure and shape [Big and Little Squaw Mountains]. We were no sooner out of the second lake, than we found ourselves again in rapids [very rough rapids called "the Hulling Machine" by loggers]. . . . We quitted the river and struck into the woods . . . This night encamped in the woods at some distance from the river, after a very laborious march, for there were hardly any marks to be found of a carrying place. [They must have taken the "Carry Brook" portage south of the river.]

3rd July. Continued the portage through the woods. After walking about [blank] we launched the canoes into a muddy creek in the middle of a marshy savanna [a flat treeless grassland]. Upon this creek we advanced [a few] miles, and opened a vast number of beaver dams, which were of some use to us. It seems the governor of Canada had been formerly acquainted with this, and all hunters were by his edict forbidden to molest the beavers in this part of the country. These marshes are of great extent and are often cut by deep gullies or pools of water. We had all along been much annoyed by the mosquitoes, but never suffered so much from them as here. Though much fatigued we made but small progress this day. Towards night we reached the end of the marsh, where our muddy creek changed to a small [stream] and took its course down the [slope] of the hill to the Arransoak. Here we encamped.

4th July. Began another portage, steering [northward]. After having walked about two miles we descended a steep hill and came to the river, into which we launched our canoes. Though less confined and rapid than before, the Arransoak still continued dangerous, till after having gone about three leagues [9 miles], we came to the north branch, called the [Dead] River. Here the country began to wear a better face, and the current to be more moderate; so that it may be looked upon as the end of the steep and rocky stage which prevails from this to the height of land. The Indians told us that in the spring this river is less difficult; for, being then full of water, they were able to keep close to the shore without being in the rapidity of the current. After passing the [Forks], we went at a great rate. At sunset encamped on the south shore. Went this day, in all, not less than [blank] leagues.

5th July. The current still inclining to be rapid; the land mountainous, running in short ridges, like that on the Chaudiere; the course of the river is southerly. The country is now open and very beautiful. The woods [are] full of large and noble trees. The river abounds in salmon, trout, etc. We saw a great many bears, moose, deer, wolves, etc., several of which we killed. The river hereabouts forms many islands and receives the [blank] which comes from the west. [These islands are just south of Bingham and the stream from the west, probably Houston Brook, is famous for its beautiful waterfall.]

The Arransoak afterwards takes a long circuit to the east before it returns to its proper course. We saw this day the falls of Carrartoank or Devil's Falls, where it contracts itself to a few yards in breadth and shoots about twelve or fifteen feet perpendicular. [Caratunk Falls at Solon.]

July 6th. After having gone about [15 miles] we came to a deep fall, where begins a carrying place of about two miles in length, the river being too rapid for canoes. This bears the name of the Falls of Arransoak [now Madison Falls], from a village of the Abenakis so called by them in the beginning of the war. It is on the left hand shore half a mile below the rapids. Opposite to this village the Arransoak receives a large river [Sandy River]. It now makes a noble appearance, very broad and deeper than any we have yet met with. Its current is very gentle to the nine mile falls [named thus by the Indians of the village as it was nine miles by trail from there]; here it precipitates itself with great fury over high rocks, and being confined by high and rocky banks, runs a quarter of a mile with vast rapidity, below which it forms a large basin, and then directs its course to the south. We encamped on an island half a league below the falls. [The nine mile falls are at Skowhegan.]

July 7th. Continued our voyage, and after sailing about three leagues with much difficulty, the river being often very shallow and rapid, we came to Ticonic Falls, which are immediately above Fort Halifax. We left our canoes above the falls and went into the fort. Fort Halifax was built by Mr. Shirley in 1754, to awe the Indians and cover the frontiers of New England. It stands on the east branch of the river at the [influx] of the [Sebasticook] into the Arransoak. It is square; its defense a bad palisade [flanked] by two block houses, in which there are some guns mounted, but as the fort is entirely commanded by a rising ground behind it, they have been obliged to erect two other block houses and to clear the woods for some distance around. They are capable of making a better defense, and it must be confessed that either of them are more than sufficient against an enemy who has no other offensive weapons than small arms. The fort is garrisoned by a company of New Englanders and supplied from the settlement below. The tide brings sloops as far as Fort Western, six leagues below Fort Halifax. From this fort to where the Kennebec [the first time Montresor gives the Kennebec its rightful name] empties itself into the sea, a little eastward of Casco Bay, is about forty-one miles. We continued here at Fort Halifax two days to refresh ourselves and renew our provisions. That done, on the evening of the 9th, we remounted the river about two leagues.

10th, 11th, 12th, continued to go up the river. Through the excessive heat and dryness of the season, the waters are visibly decreased.

[July] 13th. We had now remounted the river about twenty-three leagues and drew very nigh the great Fourche [the Forks]. We came this day to where we were to begin our portage across the county westerly to the western branch of Kennebec River, called the Dead River, which western branch [swings to the north just before joining the Kennebec]. The [north-swinging portion], before it joins the eastern branch of the Kennebec, has a great many windings, is full of islands, shallow and rapid. To avoid these inconveniences it is usual to carry the canoes through the woods till you meet the river, where it is of great depth and its current hardly perceivable. This portage is divided by three different lakes, each of which is to be passed before you can arrive at the Dead River . . . It has been formerly mentioned that although the French made use of the eastern road to go into New England, yet this was always looked upon, both by them and the English, as the most eligible road to enter Canada. In order, therefore, to make these portages more remarkable, we took care to blaze all the portages from the Kennebec to Lake Megantic in such a manner, as to make the way much less difficult for whoever may follow us. A little above the portage a remarkable brook falls into the river [from] the first or nearest lake [Carrying Place Stream from East Carry Pond].

July 14th. We took leave of the Arransoak or Kennebec River, and early in the morning entered the woods, advancing but slowly, the way being difficult to find; the ascent very great and the weather sultry. Our course was [west 27 degrees north]. After walking about eight miles [Montresor was mistaken; the distance is 3¼ miles], we came to the first lake [East Carry Pond]. It is the least considerable of the three, not being above six hundred yards in length and four hundred in breadth. Our course over it was [due west]. We entered on the second portage steering [due west] and in an hour came to another lake [Middle Carry Pond]. This extends itself about three-fourths of a mile from [east to west], but of no great breadth. Our course over it was [due west]. When we came to the other side we paddled through the rushes to the mouth of a large creek, into which we went. After carrying us about five hundred yards, it took a second sweep to the right, inclining backwards towards the lake. Here we landed and after a long search found the portage. No nation having been more jealous of their country than the Abenakis, they have made it a constant rule to leave the fewest vestiges of their route. The course over this portage is [west, and] as it is not long, we soon came to the third lake. We had made a long and fatiguing march; the night came on, the weather threatening, so that we made no attempt to pass over, but encamped.

[July] 15th. Next morning set out early. The lake seemed to be in breadth [3 miles] and in length extending [2 miles] from the opposite bank. The land rose to a ridge of hills, over which appeared the mountain [later named Bigelow] rising to a great height. As we passed the lake we were overtaken by a heavy shower; what was more disagreeable we could find on the shore no marks of a portage. In vain we coasted along the lake and examined every opening; we were obliged to send Indians into the woods, and it was not till after a long search that they found any way. Our course over the lake was [west,] our course now over the portage was [northwest]. We ascended the hill, the portage conducting through the gap or breach. Its whole length cannot be less than [2¾ miles]. After descending, we winded a long time along the foot of the hill, till we came at last to a low savanna, where we halted. The brooks were all dry from the excessive heat of the season. After crossing this savanna, we continued our course through the woods till we arrived at a second, more swampy than the first. This gave rise to a large brook [Bog Brook] into which we put our canoes. We followed the stream which in a few minutes brought us to the river [Dead River]. This noble river more than answered our expectation. We found it about sixty yards in breadth, uniformly deep and gentle in its current. The land on both shores is rich and beautiful, and by the prints on the sand, must be full of game. We were now very near the mountains from which this river takes its name, but we had not gone far, when a violent shower obliged us to encamp.

July 16th. Continued our voyage; course for two leagues nearly [west]. We had now passed the mountain, but the river, by its extraordinary windings, seemed unwilling to leave it. Two hours passed away and we had gained nothing in our course, but at last by slow degrees it became more regular and returned to its proper course. When we had gone four leagues we found the river parted into two branches, the chief of which we left on the left hand [confluence of north and south branches of Dead River]. . . . The other which we followed has a few rifts a little above the fork, but the river soon became deep and gentle as before, though its breadth is greatly diminished.

July 17th. We gained this day four leagues further up the river. We had more difficulty than before, as we met with two falls and some rapids, though not considerable [Shadagee and Sarampus Falls].

18th. The river being extremely diminished, we divided; some striking into the woods, the others leading the canoes up the shallow rapids. After having gone about two leagues with much fatigue, we launched the canoes into a large beaver dam which leads into the first lake [Chain of Ponds].

These lakes are of a great depth and entirely surrounded by mountains. The first is about half a mile in length, but of a very small breadth. In one place, where it contracts itself, the current is easily perceivable. The further end is marshy. Here we again found the brook, and after having gone on it about a quarter of a mile, we came to the second lake. This is larger than the first, though little different in appearance from it. We had a view of the mountains of the height of land. . . . We continued to lead our canoes in it, till at length we arrived at the long looked-for portage. Here the river turns off to the [northwest] although a rivulet which falls into it here, springs from lakes I have yet to mention. The appearance of the country here, though inferior to what it was below, is still very beautiful. We were now four leagues from Lake Megantic and divided from it by the height of land; but though we could have no further assistance from rivers, we had still a chain of lakes to conduct us the great part of the way.

July 19th. Set out very early. Just by us we found a small lake bearing from the portage [Lost Pond]. . . Having passed it, we again entered on the carrying place. Our course was [northwest]. After walking about [1 mile] we came to a very beautiful lake about seven hundred yards in length and two hundred and seventy in breadth. The brook which falls into [Horseshoe Pond] passes through it. Leaving the brook, which has a cascade, on our right hand, a portage of five hundred yards brought us to another lake [Mud Pond]. This is much smaller, its form very regular, the shore rocky. We passed over and landed at the mouth of the same brook, to the source of which we now drew nigh. A short portage brought us to the last and most considerable lake [Arnold Pond]. We entered on it nigh the source of the brook; it is about three-fourths of a mile in length and almost five hundred yards wide. Our course over it carried us its full length. Bidding adieu to the southern waters we entered on the portage of the height of land. Our course was nearly [westerly,] the ascent very considerable. After walking two miles we gained the greatest height and began to descend. Three miles further brought us to a low, swampy ground, where the river Megantic takes its rise. We were here a long time at a loss for the path, but at last happily found it. Having crossed a large brook we came into a most beautiful meadow, much excelling any we had yet seen, and still more beautiful from the disagreeable tract we had just left. Keeping a [northerly] course we soon arrived on the banks of the river Megantic [Seven Mile Stream]. It is only a large brook, but the descent being very gentle, the canoes made good progress. The New

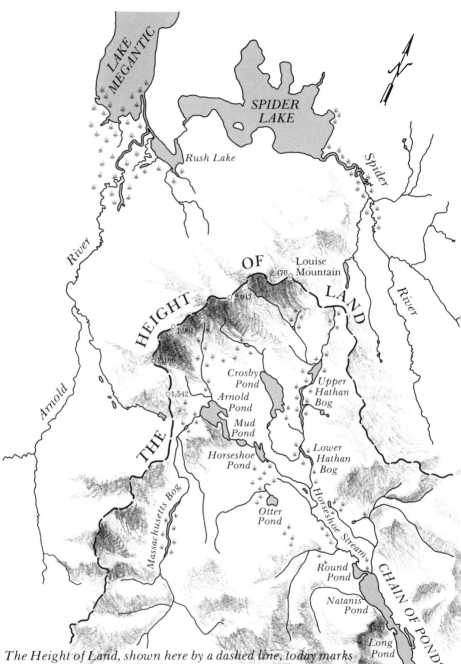

The Height of Land, shown here by a dashed line, today marks
the boundary between Maine and the province of Quebec. Ele-
vations are given in feet. Map by Suzanne A. Gabel.

308

Englanders who measured this carrying place, call it a little more than four and a half miles. This must be understood only from the last lake to the river Megantic; though even that did not seem less to us than six miles. . . . We had gone down the river about four miles, when night overtook us; but being resolved to reach the lake, we still pushed on. Two miles more and we entered the lake Megantic. Our guides kept still rowing and passed over to the opposite shore, where we encamped.

The fact that they made this part of the journey after dark may explain why Montresor failed to mention the swamps at the mouth of Seven Mile Stream (now called Arnold River), and this oversight would result in disaster for many of Arnold's men fourteen years later. The journal ends soon after this point.

John Montresor spent a total of 24 years in America with the British army, part of the time fighting against the Americans in the Revolution, and he knew the country better than any other British officer. He had developed a good rapport with the Indians and from them learned to be an expert at wilderness marching and fighting. We Americans should feel fortunate that his advice was not sought as to the best methods of fighting our minutemen.

The year 1764 saw an awakening of interest in the old Indian trail, when Governor Francis Bernard sent an expedition led by a surveyor named Joseph Chadwick to look into the feasibility of building a road from central Maine to Quebec. An account of the survey expedition was called "Of a survey through the interior of the country from the Penobscot to Quebec, by order of the Governor of Massachusetts." Unlike Montresor, Chadwick ended in Quebec instead of starting there.

The Chadwick party left Fort Pownal on the Penobscot River on May 7, 1764, going early in the season to avoid black flies and mosquitoes. In addition to Joseph Chadwick, surveyor, there were John Preble, interpreter, Dr. William Crawford, second surveyor, and Philip Nuton, assistant. John Preble was the famous Indian interpreter later employed during the Revolution to deal with the Indians. Dr. Crawford after this trip became the surgeon, chaplain and justice of the peace at Fort Pownal (now Fort Point), and died there at age 46 on June 15, 1776.

At Persodunk (present-day Passadumkeag) fifty Indians met the four men and escorted them to their governor's habitation. Chieftains present were Tomah, Odohando and Orono, richly dressed in ceremonial regalia. They were seated on piles of beaver skins, with which the walls were also covered. The Indians had always regarded the beaver's fur as superior to all others. A rare glimpse of Indian life at that time can be seen in Chadwick's observation of "Mederwomkeag" ". . . an Indian town and a place of residence in time of war, but is now mostly vacated. In the mess house are sundry large books and other things. On the house hangs a large bell which the Indians take care to preserve."

The conference with the Indians was to inquire whether they thought the proposed route over the old trail would be practical and the most direct for a road to Canada. Whatever the Indians answered, it was decided to go ahead with their plans. Among the

Indian guides hired was Joseph Aspegueunt, a Penobscot chieftain whose name occurs often in the James Phinney Baxter manuscripts as a delegate to Boston, signer of peace treaties and other documents. Baxter speaks of him as one of the most important sagamores; however, Colonel Goldthwait of Fort Pownal called him "very sulky and deceitful." Soc Tomah was another guide, an "old villain" according to the same Goldthwait; Auson and French Messer (later called Mitchell) were represented as being very friendly. Others were Soc Alexis, Joseph Marey (no doubt Joseph Mary for whom Jo-Mary Mountain was named), Sakabis and Francis.

Trouble arose almost at once as the Indian guides became suspicious and fearful at the idea of their forests being surveyed and recorded. Three of them refused to go further at Penobscot Island (Old Town) and started a dispute that went on for two days and threatened to disrupt the trip. Chadwick's journal gives an exact account of the dispute which arose with the Indian guides.

"The Indeins are so jealous of their country being exposed to this survey: as made it impractable for us to perform the work with acqurice [accuracy], altho they waer ingaged in the service by the large wages . . . three of the party refused to go forward . . . And the disput between our party and the other Indeins was so great as to come to a fray. Which after two days dispute the result was that I should make no draughts of an lands but only wrightings. And saying that when they were among English Men they obayed their commands and best way you do obay Indein Orders."

Chadwick, in other words, was told that the white men were outnumbered and that the Indians would give the orders. One order was that no maps would be made.

It would seem that because of the disturbed times and distrust on both sides some of the leading men of the tribe joined the party to keep an eye on what was going on. Also, the Indians did not overlook the fact that the pay was good. Guides' wages at that time was three pounds, ten shillings or about seventeen dollars per month.

Chadwick's journal, although interesting, is rather sketchy and gives no description of the trail after leaving Seboomook. Perhaps he was further intimidated by his guides, admittedly a very aggressive bunch of Indians. There are, however, several sections worthy of note, if only to inspire wonder at Chadwick's originality in spelling and also his methods of surveying.

Starting on the Penobscot, Chadwick took his party up the "Perscatiequess" River, to Soback Pond, then to "Obernestzamebooh" (Lake Onawa), where he wrote of a "remarkable mountain" now called Boarstone. From there they took Wilson Stream to Wilson Pond, and continued to "Moose Hills Lake" (Moosehead Lake), so called, he said, by being environed with large mountains and rocks. They paddled the length of the lake to reach Northwest Carry, where they proceeded to the West Branch of the

Penobscot by way of a carrying place and small pond (Carry Pond).

Especially interesting is the description of Chesuncook Lake as it was before the dams were built. "Gesoncook Lake was very shole water and a mud bottom. In most parts of the lake our canoes could not pass within a hundred yards of the shore by which we had not a very good view of the shore and land. The ground appears to be ded level. Large tracts of grass land and at sum distance backwards riseing with esey ascent grows a thick growth of young trees."

A dam built later at the foot of Chesuncook Lake was to raise the water level, and the meadow river with its soft shores and grassy lowlands was flooded back to a hard shoreline. Each time the dam was rebuilt and raised the shore and forest were further pushed back. Later, when Ripogenus Dam was built, the shoreline was changed still further and part of the village of Chesuncook was flowed out.

Chadwick described Mount Katahdin in what is probably the first English description of it. He called it Satinhungermoss Hill, a remarkable hill for height and figure. "The Indines say that this hill is the highest in the Country . . . That they can ascent so high as any greens grow and no higher. That one Indine attempted to go higher but never returned. The hight of vegetation is as a Horizontal line about half the perpendicular hight on the hill and intersects the tops of sundry other mountines. The hight of this hill was very apparent to us as we had a sight of it at sundre places easterly and westerly at 60 or 70 miles distance . . . So lofty a pyramid." He mentioned rainbow hues in Abol Stream.

It is surprising that Chadwick achieved any "acqurice" at all considering the primitive methods of surveying he used. The governor did not order a measure by chain but wished the survey to be performed by the most expeditious method. So they used the method used in plain sailing. "As we passed in birch canoes; the distance is found . . . from a fishing rod a fine silk cord was suspended. The cord was 8 ft. 3 inches long. A small piece of brass the bigness of a sixpense being properly balanced shows the number of rods run in one minute etc.. but in rapid water and land the distance was estimated . . ."

Joseph Chadwick went successfully through to Quebec, the expedition taking six weeks. His report to Governor Bernard was shelved, however, as Massachusetts had other problems to cope with, and after all there were very few white inhabitants on the Penobscot River at that time. There were only eighteen incorporated towns in the whole district of Maine before 1764 and they were all on or south of the lower Kennebec and Androscoggin rivers; the Massachusetts government could see no reason yet for building such an ambitious road. And so, for some years after Chadwick's visit, the history of Moosehead Lake and the upper Kennebec valley remains obscure, with only the archaeologists interested in Indian artifacts able to piece together portions of the puzzle.

Scotland provided us with the third man to explore the Penobscot-Chaudiere route with the express purpose of finding a convenient location for a Quebec-to-New England thoroughfare.

Hugh Finlay had been appointed surveyor of post roads on the continent of North America in December of 1771. This seems like a tall order for one man; however, when we stop to think we realize that even New England was largely a wooded wilderness before the Revolution. As for the district of Maine, colonists were few and far between; and the west and the south of North America were completely unexplored, as far as the British were concerned.

Finlay was extremely well qualified for the position. He had left his native Scotland in 1763 at the age of 19, already assured of the job of postmaster at Quebec, which had only lately been conquered by the British. He spoke French fluently, which was a great help. His commission as postmaster at Quebec was signed by Deputy Postmaster General Benjamin Franklin. (The certificate has been preserved and may be seen at the Maine Historical Society in Portland.) In 1774 Hugh Finlay was appointed deputy postmaster general to take Franklin's place, and directly after the exploration for the Penobscot-Quebec road he went to New York to take over that job. Later, in 1784, he was appointed deputy postmaster general of Canada, Nova Scotia and New Brunswick. He was one of the most remarkable men in the postal history of the two countries and became known as the father of the Canadian postal system.

Hugh Finlay

This then was the man who explored the Penobscot, Moosehead Lake, and Kennebec regions in
order to find a short and easy route, unobstructed by
lakes or large rivers, for a road from Quebec to Falmouth on Casco Bay.

The post route at that time was by way of Lake
Champlain. It had proved to be slow and beset by
difficulties, especially in the spring when it became
impassable with the breaking up of the ice and spring
floods.

Sufficient money for the trip was raised by private
contributions within twenty-four hours after the sub-
scription papers were distributed. Four Indian
guides were hired, and arrangements were made for
an interpreter of the Abenaki language to meet the
party at the last settlement on the Chaudiere.

The party crossed the St. Lawrence River and proceeded to the last farm on the Chaudiere on the 13th
of September, 1773. There they met the Indian
guides. Finlay noted in his journal that the road was
passable for carriages, and the inhabitants were
working to further improve it. On the fifteenth they
boarded the canoes with twenty days' allowance of
pork, flour and hardtack; they intended to depend on
their guns and fish hooks for extra food. The first
night was spent at the mouth of La Famine River
where they found huts inhabited by two families
engaged in clearing homesteads. Finlay remarked
that the soil was rich and had produced excellent
wheat. The Canadian farmers made them welcome
and prepared a meal of roasted Indian corn, baked

pumpkin and milk.

The Indians recommended going by way of the Rivière du Loup, as its length is quite free from lakes, marshes or mountains, thus providing the best terrain for a road. They pointed out that all those obstructions were to be found on the Chaudiere. Eventually, however, the main road to Quebec was built over the Dead River, Chain of Ponds, Chaudiere trail.

The Rivière du Loup is about 40 yards wide at the mouth, and was very shallow at that season. Finlay's journal states that there their troubles and fatigue began. The water in fact was so low that they had to wade and haul the canoes along. Their feet became so waterlogged and tender that they kept falling on the rough rocky stream bed. They camped at the foot of a waterfall which fell over a bed of rocks ten feet high. The birch canoes were set near a fire to dry out, and they then built a hut of branches. Finlay describes the shelter as follows: "The floor of our wigwam we laid with tender sprigs of the aromatic spruce tree, which comforts the lungs, and defends the breast from obnoxious night vapors; this makes a soft and agreeable bed. After this was arranged we hung our kettle to the fire and boiled pork in sufficient quantity for supper, and to last us all next day till evening when the same work is done again. After supper each man wraps himself in his blanket, lays himself down on his spruce bed with his feet to the fire, and passes the night in sound and refreshing sleep."

They found trout, ducks and partridges everywhere, so they did not lack for food. Every evening after supper Mentowermet, the chief guide, would draw a sketch of the next day's route on a sheet of smooth birch bark, using a piece of charcoal. He marked ponds, marshes, ascents and descents and made a dotted line for the proposed roadway. Finlay then copied these sketches on paper, putting in the distances himself. He noted that the Indians were very correct in everything but that. As they approached the boundary between Canada and Maine they made a long difficult portage over the pass, traveling nine miles in nine hours. As they left Portage Lake in Canada to go to Penobscot Lake across the border Finlay noted that they were 98 miles from Quebec and 46 miles from the last house on the river Chaudiere.

The description of the trip down the Penobscot is somewhat like Montresor's; he followed exactly the same trail. When the party reached Moosehead they found that the lake was extremely stormy with high surf. Nevertheless, they started out, keeping to the right-hand shore, paddling seven and a half miles right into the eye of the storm. When the canoes were almost filled with spray and the food was getting soaked they put ashore and made camp.

The storm let up before daybreak and they went on in spite of the large swells remaining, being anxious to start their trip down the Kennebec. Mentowermet and the other Indians apparently knew the territory well; they made all the necessary portages around the falls and dangerous rapids in the Kennebec Gorge,

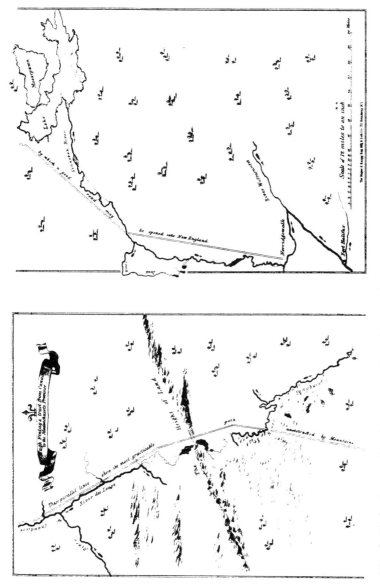

Hugh Finlay's map for the proposed road to Quebec. At left, the northern half; at right, the south-ern half, showing the Kennebec River from Moosehead Lake to Fort Halifax.

319

and reached the Forks and then the Carrying Place with no trouble.

The guides were well acquainted with the route over the Carry Ponds, the "Great Carrying Place" made famous by the Arnold expedition a few years later. The party went ashore here to leave a cache of food, including pork and flour, which were well wrapped in birch bark and hung high up in trees to keep them from the wild animals. As soon as the guides and interpreter had conducted the party well out of the wilderness, they would return to Canada by way of the Dead River trail and pick up the food left at the Carry. Finlay wrote: "The country here begins to wear a more smiling aspect, and continues for 5 miles winding as before, down to a charming island where the country is past description, enchanting. The Indians much frequent this tract, on account of the incredible quantity of game with which the woods are stored, and the river here swarms with salmon, trout and other fish."

The explorers were now in the vicinity of Caratunk, Moscow and Bingham, which is still a very scenic area, although changed by the formation of Wyman Lake. Finlay is correct about the presence of the Indians also, as many artifacts and evidences of Indian camping grounds have been found, especially around the mouth of Austin Stream. Tradition has it that there are some ancient Indian graves in the Bingham cemetery.

They went on until they arrived at a waterfall. Hugh Finlay's description of it is so graphic that it shows him to be not only a successful businessman and master surveyor, but an excellent writer, and a lover of natural beauty.

"The fall was about eight feet perpendicular, most romantically beautiful: the river is confined between two rocks, and rushes over in a surprising manner foaming with incredible fury; it falls into a fine rock-bound basin perfectly circular and full of fish; we encamped on the side of this basin with the fall in front, and we caught a great quantity of fish here in a few minutes."

The waterfall was Caratunk Falls at Solon, called "The Devil's Falls" by the Indians. A dam and power plant have been built at this location; however when the gates have been opened at flood tide in the spring, the sight is still wildly beautiful, and the pool and rocky basin at the foot are still there.

It was by now the 25th of September and the journal for that day mentions that it froze hard during the night. They left their camp at the foot of the falls and continued down river. After passing Weston's Island, just north of Madison, Finlay writes that they came to some rapids where they were forced to make a carry of a mile southerly past a large grove of pine trees. This rapid must have been what is now Madison Falls, then known as Norridgewock Falls, named for the Norridgewock Indian village just a mile below. The large grove of pines is still there, although probably now much smaller in area.

After embarking at the foot of the rapid, they came upon a cleared point of land on the left-hand shore, opposite the entrance of a river. Finlay knew about the old Indian village and wrote that not a vestige of it remained. He said that it was a village of the Abenaki Indians, called Aronsoak, now Norridgewock. They saw some haystacks on the banks of the Sandy River, and at Old Point came to a hut; there two men who had cleared several acres of land, had sowed it with wheat and rye and planned to build a house the next year.

The histories of Norridgewock and Madison confirm that there were settlers around Old Point at that time. James Waugh had bought land at the mouth of the Sandy River in 1772, cleared it, built a cabin and brought his bride there in 1773. Sylvanus Sawyer and his son Luke arrived in 1772 also, although apparently the Finlay party visited before they had built a permanent residence. These were the first inhabitants the Finlay group had seen since leaving the Chaudiere River in Canada.

The next inhabitants, according to the journal, were 10 miles down river. The travelers stopped at Captain Jonathan Oak's farm, located in the present town of Skowhegan. He had been there only a year but had already stored 300 bushels of grain in his barn. He informed Finlay that it was 78 miles from his house to Seguin Island at the mouth of the Kennebec. They found that in spite of the settlements no roads had been opened, only paths through the woods from house to house. At this place Finlay discharged his Indian guides and interpreter. He gave them instructions to return to the Great Carry where provisions had been left for them. He also gave the interpreter written instructions on taking the courses, computing distances and noting the remarks of the Indians as to the character of the country as they went along. He reminded him that the purpose of the whole trip was to ascertain the best route for a road.

Finlay apparently had a very good relationship with his guides, unlike Chadwick, and mentioned that at this place he parted from his Indian friends. Their trip down the Kennebec was continued in wooden canoes as far as Merrymeeting Bay, then up the Androscoggin to Brunswick. From there they traveled overland four miles to Casco Bay, and by canoe to Falmouth, arriving there on Thursday the 30th of September, having taken five days to come from Captain Oak's house — 98 miles. It had taken them 16 days to go 310 miles, traveling at not quite 20 miles per day.

Finlay apparently realized that the route he surveyed might not meet with much success because, he wrote, the lands he had surveyed were owned by some gentlemen known by the name of the Plymouth Company, and they were not disposed to give any encouragement to open a road. The Assembly on their part announced they would not grant one shilling toward opening a road over that route into Canada. The public was heard from also; the people said that they were not interested in improving the Plymouth Company's lands to make their estates more valuable, and that rumors were afoot that all the country east of New Hampshire might be taken from Massachusetts Bay and made into a province bounded by Nova Scotia.

The prophets were quite right, as the Continental Congress divided Massachusetts in 1775 and the District of Maine became a reality.

Arnold's March to Quebec

An epic story of courage and disaster.

T HE SHOT HEARD 'ROUND THE WORLD had been fired, and the American colonies were in an active state of rebellion against Great Britain; Canada was now an English colony, having been wrested from the French on the Plains of Abraham in 1759; England was lord and master of the North American continent and intended to remain so. Lord Sandwich spoke as follows in the House of Commons: "Suppose the Colonies do abound in men, what does that signify? They are raw, undisciplined, cowardly men."

This was the setting in the spring of 1775 when the war for independence was in its first stages. Sam Adams' Boston Tea Party had given the British a taste of what was coming. In April Paul Revere made his famous ride, and the fighting started at the bridge in Concord; May saw the capture of Fort Ticonderoga by colonial troops, then Crown Point fell to an army commanded by Benedict Arnold; June brought

Bunker Hill, with neither side a clear victor, and George Washington was appointed commander of all American forces on June 15, 1775.

The next logical move was for the colonials to make a bold offensive aimed at the city of Quebec. The plan was that General Philip Schuyler would proceed with a force to conquer Montreal, after which his army would head toward Quebec. There they would join forces with a detachment led by Benedict Arnold northward through the wilds of Maine. The combined army would then crush the ancient fortress, and Canada would be annexed as the fourteenth colony.

Benedict Arnold, at the time of the expedition to Quebec, was an experienced officer with a brilliant record for bravery. At the news of the first shots fired at Lexington, he had gathered a company of men in Connecticut and marched to Cambridge. He was given the rank of colonel in the new army. Joining forces with Ethan Allen of Vermont, and leading only 83 men, he captured Fort Ticonderoga and then Crown Point. Arnold immediately sent spies into Canada and also some Stockbridge Indians to conciliate the Caughnawaga Indians north of Montreal.

Arnold's knowledge of the region was great because of his visits in civilian life as a trader, and his record at Fort Ticonderoga and Crown Point made him the logical man to head an expeditionary force against Quebec. He may have actually suggested the plan to General Washington. If not, he certainly entered into the plan wholeheartedly.

The first part of the plan worked like a charm. General Schuyler, becoming ill, stepped down in favor of his second in command. Under the brave and talented leadership of young Richard Montgomery, the northern army captured Montreal and moved toward Quebec as planned.

The second part of the plan looked fine on paper. Raise an army of 1100 men, equip them with supplies and dory-like river boats, called *bateaux* even today, and send them north along the old Indian trail up the Kennebec. But when this part of the plan proceeded, much time had been lost, which was to prove disastrous to the final result of the operation. Nature also seemed to conspire against the march through Maine, with early severe snowstorms and floods. John Codman, in *Arnold's Expedition To Quebec,* says that no previous expedition had been obliged to follow a path so dimly traced through almost unexplored wilderness, or to meet the hardships and perils which were in store for Arnold's devoted band.

Benedict Arnold, when entrusted with the leadership of the eastern prong of the pincer operation to capture Canada, was 34 years old, rather short of stature, thickset, muscular, with dark hair and a florid complexion; he was called handsome by the ladies, with whom he was a favorite. He was an expert horseman, a sailor, and a good marksman with either rifle or pistol. At the time of his departure for Quebec, he was a widower with three children. His house and children were cared for by his devoted sister, Hannah, during his absence.

Arnold's March to Quebec

Arnold's army of 1100 men were mostly chosen from forces already stationed in Massachusetts. Among them were seasoned woodsmen and frontiersmen such as Captain Daniel Morgan, who had fought in the French and Indian wars under Washington; Captain Henry Dearborn of New Hampshire; Lieutenant Colonel Christopher Greene of Rhode Island; young Aaron Burr, the nineteen-year-old son of the president of Princeton College; and Dr. Isaac Senter of Rhode Island, who at the age of twenty-two was already a surgeon, with experience in the army during the siege of Boston.

On the day appointed for the start of the expedition Arnold and his army gathered in Cambridge. Here is the account of Abner Stocking, one of the soldiers, as taken from his journal for September 13, 1775:

> All things being in readiness for our departure, we set out from Cambridge, near Boston, on the 13th Sept. at sunset, and encamped at Mistick at eight o'clock at night. We were all in high spirits, intending to endure with fortitude all the fatigues and hardships that we might meet with in our march to Quebec.

The army next camped at Danvers, then at Newburyport, where they spent several days making preparations for their voyage to the mouth of the Kennebec River.

> September 18th. We this day embarked at six o'clock in the afternoon. Our fleet consisted of eleven sail, sloops and schooners. Our whole number of troops was 1100 — 11 companies of musketmen and three companies of riflemen. We hauled off into the road and got ready to weigh anchor in the morning if the wind should be favorable.
>
> September 19th. This morning we got under way with a pleasant breeze, our drums beating, fifes playing and colors

Plate IX: Mount Bigelow, elevation 4,150 feet, is the fifth highest mountain in Maine, presenting a formidable climb of over three thousand feet.

Plates X and XI: In the fall of 1975, the Arnold Expedition Historical Society reenacted Benedict Arnold's 1775 march to Quebec. Hundreds of Americans enthusiastically took part, equipped with authentic costumes, bateaux, firearms and tools.

They traveled up the Kennebec River, across the Carry Ponds, up Dead River and across the Height of Land, then down the Chaudiere River to Quebec, where they were cheerfully defeated in mock battle by the Canadians.

Plate XII: Cathedral Pines in Eustis was one of the campsites for the Arnold expedition in 1775.

(Plates IX-XII are photographs taken by the author.)

flying.

Many pretty girls stood upon the shore, I suppose weeping for the departure of their sweethearts.

At eleven o'clock this day we left the entrance of the harbor and bore away for the Kennebec River. In the latter part of the night, there came on a thick fog and our fleet was separated. At break of day we found ourselves in a most dangerous situation, very near a reef of rocks. The rocks indeed appeared on all sides of us, so that we feared we should have been dashed to pieces on some of them. We were brought into this deplorable situation by means of liquor being dealt out too freely to our pilots. Their intemperance much endangered their own lives and the lives of all the officers and soldiers on board; but through the blessing of God we all arrived safe in Kennebec River.

The lower Kennebec River was described in the journal of Captain Henry Dearborn of New Hampshire, then twenty-four:

[September] 21st. Put up the river as far as Swan Island, at the upper end of Merrymeeting Bay, where we run on shore and came to an anchor. I went on shore with some of my officers and stayed all night.

September 22nd. Proceeded up the river. We passed Fort Richmond at 11 o'clock, where there are but few settlements at present. This afternoon we passed Pownalborough, where there is a courthouse and jail, and some very good settlements.

In 1775 Pownalborough (now Dresden) was the Lincoln County seat. The county at that time extended north to encompass the present Somerset County. By the time the expedition arrived, Pownalborough had had a varied and troubled political history. The pioneer minister, Reverend Bailey, a staunch Tory, had been expelled from the colony by zealous patriots of the region. John Adams, then a young law student from Quincy, Massachusetts, had ridden his horse through the woods to try cases in the courthouse on the bank of the Kennebec. Pownalborough Courthouse is now owned by the Lincoln County Cultural and Historical Society and is one of the finest pre-Revolutionary buildings in Maine. Guided tours are conducted during the summer.

The fleet next proceeded up river to Gardinerstown (now Pittston) where feverish activity was under way. Major Reuben Colburn, the owner of a shipyard there, had received a directive from General Washington some three weeks before to build 200 bateaux, outfit them with food and supplies, and have them ready in time for the army's arrival.

This was an immense undertaking for a frontier outpost boatyard, but Major Colburn rushed into production at once, using green wood, which was all he could secure in the short time allotted. When Arnold's fleet arrived at the Colburn home and shipyard on the east bank of the river, they were greeted by Colburn himself and the workers who were still putting the finishing touches on the bateaux. As the boats were lined up on the river bank and loaded with foodstuffs, the soldiers were divided into crews to man them. The activity went on at a frantic pace with Arnold everywhere directing and organizing. Finally the army was actually on its way up river to its next stop, Fort Western in present-day Augusta, where they would spend a few days regrouping.

From the journal of Dr. Isaac Senter:

> Saturday, [September] 23rd. . . . Arrived at Fort Western at 10 o'clock in the morning. We were now come to a rapid in the river, beyond which our transports could not pass, nor

Henry Dearborn. This etching is in the J. S. H. Fogg Autograph Collection of the Maine Historical Society, Portland, Maine. Photograph reproduced by permission of the Maine Historical Society.

could they all get up as far as this. [This was where they encountered the first falls in the Kennebec, the present location of the dam and the Edwards Paper Mill in Augusta.] Most of [the sailboats] were left at Gardinerstown, where the bateaux were built . . . Headquarters [here] were at Esquire Howard's, an exceeding hospitable, opulent, polite family.

Descendants of the hospitable Mr. Howard, the Gannett family of newspaper fame, were instrumental in restoring Fort Western to its present fine condition with many eighteenth-century furnishings. It may be visited during the summer for a nostalgic trip back to the 1700s.

Sunday, [September] 24th. Early this morning was called to attend a wounded soldier, who was shot through the body last night by a malicious drunken fellow belonging to the army. The hemorrhage was great inwardly, which soon occasioned his death. . . .

Monday, 25th. This morning search being made for the fellow who was imagined to be the murderer — found and condemned by a court martial to hang. [He was, however, given a reprieve and conveyed back to Massachusetts for General Washington to consider the matter.]

After leaving Fort Western the fleet of bateaux continued up river for eighteen miles to Fort Halifax, in present-day Winslow. This fort had been built in 1754, the same year as Fort Western. It stood on a point of land at the confluence of the Kennebec and Sebasticook rivers. Two blockhouses and a large barrack were enclosed by a high fence. The fort was surrounded by a few settlers' homes.

Fort Halifax was the center of a small settlement that included a flour mill and trading post. Montresor had replenished his supplies here on his trip in 1761. The first five settlers of Norridgewock made a trip to this mill around 1773 that was to end tragically. The five men gathered all their wheat and loaded it in a boat for the voyage to Fort Halifax. Near Skowhegan at the bend of the river the boat was wrecked on a dangerous rock in the rapids. Four men were drowned, leaving one to return to Norridgewock with the sad news that all the other husbands and fathers in the settlement had been lost.

Arnold's men would also find this a dangerous area, and these rapids, combined with the double falls at the island, made this one of the most hazardous portages on the Kennebec River. Overturned bateaux, soaked clothing and supplies were the lot of all of them before they reached the comparative calm of the island.

Above Fort Halifax the river became more rapid and many of the boats took on water as the crews negotiated the "Five Mile Ripples." Just beyond the rapids Major Return Meigs bought an ox from a farmer, which he had dressed and distributed among the men as they came by. They ate well that night.

Three miles down river from the present town of Skowhegan the soldiers passed the Weston homestead. Joseph Weston, the first settler of Skowhegan, had brought his family here in 1770 to farm the rich intervale land. Colonel Arnold and some of his officers were entertained here at dinner. And since Eunice Weston's fame as a cook has come down through the years, it is certain they dined well — no doubt on salmon, grouse and venison.

It was here that Benedict Arnold received his first

offers of help from the settlers. Joseph Weston and two of his elder sons volunteered to go along with the army as far as Norridgewock Falls, in what was then known as Barnardstown (now Madison), to help the army over the carry with a team of oxen. The Westons knew the difficulties ahead not only on the Skowhegan carry but on navigating the two falls nine miles up river.

This trip proved to be a tragic one for the Weston family, as Joseph caught cold due to exposure in the cold river water and rainy weather. The cold quickly turned into pneumonia, which caused his death within a week after his return home. He was a war casualty as surely as any of Arnold's soldiers who died in the Canadian campaign.

Arnold's men were now approaching Skowhegan Falls. Half a mile from the falls there was a right angle turn with whirlpools caused by the narrow channel above. Here the bateaux slammed against the many rocks. Above this there was a half mile of very rough rapids and then the falls. Kenneth Roberts' description of this carry in *Arundel* is graphic:

"The falls were on each side of a craggy island in midstream. The face of the island is six times the height of a man; and in the middle of it is a cleft, which the Abenakis say was made by the tomahawk of the great god Glooskap. This cleft is the route for carrying canoes over the falls."

To get the bateaux over the carry through the cleft in the sheer rock walls, one man had to drag, and another must push, pressing himself against the walls like a snail. Dr. Senter's journal of the expedition states: "These were a very high water fall, and exceeding difficult carrying by. . . . With a great deal of difficulty we passed this, but not without coming very nigh losing one of my hands."

When the soldiers had gained the calm of the island, they found several settlers with whom they traded. They were glad to get provisions even though one of the journalists called their prices exorbitant. The soldiers bought salted moose and deer meat and salmon in abundance. They noted that the land around the town was dark and rich looking, "a veritable Canaan," which was the name of the town at that time. A settler named Copeland was building a mill.

The main army was by this time moving between Skowhegan, or Nine Mile Falls as the Indians called them, and Norridgewock Falls. Arnold and one or two other journalists mentioned stopping overnight halfway between, at a small settlement then called Oosoola and later Norridgewock. Arnold lodged at the Widow Warren's home, her husband being one of the men drowned on the trip to the grist mill at Fort Halifax. Meigs reports that he called at a house where he saw the first white child born in the village of Norridgewock, a boy then fourteen months old.

J. W. Hanson, in his history of Norridgewock, says that the villagers were flabbergasted at the sight of a stream of bateaux and soldiers going up the river for hours, and we can imagine that an army of 1100 men passing up the river was quite an event in the lives of the few residents there. A man who lived on the bank of the river told of watching boats and men go by his house for hours. They were also eager to talk to the soldiers and get news of the outside world, including the progress of the war. One Norridgewock man became so fired with the cause that he enlisted on the spot and joined the march to Quebec. He took part in the battle of Quebec, was imprisoned, and then made his way back home, never to leave again, it was said.

The straggling parade reached Bombazine Rips after miles of calm water. These rapids signaled the beginning of some very hard going. The river was to get wilder and wilder as they progressed. Dr. Senter told of hiring two Indians to take the bateau the last stretch before Norridgewock Falls, as the water was so fast (there are still continuous rapids, although somewhat reduced now because of the two dams in Madison). The Indians brought the boat safely to the foot of the falls, where several ox teams owned by the inhabitants were hauling the bateaux up the steep carry around the falls.

Just before reaching Norridgewock Falls, they passed the site of the old Abenaki Indian village and noticed, in Arnold's words, "some small vestiges left of an Indian town . . . the foundations of an old church and altar, the monument over the fort St. Francis, the founder of the church, and the whole tribe we are told are extinct except two or three." There was a spring on the bank of the river with the remains of a covered walkway leading down to it.

The spring is still there, producing delicious clear water, and many Madison families wouldn't drink anything else.

There were three farmers in the area, two at Old Point, Sylvanus Sawyer and a Mr. Fling. James Waugh, the first settler in Starks, had bought a farm near the mouth of the Sandy River just across from Old Point. Being the most prosperous, he owned the only team of horses in the area, which were pressed into service to help move supplies and bateaux over the carry.

Benedict Arnold gave a good account of their week's stay at Norridgewock Falls. The long stop was necessary because of bad weather, the difficulty of the portage, and leaky bateaux. The commander and his company arrived at the foot of the Great Falls on October 2 to find Captain Morgan's riflemen moving their baggage over the carry. Their difficulties here were compounded by the fact of the double falls, the rainy cold weather, leaky bateaux and consequent loss of much of their food. Everything was soaked — bread, peas and flour. The length of the carry was one and a quarter miles, and very steep the whole way. The deterioration of the food supplies was described by Dr. Senter in his journal for October 5:

> . . . A quantity of dry cod fish, by this time was received, as likewise a number of barrels of dry bread. The fish lying loose in the bateaux, and being continually washed with the fresh water running into the bateaux. The bread casks not being waterproof, admitted the water in plenty, swelled the bread, burst the casks, as well as soured the whole bread. The same fate attended a number of fine casks of peas. These with the others were condemned. We were now curtailed of a very

valuable and large part of our provisions, ere we had entered the wilderness, or left the inhabitants. Our fare was now reduced to salt pork and flour. Beef we had once now and then, when we could purchase a fat creature, but that was seldom. A few barrels of salt beef remained on hand, but of so indifferent quality, as scarce to be eaten, being killed in the heat of summer, took much damage after salting, that rendered it not only very unwholesome, but very unpalatable.

Colonel Arnold remained at Norridgewock Falls for seven days, October 2 to 9, in rain and cold, whistling winds, and stormy skies; driving each division at top speed, repairing bateaux, repacking wet provisions and carrying up the steep sides of the falls. On October 9 the last bateau was hoisted up the steep hill and around the falls. They were only a third of the distance to Quebec, and would not find a dwelling or road, only unbroken forests which had never seen an axe, until they reached the villages along the Chaudiere River in Canada.

From Dr. Senter's journal:

Saturday, [October] 7th. We were still at Norridgewock, where was now most of the army. By a council of the officers, it was thought advisable to send letters into Quebec . . . After the dispatches were wrote it was concluded to send one Mr. Jackquith, inhabitant of this river and native of Germany, who spoke the French language, in company with two Penobscot Indians, by name Sabatis and Eneas, who were well acquainted with the wilderness through, as well as the inhabitants of the country where they were going. Accordingly they were dispatched in a bark canoe, taking a sufficient quantity of provisions for the purpose.

Some historians have questioned whether it was wise to send important letters by Indians, but we must remember they were the only couriers available who knew both the wilderness and the villages of Canada.

Also, Dr. Senter called the two Indians Penobscots. They were Abenakis, Sabatis belonging to the Norridgewock clan. His main residence was a cabin on the South Branch of Dead River.

An unusual rock seen at Norridgewock Falls was described in the journal of John Joseph Henry. He was only sixteen years of age when he started on the expedition, serving in Captain Smith's company of Pennsylvania riflemen. Henry's journal was written years after the march as a gift to his children, to acquaint them with his adventures and the privations he had gone through.

> . . . a rock, as we passed it, drew my attention very particularly; it was standing in a conical form, five feet in perpendicular height, and ten or twelve feet in diameter at the base. I observed that next the water, the face of the rock, which was a bluish flint, was, as it were, scalloped out, down to the water's edge. Asking Getchel how this had occurred, his reply was that the Indians in former times had from thence obtained their spear and arrow points.

Since the carry was on the west bank of the river here, presumably the landing and rock were on that side also. Another journal described the rock as being a dark blue hard flint, which is rather unusual for this region. I have never seen or heard of such a stone near the falls, even though I lived in Madison. The area may be the spot where the Great Northern Paper Company power plant was built in 1923 in Anson (west side of the falls), so if the flint rock was still there at that time, it probably was destroyed by blasting.

Arnold described the Kennebec above the falls as having a remarkable bend to the east northeast for about three quarters of a mile, then turning west by north about three quarters of a mile, after which it returns to its proper northward course.

After passing the two river bends, Seven Mile Brook (the Carrabassett River at North Anson), and some islands just south of the present town of Solon, the army found another waterfall in their path, called Caratunk Falls. This fall, although known as Devil's Falls to the Indians, was not as difficult to carry by as either Skowhegan or Norridgewock Falls. The journalists varied in their opinions both of the size of the fall and of its proper spelling. Arnold estimated "Curratunk falls" to be about 15 feet high with a 50-rod portage. Dearborn, in his journal, called the portage 95 rods around "Carritunkus-falls." "Carry-tuck," according to Simeon Thayer, was about 16 feet high with a carry of only eight rods, although frozen and difficult. At this place the army was spread up and down the river for a distance of 10 or 12 miles.

They were now getting close to the Great Carrying Place, the shortcut trail across the Carry Ponds to Dead River. This route would enable them to avoid many miles of the twisting West Branch or Dead River. Carrying Place Stream, the outlet waterway of East Carry Pond, marks the starting point of the Great Carrying Place. The trail across the carry actually starts about a quarter mile south of the mouth of the stream.

Today we can stand on the high eastern river bank regarding the broad river below from a scenic lookout on Route 201, about five miles south of Pierce

Pond Stream and the village of Caratunk. Arnold Trail markers describe this historic spot and show us where to look to see the starting point of the terrible journey. The river here flows between two ranges of wooded hills and from our viewpoint the western bank of the river looks much the same as it must have appeared in 1775, as Arnold's weary men, with their leaky bateaux, prepared to cross the river and enter the trackless forest.

By means of Arnold's journal, himself a master reporter, and those of several of his men, we can turn back the clock and imagine that we are traveling over the forest trail with the little army. Over all these carries the 400-pound bateaux would have to be carried, cutting cruelly into the flesh of the men's shoulders. Exhaustion, starvation, disease and defeat were still ahead of them.

This is Arnold's account of the journey from the Great Carrying Place to the Canadian border, following the version published by Kenneth Roberts in *March to Quebec*:

> Wednesday, Oct. 11th, 1775. We embarked early this morning and proceeded up the river, the stream very rapid indeed. At 10, arrived at the Great Carrying Place which is very remarkable, a large brook emptying itself into the river just above, which comes out of the first lake. When abreast of the carrying place in the river, you will observe at about 400 yards above you a large mountain in shape of a sugar loaf, at the foot of which the river turns off to the eastward. This mountain, when you are at the carrying place, seems to rise out of the middle of the river. Here I overtook Capt. Morgan and his division, Col. Greene and division; part of each had proceeded as far as the second lake. Major Meigs arrived just before me. Met Lt. Church who had been at the Dead River on

a survey and reports as follows: from Kennebec over the portage to the first pond or lake, course west 27 degrees north, distance 3¼ miles, rising ground, bad road but capable of being made good.

Over the first pond half a mile, which pond is 1¼ miles long. Here our people caught a prodigious number of fine salmon trout, nothing being more common than a man's taking eight or ten dozen in one hour's time, which generally weigh half a pound apiece. [Roberts notes, "This means catching a half-pound trout every thirty seconds for an hour."] The second portage is west 6 degrees north, half a mile and 20 rods, very hard but rough roads. The second pond is in length from north to south 2½ miles long, and ¾ mile wide.

The third carrying place is ¼ mile and 40 rods, the road very bad, course west 10 degrees north.

The third pond is in length from north to south 3 miles, width 2 miles, course over west by north.

The fourth or last portage is west 20 degrees north, distance 2¾ miles and 60 rods, the first part of the road tolerable good, the last mile a savanna, wet and miry about six or eight inches deep.

Thursday, Oct. 12th. Lt. Steele returned from Chaudiere Pond and says he discovered no Indians, that the Dead River from the last carrying place he judges to be 80 miles; most part of the way a fine deep river, the current hardly perceptible; some five falls and short carrying places, and rapid water; the carrying place from the Dead River to Chaudiere Pond about 4 miles; very good . . . ground most part of the way and plenty of moose and other game on the river. This day employed Capt. Goodrich's company in building a log house on the second carrying place to accommodate our sick, eight or ten in number, who we are obliged to leave behind; also a party at the east side of the first portage to build a small log house for men and provisions.

Arnold's hospital was hurriedly thrown together to house the deathly sick and exhausted men. The site is between East and Middle Carry Ponds, and many sad mementos have been found there by scholars of

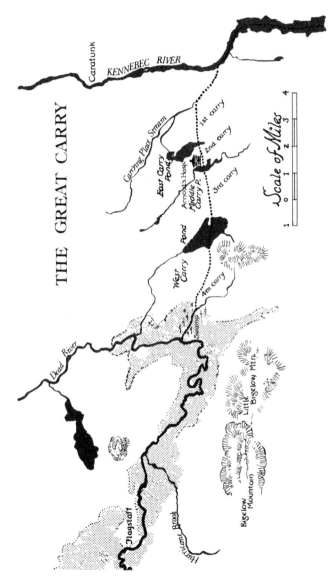

THE GREAT CARRY

Caratunk

KENNEBEC RIVER

Carrying Place Stream

1st carry

2nd carry

East Carry Pond

Arnold's Hosp.

Middle Carry P.

3rd carry

Scale of Miles

1 0 1 2 3 4

West Carry Pond

4th carry

Swamp

Dead River

Bigelow Mtn.

Little Bigelow Mountain

Bigelow Mountain

Flagstaff

Hurricane Brook

This map shows the route the Arnold expedition took across the Carry Ponds to Dead River. The area shaded in dots shows where Flagstaff Lake has since flowed out Dead River. Map by Ruth Lepper Gardner.

343

the expedition. Dr. Senter described the log hut in his journal:

> Monday, [October] 16th. We now found it necessary to erect a building for the reception of our sick, who had now increased to a very formidable number. A block house was erected and christened by the name of Arnold's Hospital, and no sooner finished than filled. Not far from this was a small bush hut provisionally constructed by Morgan's division of riflemen, who were gone forward. In this they left a young gentleman by name Irvin, a native of Pennsylvania, brought up a physician in that city, and serving as an ensign in the company under Capt. Morgan. The case of this young gentleman was truly deplorable. In the first of our march from Cambridge, he was tormented with a dysentery, for which he never paid any medical attention. When he came to wading in the water every day, then lodging on the ground at night, it kept him in a most violent rheumatism I ever saw, not able to help himself any more than a new born infant, every joint in his extremities inflexible and swelled to an enormous size. Much in the same condition was Mr. Jackson of the same company, and Mr. Greene, my mate. The last of whom was left at Fort Western. All these three gentlemen were afflicted with the same disease during the beginning of our march, nor would arguments prevail on them to use any medicine. Flattered as they were that nature would relieve them, yet for once they were mistaken.
>
> Tuesday, 17th. By this, the remainder of the army had now come up, in consequence of which I quit my hospital business and proceeded with them where I left poor Dr. Irvin, with all the necessaries of life I could impart to him. He was allowed 4 men of his company to wait upon him, but as they'd nothing to do with, they could be of little service, except keeping him a good fire, turning him when weary, etc. His situation was most wretched, overrun with vermin, unable to help [himself] in the least thing, attended constantly with the most violent pain. . . .

There in that rude shelter many would perish. In later years, woodsmen found graves with rustic wooden crosses, and at least one body was moved to

the cemetery in Moscow where can be seen a stone
with this inscription:

JOHN KIRK

ONE OF ARNOLD'S MEN

Arnold's journal continues for October 12:

Ordered Lts. Steele and Church with 20 ax men and a
surveyor to Chaudiere Ponds to clear the portages and take a
survey of the country; Lt. Steele to go down the Chaudiere
near the inhabitants and examine the falls, portages, etc., and
return to the pond as soon as possible. Our men are much
fatigued in carrying over their bateaux, provisions, etc., the
roads being extremely bad; however their spirit and industry
seems to overcome every obstacle and they appear very cheerful. [Arnold often shows his sympathy for his army's hardships and admiration for their fortitude.] We have had
remarkable fine weather since we left Cambridge, and only
one death has happened, and very few accidents by water,
which is the more remarkable as there seldom passes a season
without some people being drowned in the Kennebec, which
is very difficult and dangerous to ascend.

Oct. 13th. This morning dispatched one Eneas and
another Indian with letters to some gentlemen in Quebec and
to Gen. Schuyler. Sent a white man with [Eneas] who is to
proceed as far as Sartigan and after discovering the sentiments of the inhabitants, and procuring all the intelligence
he can, is to return to us at Chaudiere Pond where we expect
to meet him in about 7 or 8 days. Two divisions have this day
reached the Dead River.

N.B. The foregoing transmitted to Gen. Washington.

Colonel Arnold and Dr. Senter seem to disagree on
the date and place of this event. Senter's journal has a
more complete account of a council meeting of the
officers held on October 7 at Norridgewock Falls.
Senter also gives the names of all three men, while
Arnold mentions Eneas, another Indian and a white
man. The white man, Jackquith, I believe would

more likely have been at Norridgewock than on the Great Carry, but this is just conjecture. It may well be that the course of action was decided at the council on the October 7, while the actual letters were written and sent on the 13th.

Saturday, Oct. 14th, 1775. Left our encampment at 4 p.m., carried over the portage, which according to Lt. Church's survey is west 6 degrees north, ½ mile and 20 rods, ground hard. We soon arrived at the second pond, which makes as desolate an appearance as the first does bountiful, the lake being very irregular, long and narrow, the trees all dead and full of moss, the water very thick and muddy. Our course over it for about ½ mile was west, then stand north by west about ¾ mile up a narrow creek or arm of the lake. Our course over the third portage was west 10 degrees north, 1⅜ of a mile; road extremely bad, being choked up with roots which we could not clear away, it being a work of time. Reached the third pond or lake; there the prospect is very beautiful and noble, a high chain of mountains encircling the pond, which is deep, clear and fine water, over which a forked mountain [Bigelow] which exceeds the rest in height bearing northwest, and covered with snow, in contrast with the others adds greatly to the beauty of the scene. It being late, made no attempt to cross but encamped for the night.

Sunday, Oct. 15th, 1775. At 10 a.m. we embarked and proceeded over the lake. Our course was northwest. This lake appears to be 3½ miles long and 2½ broad, very uniform, a small elbow running into it from the southeast on the west side of which it empties itself. We entered on the portage at 1 o'clock p.m. We ascended the hill about one mile, the portage conducting us through the gap or breach in the mountain. After descending the hill a mile we came to a low savanna, where we encamped for the night.

Monday, Oct. 16th. Early in the morning continued our route over the savanna which is divided by a small wood not exceeding 100 rods. The road excessive wet and miry, being near up to our knees, (but thanks to our boots) we got over without being much wet. Our course was nearly west 20 degrees north, 2¾ miles and 60 rods. Here the men had a most fatiguing time in getting over their bateaux, baggage etc. At half after one p.m. we arrived at a small brook [Bog Brook], where we launched our bateaux and after rowing about one mile arrived at the Dead River, which is about 60 yards wide, uniformly deep and gentle with current. Prior to which ordered 10 men of each company of Major Meigs' division to work on the roads, that the rear might pass with less difficulty. Continued our voyage up the river. We were now near the large mountain mentioned the preceding day. Here the river by its extraordinary windings seemed unwilling to leave it. Two hours had passed away and we had gained nothing in our course, but at last by slow degrees it became more regular and returned to its proper course. [This passage is identical to Montresor's describing the same location.] When we had got 3 leagues we found a small fall [Hurricane Falls], the portage over 40 yards. The course this 3 leagues [approx. 9 mi.] was nearly southwest. Here we passed Capt. Morgan's company and continued our course 2 leagues where we found an Indian house. One league further up we overtook Capt. Green and division, with whom we encamped much fatigued. Our course was about west northwest.

Captain Dearborn's journal for the next day also mentions this Indian house:

[October] 17. We proceeded up the river 10 miles and came to an Indian wigwam, said to belong to an old Indian called Natanis. It stands on a point of land beautifully situated, there is a number of acres of cleared land about it; the river is very still and good land on each side of it a considerable part of the way. . . . Here we encamped.

At this point Arnold's division was only a day or two ahead of Dearborn. He had camped at this place on the 15th or 16th and had raised a flagpole. This later became the location of the village of Flagstaff, which was named in honor of that event. The Mount Bigelow range dominates the landscape here, over four thousand feet high and twelve miles long. Flagstaff village was entirely flowed out by Long Falls

Arnold's March to Quebec

Dam, built in 1950. Now in place of the winding river and village there is a large lake, also named Flagstaff. Arnold's journal continues:

Tuesday, Oct. 17th. Finding Col. Greene's division short of flour (great part of their bread being damaged) ordered a subaltern, 2 sergeants and 29 privates out of each company, under the command of Major Bigelow, to return and assist the rear in bringing up their provisions, the remainder of the division to be employed in making up their cartridges. [Roberts explains, "Cartridges were made by opening a keg of powder, rolling cartridge paper into cylinders, filling the cylinders with powder, twisting the ends, and packing the cylinders in cartridge boxes. When loading with such a cartridge, a musketman bit the paper from one end, poured the contents into his musket; then used the cartridge paper as a wad."] Caught a number of fine trout on the river. At 12 o'clock Capt. Morgan's division passed us and went on for Chaudiere Pond.

Wednesday, Oct. 18th, 1775. At 10 a.m. Capt. Goodrich's and Dearborn's companies arrived. Gave orders for their making cartridges as well as those who are up. At 5 p.m. Major Meigs arrived with the last of his division.

Oct. 19th, Thursday. Small rains the whole of this day. At 3 p.m., the storm abating, Major Meigs went forward with his division, and soon after followed and proceeded on our way about 2½ leagues to the second carrying place. Our course was various; part of the way was southwest and gradually shifted to southeast with many turnings and windings. We passed 6 small rips, very swift water and shallow, which brought us as near the mountain as we had been at any time before. The course over this carrying place is south 35 degrees east, distance 15 perches. Night coming on and the rain increasing, we encamped on the portage and caught a plenty of fine trout near the falls.

N.B. Rained very hard all night. The whole country since we came into the Dead River appears flat for a great distance to the northward and eastward, tolerable land and some part well wooded, but in general covered with spruce, cedar, fir, birch, etc., the soil cold and in general barren.

348

Friday, Oct. 20. Rainy morning. At noon Major Meigs' division came up, and being very wet and the storm continuing, they proceeded on, intending to encamp early. Continues rainy the whole of this day, wind to the southwestward.

Saturday, Oct. 21. Storm continues though something abated, a prodigious fall of rain for two days past — has raised the river upwards of three feet . . . At 7 a.m. embarked and proceeded up the river 3 leagues when we came to a small fall of water, the portage over west northwest about 10 rods. About ½ mile higher up came to another fall more considerable. Portage over about 26 rods, course west northwest. Continued our route up the river for about half a mile and came to another fall; the portage 75 rods, course over west northwest. About 90 rods higher up met with a fourth fall, very considerable and long [Long Falls]; portage over west northwest, distance 73 rods. Here we overtook Capt. Morgan and his division, but as his encampment was bad proceeded about one mile higher up, very wet and much fatigued, having paddled up near four leagues, through the rain which continued incessantly. It was now quite dark so that we had little time to encamp, and it was near 11 o'clock before we could dry our clothes and take a little refreshment, when we wrapped ourselves in our blankets and slept very comfortably until 4 o'clock in the morning, when we were awaked by the freshet which came running on us like a torrent, having rose 8 feet perpendicular in 9 hours, and before we could remove, wet all our baggage and forced us from our comfortable habitation. Very luckily for us we had a small hill to retreat to, where we conveyed our baggage and passed the remainder of the night in no very agreeable situation. [Roberts notes, "In the opinion of the United States Weather Bureau, this storm was a wandering West Indian hurricane."]

Sunday, Oct. 22nd. This morning presented us a very disagreeable prospect, the country round entirely overflowed, so that the course of the river being crooked, could not be discovered, which with the rapidity of the current renders it almost impossible for the bateaux to ascend the river, or the men to find their way by land or pass the small brooks, arms of the river, etc. Add to this our provisions almost exhausted, and the incessant rains for three days has prevented our gaining anything considerable, so that we have but a melancholy prospect before us, but in general in high spirits. At 9 a.m. Capt. Morgan with his company passed us up the river, and at 5 p.m. Major Meigs with part of his division came up with us. Were employed the whole of this day in drying our baggage, etc., the whole of which was sometime under water (last night) and very wet.

Monday, Oct. 23rd, 1775. At 7 a.m. Capts. Smith, [Hendricks], and Major Meigs with his division came up and passed on. At 10 a.m. embarked and proceeded up the river, the stream by reason of the freshet very quick; in about 3 miles we came to the crotch of the river [junction of Alder Stream and Dead River]. Our course was about west. Here we found that the land [party] had by mistake taken the southwest or wrong course, which we rowed up two miles, and sent men ahead to inform them of their mistake, and direct their march. This mistake occasioned a detention of the bateaux and whole division near two hours. When the whole were formed we proceeded up the river against a very rapid stream about 3 miles to the seventh carrying place, course over north 35 degrees east, distance 7 perches. Here we had the misfortune of oversetting 7 bateaux and losing all the provisions. Here the whole division encamped [Shadagee Falls]. The river continues high and rapid, and as our provisions are but short and no intelligence from Canada, I ordered a council of war summoned of such officers as were present, who came to the following resolutions.

Tuesday, Oct. 24. Sent back the sick, 26 in number, and ordered Col. Greene and Col. Enos to send back as many of the poorest men of their detachment, as would leave 15 days' provision for the remainder, who are to follow on as fast as possible. [This order, its meaning quite specific, occasioned much controversy in light of Col. Enos' later return to Massachusetts with his complete company.] Capt. Hanchet with 50 men set out early for Chaudiere Pond, in order to forward on provisions from the French inhabitants of Sartigan for the use of the army. Dispatched the division inward and at noon set forward. Went about 7 miles, very rapid water, when we came to two falls. The portages over the first was north 20 degrees west, 12 perches; the second which was about 100 yards above the first was north 12 degrees east, 6 perches. N.B. This is the tenth carrying place since we entered the Dead River. We are now about 20 miles from Chaudiere Pond. We proceeded about 1 mile higher up, when night coming on, and the rain increasing, which had begun about an hour before, we encamped. It continued raining and snowing all night. At 4 in the morning the wind shifted to north and it cleared up. About two inches now on the ground.

Wednesday, 25th Oct. We embarked early this morning and proceeded up against a rapid stream; about 1½ mile came to a portage of about 40 rods, course about northwesterly, the fall very inconsiderable. About 1 mile higher up found another fall, the portage over 100 rods, northwest [Sarampus Falls]. Water continues rapid ½ a mile, when we entered the first lake [Lower Pond] which is about ½ a mile wide, but contracts itself in several places. We rowed about 2 miles when the lake is no more than 2 rods wide, when it again opens to its former length [Bag Pond]. One mile and a half brought us to a marshy ground. Passed on in a small rivulet for half a mile which brought us to a lake about five miles long and ¾ wide [Long Pond and Natanis Pond]; several points make out into it. All these lakes are surrounded with a chain of prodigious high mountains. At the cut of this lake which lies north and south, we found it contracted to about 3 rods wide for a short distance which brought us to a small round pond or rather the north end of the lake [Round Pond. These first five ponds, Lower, Bag, Long, Natanis, and Round, are now called Chain of Ponds]. Here we were a long time at a loss for the portage. At length we found a small brook [Horseshoe Stream] which we entered and rowed up about 1½ miles with much difficulty, being obliged to clear away the drift logs in many places. Snowed and blowed very hard, the wind at north. All this day in the last lake the sea ran so high we were obliged to go on shore several times to bail our bateaux, which was with much difficulty kept above the water. Night coming on and we being much fatigued and chilled with the cold, we were obliged to encamp without being satisfied whether we were right or not, as our guides gone forward had made no marks or we had missed them. We

351

made it 11 o'clock before we could get comfortable to lie down. The whole distance this day appeared to us near 14 miles, but as we rowed against sea and wind we might possibly be deceived 3 or 4 miles in the distance.

John Joseph Henry, years later, gave the best description of the forests of any of the journalists, expressing a real appreciation for the beautiful scenery they saw, though often in uncomfortable circumstances. His extreme youth was in his favor as far as enduring discomfort, and he obviously enjoyed adventure.

The timber trees of this country are in a great measure different from those of our own [in Pennsylvania]. Here are neither oaks, hickories, poplars, maples or locusts; but there is a great variety of other kinds of excellent timber, such as the white and yellow pines, hemlock, cedar, cypress, and all the species of firs. These trees, in the low grounds, grow to a very large size. On the hills, as we approached northwardly, they seem to dwindle, particularly as we come to the "height of land"; but again rise to a superb height as we descend into the intervale, on the streams running into Canada.

Among the trees of this country there are two which deserve particular notice, because of their remarkable qualities. These are the balsam fir (Canada balsam, Balm of Gilead fir, or *balsamum Canadense pinus balsomea*, which produces the purest turpentine), and the yellow birch. The first, as its vulgar name imports, yields a balsamic liquid, which has been, and perhaps is now, much esteemed by the medical profession. The bark is smooth, except that there are a vast number of white and lucid protuberances upon it, of the size of a finger or thumb nail, bulging from the surface of the bark. This tree grows to the size of from 15 to 20 inches in diameter. From the essays made, it seemed to me that a phial containing a gill might be filled in the space of an hour. Getchel, our guide, taught me its use. In the morning when we rose, placing the edge of a broad knife at the under side of the blister, and my lips at the opposite part, on the back of the knife, which was declined, the liquor flowed into my mouth freely. It was heating and cordial to the stomach, attended by an agreeable pungency. This practice, which we adopted, in all likelihood contributed to the preservation of health — for though much wet weather ensued, and we lay often on low and damp ground, and had very many successions of cold atmosphere, it does not now occur to me that any of us were assailed by sickness during this arduous excursion.

The yellow birch is useful in many particular instances to the natives. They form the body of the tree into setting-poles, paddles, spoons and ladles. The bark, its better property, serves as a covering for the frame of the canoe, much in the same manner as the Eskimos and Greenlanders apply the seal skin. . . . From the bark of yellow birch, the Indian also forms bowls and baskets of a most beautiful construction, and it even serves as a wrapper for any nice matter which it is wished to keep securely, much in the manner we use brown wrapping paper. The appearance of the yellow birch tree at a distance is conspicuous. Approaching near it, in the autumn, it seems involved in rolls, something resembling large circular rounds of parchment, or yellow paper.

Arnold's journal continues toward the Canadian border:

Thursday, 26th Oct. Early in the morning dispatched one of my men up the small stream to see if he could discover any signs of a portage while we got breakfast, and packed up our baggage. He returned without making any discovery; we continued our route up a narrow and very crooked and rapid brook about 3½ miles which brought us to a portage of 12 perches, course west 20 degrees south to a small lake about 80 rods long and 30 broad [Lost Pond]. In a few minutes we arrived at another portage, course west 35 degrees north, distance ¾ of a mile and 53 rods. Carried over and entered another lake [Horseshoe Pond] ½ a mile in length; another carrying place of 74 rods, course west 5 degrees north, brought us to another lake [Mud Pond] of about ½ a mile long. Another portage of 44 rods, course west, brought us to the last lake [Arnold Pond], which is 1½ miles in length and ½ a mile broad. At 4 p.m. entered on the great carrying place into Chaudiere Pond, the length of the portage 4 miles and 60 rods; the first two miles about north, 1½ miles west 10 degrees south, then north to the brook. About 2 miles of the first part of the portage you ascend, which brought us to the Height of Land at an elevation of about 35 degrees; from that we then descended the hill to the brook. We advanced on the portage about 3 miles this evening (at dusk) much fatigued.

Arnold understated the difficulties of this portage, which even today is almost impassable, full of thick forest and blowdowns, swamps and precipices. George Morison, a private in Capt. Hendricks' company of Pennsylvania riflemen, described it as

. . . the *Terrible Carrying Place;* a dismal portage indeed of two miles and fifty perches; intersected with a considerable ridge covered with fallen trees, stones and brush. The ground adjacent to this ridge is swampy, plentifully strewed with old dead logs, and with every thing that could render it impassable. Over this we forced a passage, the most distressing of any we had yet performed. The ascent and descent of the hill was inconceivably difficult. The boats and carriers often fell down into the snow, some of them were much hurt by reason of their feet sticking fast among the stones. . . . We now determined to leave our boats in the woods, as the oppression of carrying them was becoming absolutely intolerable.

Even as the vanguard of the army was beginning to make its way over the Terrible Carry, the troops at the rear were giving up. The story of the unauthorized return of Lt. Col. Roger Enos is perhaps best told in Dr. Senter's journal:

Wednesday, [October] 25th. Every prospect of distress now came thundering on with a two fold rapidity. A storm of snow had covered the ground of nigh six inches deep, attended with very severe weather. We now waited in anxious expectation for Col. Enos' division to come up, in order that we might have a recruit of provisions ere we could start off the ground.

An express was ordered both up and down the river, the one up the river in quest of Col. Arnold, that he might be informed of the state of the army, many of whom were now entirely destitute of any sustenance. The colonel had left previous orders for the two divisions, viz: Greene's and Enos', to come to an adjustment of the provisions, send back any who were indisposed, either in body or mind, and pursue him with the others immediately. The other express went down the river to desire Col. Enos and officers to attend in consultation. They accordingly came up before noon, when a council of war was ordered.

Here sat a number of grimacers — melancholy aspects who had been preaching to their men the doctrine of impenetrability and non-perseverance. Col. Enos in the chair. The matter was debated upon the expediency of proceeding on to Quebec. The party against going urged the impossibility, averring the whole provisions, when averaged, would not support the army five days.

The arrangements of men and provisions being made at Fort Western, in such a manner as to proceed with the greater expedition. For this end it was thought necessary that Capt. Morgan's company with a few pioneers should advance in the first division, Col. Greene's in the second, and Enos, with Capt. Colburn's company of artificers, to bring up the rear. The advantage of the arrangement was very conspicuous, as the rear division would not only have the roads cut, rivers cleared passable for boats, etc., but stages or encampments formed and the bough huts remaining for the rear. The men being thus arranged, the provisions were distributed according to the supposed difficulty, or facility, attending the different dispositions. Many of the first companies took only two or three barrels of flour with several of bread, most in a small proportion. While the companies in the last division had not less than fourteen of flour and ten of bread. The bread as mentioned before, was condemned in consequence of the leaky casks, therefore the proportion of bread being much greater in the first division, their loss was consequently the greater. These hints being premised, I now proceed to the determination of the council of war.

After debating upon the state of the army with respect to

Bateaux similar to those used by Arnold's men were built for the 1975 bicentennial reenactment of Arnold's march to Quebec. On the original march, the bateaux were used mostly for transporting foodstuffs. Photograph by the author.

provisions, there was found very little in the division then encamped at the falls (which I shall name *Hydrophobus*). The other companies not being come up, either through fear that they should be obliged to come to a divider, or to show their disapprobation of proceeding any further. The question being put whether all to return, or only part, the majority were for part only returning. Part only of the officers of those detachments were in this council. The number and opinions of those present were as follows:

For proceeding: Lt. Col. Greene, Major Bigelow, Capt. Topham, Thayer, Ward, Lt. Col. Enos.

For returning: Capt. Williams, McCobb, Scott, Adjutant Hide, Lt. Peters.

According to Col. Arnold's recommendation the invalids were allowed to return, as also the timorous. One bateau only for each company to proceed, in order to carry the military stores, medicines, etc. Expresses returned, but no word from Col. Arnold, as he was now in the advanced part of Morgan's division, equipped in the best manner to go in to the inhabitants as soon as possible. He carried no other stores except a small quantity of specie, attended with a good pilot in a British canoe, hands sufficient to carry every thing over the various carrying places, and proceeded by water with great expedition. But to return: the officers who were for going forward, requested a division of the provisions, and that it was necessary they should have the far greater quantity in proportion to the number of men, as the supposed distance that they had to go ere they arrived into the inhabitants was greater than what they had come, after leaving the Kennebec inhabitants.

To this the returning party [having already made up their minds] would not consent, alleging that they would either go back with what provisions they had, or if they must go forward they'd not impart any. [They must have known by this time of the starving condition of the company they had come up to. The day before, Senter noted that Col. Greene's division, waiting for supplies, were destitute of anything to eat except a few candles boiled in water.]

Col. Enos, though [he] voted for proceeding, yet had undoubtedly [decided] to the contrary, as every action demonstrated. To compel them to a just division, we were not in a situation, as being the weakest party. Expostulations and entreaties had hitherto been fruitless. Col. Enos, who more immediately commanded the division of *returners,* was called upon to give positive orders for a small quantity, if no more. He replied that his men were out of his power, and that they had determined to keep their possessed quantity whether they went back or forward.

They finally concluded to spare [us] 2½ barrels of flour, if determined to pursue our destination; adding that we never should be able to bring [in] any inhabitants. Thus circumstanced, we were left the alternative of accepting their small pittance, and proceed or return. The former was adopted, with a determined resolution to go through or die.

Was it desertion? Was he a traitor? Was he a coward? Or was Roger Enos acting as a prudent officer trying to spare his men, and himself, the prospect of hardship and hunger on the march ahead? Whatever the motive, the last division turned back with apparently enough food for the 350 men to cover the more than 100 miles to the settlements. They reached Brunswick in fifteen days and it was there that Enos wrote to General Washington, accounting for his action thus: "Sir, I am on my return from Col. Arnold's detachment. I brought up the rear of the whole. Captains McCobb's, Williams' and Scott's companies were assigned to my division. We proceeded as far as 50 miles up the Dead River, and then were obliged to return for want of provisions. . . ."

On Enos' return to Cambridge, Washington placed him under arrest and ordered a court of inquiry to be held. A court-martial followed on December 1, 1775. Enos was charged with leaving the detachment under Colonel Arnold, and returning home without permission from his commanding officer.

The defendant stated that although it was true that he had left the expedition without permission from his commanding officer, the circumstances were such that he was obliged to do so. The witnesses for the defense were his own officers, who to a man had voted to leave the march at the council meeting on Dead River.

There were no witnesses for the prosecution, since Arnold's army were extremely busy before the gates of Quebec on December 1, and effectively out of touch with headquarters in Massachusetts.

After the last witness had testified, the court was cleared, and Brigadier General John Sullivan and twelve field officers retired to consider the verdict. The final result was "that Colonel Enos was perfectly justified in returning with the division . . . we therefore unanimously acquitted Colonel Enos with honor."

The verdict might have been different had the court had access to the journals of some of the soldiers who went on to Quebec. Abner Stocking wrote on October 25:

> To add to our discouragements, we received intelligence that Colonel Enos, who was in our rear, had returned with three companies, and taken large stores of provisions and ammunition. These companies had constantly been in the rear, and of course had experienced much less fatigue than we had. They had their path cut and cleared by us; they only followed, while we led. That they therefore should be the first to turn back excited in us much manly resentment.

Dearborn's journal of October 27:

When we were at the great carrying place . . . from the Dead River to Chaudiere Pond, we had the unhappy news of Col. Enos, and the three companies in his division, being so imprudent as to return back two or three days before, which disheartened and discouraged our men very much, [especially] as they carried back more than their part or quota of provision and ammunition . . . Our men made a general prayer, that Col. Enos and all his men might die by the way, or meet with some disaster, equal to the cowardly, dastardly and unfriendly spirit they [showed] in returning back without orders.

Arnold's language was more restrained, as he noted mildly in a letter to General Washington on November 8: "all [men have] happily arrived (except one man drowned and one or two sick — and Col. Enos' division, who, I am surprised to hear, are all gone back) . . ."

John Codman, in *Arnold's Expedition to Canada*, describes the position of the divisions of Arnold's army on the 27th of October, after Enos had turned his back on his commanding officer and started retracing his steps down the Kennebec. Codman pointed out that an eagle soaring above the Height of Land could have seen far below:

Arnold, with four bateaux and fifteen men, having made their way across the Terrible Carry, was paddling down Chaudiere Pond.

Capt. Oliver Hanchet, with a detail of fifty men, was marching around the same lake on its eastern shore.

The rifle companies under Capt. Morgan were crossing the Chain of Ponds and working their way up the tortuous gut that led to Lost Pond and Arnold Pond.

Major Meigs, with the third division, was just entering the first pond of the Chain with four more to go.

The unlucky second division, Col. Greene's, was moving forward from the campground three miles beyond Ledge Falls where the council of war had been held. (These falls are about three miles above the present village of Eustis.) Greene's men still had long stretches of white water and falls to traverse before gaining the ponds at the head of Dead River.

And Codman's imaginary eagle could also have seen Lt. Col. Roger Enos with three companies moving at a faster pace downriver toward the Kennebec.

Although the van of the army had now reached Canadian waters, there was still disaster in store for them. Arnold's journal for October 27 describes the beginning of it:

On [Seven-mile Stream] we met Lieuts. Steele and Church with one Jakins, whom I had sometime since sent down to the French inhabitants. He left Sartigan the 22nd instant, and says the French inhabitants appear very friendly and were rejoiced to hear of our approach, that there is very few troops at Quebec, Governor Carleton at Montreal, and one small frigate at Quebec. At 4 p.m. we entered the Chaudiere Pond or rather Lake Megantic which is in length from north to south about 13 miles, and 3 or 4 wide. We rowed on about 3 miles to the east side and encamped. Here we found a very considerable wigwam. We waited here for the arrival of Capt. Hanchet and 60 men who left the carrying place with us to come on by land. At about sunset we discovered them on a point of low land on the east side about two miles from us. I immediately sent all the bateaux for them who discovered them on a low marshy ground, to gain which they had waded two miles through water to their waists. This error was occasioned by their endeavoring to keep the stream, whereas they should from the carrying place kept on the high land and steered in about north by east or north northeast, which would have brought them to the lake clear of the sunken ground. It was near midnight before all the men were brought over, as the bateaux were obliged to go three and four times each.

Many of the army had abandoned their bateaux on the Height of Land, preferring to walk along the riverbank the rest of the way to Quebec. Arnold's party, who had kept their boats, had no difficulty following the route of Montresor down the river into Lake Megantic. Montresor's map, however, did not show Spider Lake, Rush Lake and the swamps around the mouth of Seven-mile Stream; and many soldiers became lost in these swamps, disregarding Arnold's instructions to keep to high ground and not attempt to follow the stream. It was fortunate for Capt. Hanchet's marooned men that Arnold had not abandoned his bateaux.

Not all of the soldiers were so lucky. Dr. Senter's journal for the 29th of October describes the predicament of the men lost in the swamps with no food:

> From the first appearance of daylight this morn we picked up our small affairs and beat a march. Not long had we marched this course before we came into a spruce and cedar swamp, and arrived at a small pond at 11 o'clock, through the most execrable bog-mire, impenetrable *Pluxus* of shrubs, imaginable. This pond we pursued till coming to an outlet rivulet, we followed to a lake much larger than the first, and notwithstanding the most confident assertions of our pilot, we pursued this pond the most of the day, but no Chaudiere. We did not reach out of the spruce and cedar territory this day, but was obliged to encamp in the swamp, as we thought within half a mile of the Chaudiere River [Seven-mile Stream], which, according to Montresor's map, we were sure to find the way into the country without difficulty, leading us

directly to the river St. Lawrence. This day's march was computed at eighteen miles. . . .

Monday, 30th. Cooking being very much out of fashion, we had little else to do than march as quick as light permitted; half an hour only brought us to a water which we imagined to be a creek formed by the lake; laid our course more southwardly, endeavoring to go round it, but three miles march evinced our mistake; our creek proved to be a river of four rods wide. The depth and width of this river rendered it unfordable, nor [was] it possible to form a bridge, as nothing of any bigness grew on its banks. . . . This was the third day we had been in search of the Chaudiere, who were only seven computed miles distant the 28th instant. Nor were we possessed of any certainty that our course would bring us either to the lake or river, not knowing the point it lay from where we started. However we came to a resolution to continue it. In this state of uncertainty we wandered through hideous swamps and mountainous precipices, with the conjoint addition of cold, wet and hunger, not to mention our fatigue — with the terrible apprehension of famishing in this desert. The pretended pilot was not less frightened than many of the rest; added to that, the severe execrations he received, from the front of the army to the rear, made his office not a little disagreeable. Several of the men towards evening were ready to give up any thoughts of ever arriving at the desired haven. Hunger and fatigue had so much the ascendancy over many of the poor fellows, added to their despair of arrival, that some of them were left in the river, nor were heard of afterwards. In turn with Col. Greene, I carried the compass the greater part of this day. In this condition we proceeded with as little knowledge of where we were, or where we should get to, as if we had been in the unknown interior of Africa, or the deserts of Arabia. Just as the sun was departing, we brought a pond or lake, which finally proved to be Chaudiere, and soon the small foot-path made by the other division of the army, whose choice turned to their account. Our arrival here was succeeded with three huzzas, and then came to our encampment.

Tuesday, 31st. The appearance of daylight roused us as usual, and we had advanced with all possible speed till about

11 o'clock, ere we saw the Chaudiere river, which we last night imagined within a mile. Animated afresh with the sight of a stream, which we very well knew would conduct us into the inhabitants if our strength continued, we proceeded with renewed vigor. . . . We now began to discover the wrecked bateaux of those who conducted the ammunition, etc. [Morgan's company of Virginia riflemen had carried their bateaux over the Height of Land.] These were seven in number, who followed the seven mile stream into the Chaudiere lake, river, etc., and soon came to an encampment, where I found Capt. Morgan and most of the boatmen who were wrecked upon a fall in the river, losing every thing except their lives, which they all saved by swimming, except one of Morgan's riflemen. This was the first man drowned in all the dangers we were exposed to, and the third [lost] by casualties, except some lost in the wilderness, the number unknown. At this encampment was Lieut. McCleland, of Morgan's company, almost expiring with a violent *peripneumonia*. Necessaries were distributed as much as possible, with two lads of the company in charge of him. Nor was this poor fellow the only one left sick upon this river. Life depending upon a vigorous push for the inhabitants, and that did not admit of any stay for any person; nor could the two lads have been prevailed upon had not provisions been dealt out sufficient to conduct them to the inhabitants, with the promising to send them relief as soon as possible from the settlements.

The journal of Abner Stocking continues the tale:

November 1st. Our fatigue and anxiety were so great that we were but little refreshed the last night by sleep. We started however very early, hungry and wet. Knowing that our lives depended on our speedy arrival to an inhabited country, we marched very briskly all day and even until late in the evening. We then encamped in a fine grove, but in a starving condition. Captain Goodrich's company had the good fortune to kill a large black dog, that providentially came to them at that time [belonging to Capt. Dearborn]. They feasted on him heartily without either bread or salt. Our hunger was so great that many offered dollars for a single mouthful of bread. . . .

November 2nd. When we arose this morning many of the company were so weak that they could hardly stand on their legs. When we attempted to march, they reeled about like drunken men, having now been without provisions five days. . . .

Just at evening this day, we met cattle coming up the river, sent us for our relief. This was the most joyful sight our eyes ever beheld. The French people who drove them informed us that Colonel Arnold had arrived in their settlement two days before, with the advance party, and had purchased cattle as soon as possible and sent them on. . . .

November 3rd. This day we proceeded on down the river about 20 miles, wading several small rivers, some of which were up to our middles. The water was terrible cold as the ground was at this time covered with snow and ice. At evening we came in sight of a house which was the first we had seen for the space of 31 days.

Our joy was inexpressible in breaking out of that dismal wilderness in which we had been so long buried, and once more beholding a country inhabited by human beings; it was like being brought from a dungeon to behold the clear light of the sun.

The French people received us with all the kindness we could wish, they treated our sick with much tenderness, and supplied us with every thing they could for our comfort. They seemed moved with pity for us and to greatly admire our patriotism and resolution, in encountering such hardships for the good of our country. . . .

The little army had finally made it through the Maine wilderness, and legends would arise in their wake. There is, for example, a most detailed and romantic story about Aaron Burr and his romance with the beautiful Indian princess of Swan Island, Jacataqua.

Aaron Burr, the son of the president of New Jersey College, was a youth of twenty at the time of the

Quebec expedition. He is mentioned only a few times in the journals of the march to Quebec. In a letter to General Montgomery of November 30, Arnold recommends Burr as "a young gentleman of much life and activity, [who] has acted with great spirit and resolution on our fatiguing march." Later, in Arnold's letter of December 31, written immediately after the battle of Quebec, "Captain Burr" is commended, along with others, for "[behaving] extremely well."

The story goes that Jacataqua heard about the arrival of Arnold's army in the lower Kennebec River and proceeded at once to Gardinerstown in her canoe. There she caught sight of the young, handsome Aaron Burr and promptly offered her canoe and her services as a guide, so as to be near him. At one of the first camping places the two, by that time lovers, went hunting, bringing back enough bear meat for the army. A large and elaborate banquet was prepared, with not only roast bear but pies and other foods freshly harvested from September gardens.

In addition to the bear hunt and great feast at Fort Western, Jacataqua is supposed to have accompanied the army all the way to Quebec, along with her pet dog and canoe, guiding the men through the wilderness, and enduring with them the hardships of the march. When the men were starving and resorted to killing their dogs for food, that of Jacataqua was also sacrificed, much to her sorrow. On their arrival in Quebec, the princess Jacataqua found lodgings and was left by Burr in the care and protection of a young

British officer, whom he had met somewhere on the march through the woods. Just how one of Arnold's soldiers could have become acquainted with an officer of the enemy army, in the wilds of Maine or Canada, has never been adequately explained! The story goes on with the young Indian woman going to New York, there to bear Burr's child, a little daughter.

The romantic story is fascinating and it is disappointing to find that it is almost certainly not true. The great feast supposed to have been given the army at Fort Western is not mentioned, even in Dr. Senter's detailed account. The journals of Arnold's men mention Burr very little and Jacataqua nowhere. They were good story tellers and it is doubtful that every one of them would ignore such a juicy bit of gossip.

Romance was not totally nonexistent on the march to Quebec, although it was provided in a surprising manner. Two married women chose to endure the hardships of one of the most grueling army marches in history rather than be separated from their husbands. Their presence is well authenticated, having been mentioned in several journals, including Arnold's.

The women were Jemima Warner and Mrs. Grier, the wife of Sergeant Grier, both attached to Hendricks' and Smith's companies of Pennsylvania riflemen. They were regarded with respect and admiration by the soldiers; however neither asked for or received special consideration because they were women. Their reasons for making the trip were simple: they wished to be with their husbands and share their dangers, and to help in case of necessity. Mrs. Warner did all these things, in experiencing the heartbreak of watching her husband die in the Dead River wilderness, remaining with him until the end, then picking up his musket and running to catch up with the army, which was by that time twenty miles ahead.

Jemima Warner must, I think, stand at the head of America's war heroines, with the wife of Sergeant Grier close behind. Some of the most eloquent entries in the Arnold expedition journals are about these two. We read in John Henry's journal for November 1st:

> This morning . . . breakfasting on our bleary, we took up the line of march through a flat and boggy ground. About ten o'clock a.m. we arrived by a narrow neck of land to a marsh which was appalling. It was three fourths of a mile over, and covered by a coat of ice half an inch thick. At this place Simpson concluded to halt a short time for the stragglers or maimed of Hendricks' and Smith's companies to come up. There were two women attached to those companies, who arrived before we commenced the march. One was the wife of Sergeant Grier, a large, virtuous and respectable woman. The other was the wife of a private of our company, a man who lagged on every occasion [as the following events show, he was nearly dead from exhaustion and hunger]. These women having arrived, it was presumed that all our party were up. We were on the point of entering the marsh, when some one cried out, "Warner is not here." Another said he had sat down, sick, under a tree, a few miles back. His wife begged us to wait a short time, and with tears of affection in her eyes, ran back to her husband. We tarried an hour. They came not.
>
> Entering the pond (Simpson foremost), and breaking the ice here and there with the butts of our guns and feet, as occasion required, we were soon waist deep in the mud and

water. As is generally the case with youths [Henry was barely 17], it came to my mind that a better path might be found than that of the more elderly guide. Attempting this, the water in a trice cooling my armpits, made me gladly return into the file.

Now Mrs. Grier had got before me. My mind was humbled, yet astonished, at the exertions of this good woman. Her clothes more than waist high, she waded before me to firm ground. No one, so long as she was known to us, dared to intimate a disrespectful idea of her. Her husband, an excellent soldier, was on duty in Hendricks' boat, that had proceeded to the outlet of the lake with Lieutenant McCleland.

Abner Stocking's journal for November 2 tells more about Mrs. Warner and her missing husband:

The circumstances of a young Dutchman, and his wife, who followed him through this fatiguing march, particularly excited my sensibility. They appeared to be much interested in each other's welfare and unwilling to be separated, but the husband, exhausted with fatigue and hunger, fell a victim to the king of terrors. His affectionate wife tarried by him until he died, while the rest of the company proceeded on their way. Having no implements with which she could bury him she covered him with leaves, and then took his gun and other implements and left him with a heavy heart.

And now from down the narrow rocky trail comes Jemima Warner, after twenty miles of walking and running to catch up, breathless, panting, torn and disheveled, her dead husband's cartridge belt her girdle, and his musket in her hand. Faithfully she had remained with him until the end, and had then looked to her own safety and with superhuman strength overtaken the regiment.

Of the two couples who started the march, three people arrived in Quebec, the two women and Sergeant Grier. Caleb Haskell's journal records the death of Jemima Warner:

Arnold's March to Quebec

> December 11th, Monday. We have kept the enemy busy playing upon us from one part of the city, whilst we have been fortifying in another part. We have got our works almost completed. . . . Today we had a man wounded, and a woman killed by a shot from the city.

Much later, in the springtime, it was again Haskell who recorded a link in the chain of events:

> April 18th, Thursday. Our company went to headquarters to get a pass to go home. . . . a woman belonging to the Pennsylvania troops was killed today by accident — a soldier carelessly snapping his musket which proved to be loaded.

This was Mrs. Grier. In the end, Sergeant Grier was the only one of the four to survive.

After the army had been warmly received by the French inhabitants of Canada, they were confronted by a group of Indians. Dr. Senter, in his journal entry of Saturday, November 4, 1775, at Sartigan, relates the circumstances:

> The five miles march last evening brought us to [Arnold's] quarters, and this morning the savages assembled in *statu quo*, and waited on the colonel to know our reasons for coming among them in a hostile manner, pretending they were unacquainted with our intentions, among which was the two [messengers] dispatched from Norridgewock with letters to Quebec. In the assembly the savages were prepared with an interpreter. They addressed the colonel in great pomp, and one of their chiefs delivered an oration with all the air and gesture of an accomplished orator. After this being explained or translated, the colonel returned the following answer.
>
> "Friends and brethren: I feel myself very happy in meeting with so many of my brethren from the different quarters of the great country, and more so as I find we meet as friends, and that we are equally concerned in this expedition. Brethren, we are the children of those people who have now taken up the hatchet against us. More than one hundred years ago, we were all as one family. We then differed in our

religion, and came over to this great country by consent of the king. Our fathers bought lands of the savages, and have grown a great people, even as the stars in the sky. We have planted the ground, and by our labor grown rich.

"Now a new king and his wicked great men want to take our lands and money without our consent. This we think unjust, and all our great men, from the river St. Lawrence to the Mississippi, met together at Philadelphia, where they all talked together, and sent a prayer to the king, that they would be brothers and fight for him, but would not give up their lands and money.

"The king would not hear our prayer, but sent a great army to Boston and endeavored to set our brethren against us in Canada. The king's army at Boston came out into the fields and houses, killed a great many women and children, while they were peaceably at work. The Bostonians sent to their brethren in the country, and they came in unto their relief, and in six days raised an army of fifty thousand men and drove the king's troops on board their ships, killed and wounded fifteen hundred of their men. Since that they durst not come out of Boston.

"Now we hear the French and Indians in Canada have sent to us, that the king's troops oppress them and make them pay a great price for their rum, etc.; press them to take up arms against the Bostonians, their brethren, who have done them no hurt. By the desire of the French and Indians, our brothers, we have come to their assistance, with an intent to drive out the king's soldiers; when drove off we will return to our own country, and leave this to the peaceable enjoyment of its proper inhabitants. Now if the Indians, our brethren, will join us, we will be very much obliged to them, and will give them one Portuguese per month [about $8.81], two dollars bounty, and find them their provisions, and the liberty to choose their own officers."

This oratory (or the promise of pieces of gold) had the desired effect, and about fifty Indians joined the army. The fifty included Natanis, whose cabin the army had passed at Flagstaff, and Sabatis of the south branch of Dead River. It is interesting to read Bene-

Benedict Arnold. This engraving is in the J. S. H. Fogg Auto-graph Collection of the Maine Historical Society, Portland, Maine. Photograph reproduced by permission of the Maine Historical Society.

372

dict Arnold's own account of the American Revolution, knowing that many years later his name would become synonymous with treason.

The army crossed the St. Lawrence River from Point Levis on the morning of November 14. They were not discovered until they were about to land, when a frigate's barge appeared and prevented them from surprising the town. Arnold at this time had about 500 men. They had heard nothing from General Montgomery, who was on the way to join them.

A very long letter by Arnold, dated November 27 at Point aux Trembles, summarized the entire trip through the wilderness. After giving an account of their adventures on the Kennebec and Dead rivers, he wrote:

> Thus in about eight weeks we completed a march of near six hundred miles, not to be paralleled in history; the men having with the greatest fortitude and perseverance hauled their bateaux up rapid streams, being obliged to wade almost the whole way, near 180 miles, carried them on their shoulders near forty miles, over hills, swamps and bogs almost impenetrable, and to their knees in mire; being often obliged to cross three or four times with their baggage. Short of provisions, part of the detachment disheartened and gone back; famine staring us in the face; an enemy's country and uncertainty ahead. Notwithstanding all these obstacles, the officers and men inspired and fired with the love of liberty and their country, pushed on with a fortitude superior to every obstacle, and most of them had not one day's provision for a week.

On the third of December General Montgomery joined Arnold and his men at Point aux Trembles, accompanied by 300 men and supplies. They planned to occupy the town and shortly bring Governor Carleton to terms.

On December 4 the two armies arrived before Quebec and made "all possible preparations to attack the city, which has a wretched, motley garrison of disaffected seamen, marines and inhabitants, the walls in a ruinous situation, and cannot hold out long," according to Arnold. Unfortunately he was underestimating the enemy.

December 31 arrived and the battle began, with catastrophe following catastrophe. The Americans attacked the city from two sides, one army commanded by Arnold, the other by General Montgomery. Arnold was shot through the leg early in the battle and had to be carried off the field and to the hospital. There he learned of the death of Montgomery and defeat of Montgomery's troops.

In a letter to General David Wooster in Montreal, written in the hospital while the battle was still going on, Arnold expressed his great anxiety about his own soldiers.

> After gaining the battery, my detachment pushed on to a second barrier, which they took possession of; at the same time the enemy sallied out from Palace-Gate and attacked them in the rear. A field-piece, which the roughness of the road would not permit our carrying on, fell into the enemy's hands, with a number of prisoners. The last accounts from my detachment, about ten minutes since, they were pushing for the lower town. Their communication with me was cut off. I am exceedingly apprehensive what the event will be; they will either carry the lower town, be made prisoners, or [be] cut to pieces.

The army was surrounded and taken prisoner. A number of Arnold's men had been killed, including Captain William Hendricks, Captain Jonas Hubbard, Lieutenant William Humphrey, and Lieutenant Samuel Cooper. About one hundred men were wounded, including Arnold himself, the Indian Natanis, Major Matthias Ogden, Captain John Lamb, and Lieutenant Richard Steele. More than three hundred were taken prisoner, including Lieutenant Colonel Christopher Greene, Major Timothy Bigelow, Major Return Meigs, Captain Daniel Morgan, Captain Henry Dearborn, Captain Oliver Hanchet, and Captain William Goodrich.

The battle of December 31, 1775 did not end the campaign against Quebec. The severely wounded Arnold ordered his gun brought to his bedside in case the British tried to storm the hospital. Fewer than 300 American soldiers remained who had not been wounded or captured, and Arnold ordered this small force to keep the city in a state of siege. The poorly clothed and housed Americans hung on like bulldogs through the cold dreary winter. In the spring it was all over. The campaign against Canada had failed, and many other battles lay ahead before the colonies could hope for independence.

The expedition made by Benedict Arnold and his valiant army through the wilderness of the Kennebec and Dead River valleys, encountering incredible hardships, remains one of the classic marches in military history. In spite of the fact that this was one of the first military maneuvers of importance in the War for Independence, it has never received the recognition it deserves; perhaps because few of the participants came back to tell the tale, and those who did went on to other battles, where more would perish. The newly emerging nation could not be expected to dwell with pride on its defeat by the British at Quebec. Of course much later, when Arnold turned against his country, there was another reason to hush up the whole tragic story, since a true account of events could not help but reflect great credit on Arnold's courage and ability to overcome severe hardships.

Kenneth Roberts, in his novels *Arundel* and *Rabble In Arms,* and his collection of source materials entitled *March to Quebec,* made a study of the leader of the expedition. He concluded that historians have treated Arnold very unfairly, basing judgments on his later desertion and not on his conduct at the time of the expedition. At that time, the evidence shows clearly, he was a patriot willing to die for his country. He risked his life again and again, and we must remember that if he had been killed at Quebec, rather than wounded, he would have died a hero.

During the siege of Quebec, a frail woman of seventy-nine spent her days at a window of the Ursuline convent with her sewing and her memories. Sixteen years before she had watched another battle rage around the streets of Quebec. During that battle she had walked to the hospital to spend long days and nights nursing the injured soldiers as they were brought on litters from the battlefield. Most of the other nuns had been sent to the country, but she had requested active nursing duty at the hospital. When young General Montcalm was killed on the Plains of

Abraham and brought to the city for burial, she was one of those following the coffin to the grave.

Now she was a spectator at another attempt to conquer Quebec. In one of those amazing coincidences that occasionally happen in times of war, the nun, formerly Mother Superior of the convent, looked out her window at her own countrymen, come as enemies to conquer her city.

Born Esther Wheelwright at York, Maine, she had been captured by a band of Norridgewock Indians seventy-two years before, rescued from the Indian village at Old Point by Father Bigot several years later, and taken to the Ursuline convent in Quebec, where she spent the remainder of her long life. Not only were these American soldiers her countrymen, but she had covered the same Indian trail up the Kennebec River that they had, on foot, in winter, a frightened child captive, dragged along by her captor, a chieftain of the Norridgewocks.

One wonders what her thoughts must have been as she looked out the window.

NEW ENGLAND

The most remarqueable parts thus named
by the high and mighty Prince CHARLES,
Prince of great Britaine

John Smith's map of 1614
shows some of the names Maine
towns might have today if King
Charles I of Great Britain had had
his way. Still a young prince, Charles
substituted English and Scottish names
for the "barbarous" Indian originals. In
his version, the Kennebec was called the
Forth River as in Scotland, with "Edin-
burgh" about where Gardiner is, and
"Leith" in place of Bath. Confusingly,
the English "Cambridge" is midway between
them, about at Bowdoinham. Some other names:
"The Base" = Freeport, "Sandwich" = Portland, "Dartmouth" = South Portland, "Ipswich" = Biddeford, and Boston is
curiously misplaced at Kittery. Farther up the coast, "St. John
Town" = Damariscotta? and "Norwich" = Thomaston? Needless
to say, none of these names stuck. Reprinted from Justin Winsor's Narrative and Critical History of America, Vol. III, 1884.

378

Place Names of
the Kennebec Valley

A priceless heritage of
colorful and descriptive names.

THE ABENAKI INDIANS of Maine gave our rivers, lakes, streams and mountains beautiful and expressive place names, many of which are still in use today. I have gathered the following list from many sources, the most important being Chief Joseph Laurent's book *Abenakis and English Dialogues* and Henry Lorne Masta's *Abenaki Indian Legends, Grammar and Place Names.* I also found very helpful Fannie Hardy Eckstorm's book *Indian Place-Names of the Penobscot Valley and the Maine Coast.* Mrs. Eckstorm made a careful study of the subject and is considered an authority. Another valuable source, particularly for the West Branch of the Penobscot River and the upper Kennebec valley, is Lucius L. Hubbard's marvelous map and book, *Woods and Lakes of Maine.* Other sources on which I relied were *Maine Place Names and the Peopling of Its Towns,* by Ava Harriet Chadbourne, and various town histories. Stephen Laurent, a scholar of his native Abenaki language who has translated Father Rasle's French-Abenaki dictionary into English, has agreed to edit my list of names. His kind support and advice is deeply appreciated.

Joseph Nicolar pointed out some of the problems in trying to pinpoint the correct spellings and meanings of Indian words. The first white men corrupted many of the words when they tried to repeat what was said by the Indians, who were accustomed to speak in such a low voice that the unfamiliar sounds were hard to catch; furthermore, they became bored when asked to repeat words and phrases. Many of the descriptive place names are very long words.

Even considering the difficulties, Indian place names are a fascinating study. Each name is an accurate description of the place, extending over only a small area that the Indians could see at a glance or cover in a day's journey in a canoe or on foot. That explains why the Kennebec River had four names when the first white explorers visited it.

Many Abenaki words and place names are delightful to roll over one's tongue. Some have the majesty of sound found in Latin, and others are as melodic as any Italian word. Don't be afraid to try to pronounce Indian words, even the longest ones. Lumbermen in the north woods toss them off easily. The secret? Just take one syllable at a time.

We will start at the north, in the Moosehead Lake region, and work our way down the river.

MOOSEHEAD LAKE: The Abenaki Indians called it

Sebamcook or *Sebaygook,* and the neighboring Penobscots knew it as *Kzebem* or *Xsebem.* All these names have the connotation of expansive waters with the additional meaning of "high bluff" in the Abenaki version. Chief Henry Red Eagle of Greenville told of his old grandmother's trips to the "Big Sebem," which she told him she could not see across. Another name found on an early map was *Cerbon,* "great waters," and later *Orignal* on Montresor's map of 1761. With this name the meaning changed to "moose," which is *orignal* in French. Montresor's Canadian Indian guides explained that early explorers and woodsmen had noticed that Mount Kineo resembles a moose stooping. Montresor, not being quite sure what to call the lake and mountain, gave two versions on his map. He labeled the lake "Moose-Deer Lac or Lake Orignal." He was not only puzzled about the names but also the word for "lake," as he precedes the French name with the English "Lake" and vice versa. Perhaps it was a scribe's error in copying the original sketch. Mount Kineo also has two names on this map: "Mount Orignal" and "A Rocky Mountain." Joseph Laurent wrote: "Moosehead Lake is called in Abenaki: *Mozo dupi nebes,* which is the literal meaning of the English name."

MOUNT KINEO: Kineo, a mountain composed of hornblende or flint rock, was supposedly named for a famous Indian warrior named "Kineho," whose story appeared in a legend written by Mrs. Frances Mace before the turn of the century. Another legend of authentic Indian origin is about the Abenaki demigod Glusgehbeh. At Moosehead Lake he killed a large moose that became Mount Kineo; then he chased the calf, and to gain more speed he threw down his kettle, which landed upside down to form *Kokadjo* — "Kettle Mountain" or Little Spencer Mountain. Next he left his pack, which is now *Sabotawan* or Big Spencer Mountain. We will leave Glusgehbeh dashing across the north Maine woods shedding pieces of moose and equipment to give colorful names to scenes along the way. From the southern side of Moosehead Lake, Mount Kineo does seem to resemble a huge moose stooping, lying with its head toward the west, its rump toward the east, and its nose pointing to the foot of the lake. The bays and coves represent palmated antlers and the lower lake fashions the two forefeet. Tahmunt, one of Thoreau's guides, told him that the first white man to arrive saw this resemblance and named the lake "Moosehead."

SEBOOMOOK LAKE: The name is derived from Abenaki and according to one author means "shaped like a moose's head." Another says that it means "a place where the waters collect," which seems to fit better. A second spelling is *Seboomic.*

SOCATEAN STREAM: This is probably a shortened version of *Mesak ketesa gewick* (from the second, third and fourth syllables of the three Indian words), meaning "half burned land and half standing timber separated by a stream." The last syllable, *wick,* means "place."

SQUAW MOUNTAIN: The name given in Hubbard's

Woods and Lakes of Maine is *Pahn moi wadjo.*
Broken down, the meaning is: *phainem,* "woman,
femme," and *wadjo,* "mountain." This Indian name
was translated from the English, and Hubbard said
he did not know the original Abenaki name for this
mountain. However, the Montresor map of 1761
gives the name *Onguickhonta.* Montresor's guides
were St. Francis Indians, and they gave him the
names of the places along their route in the Abenaki
language. Another story of the naming of Squaw
Mountain is given in Mrs. Mace's poem "Kineo," but
it is only a legend.

WILSON POND: The ancient Indian name of this
pond near the southeast corner of Moosehead Lake is
Etas iiti, "where they had a great fight" or "destruction ground." A story tells of a great fight there long
ago during which an Abenaki village was completely
destroyed by their arch-enemies the Iroquois.

LILY BAY: *Poto bek* is probably nothing more than
the Abenaki name for "bay." *Poto* means "bulging,"
nebpe, "water," and *k* is locative: "where the water
bulges."

ROACH RIVER and ROACH POND: These were
named for an early settler who had a cabin on First
Roach Pond. Around 1917 Mrs. Irving Hamilton
petitioned the Maine Legislature to change the
names to the Indian one of *Kokadjo.* Mr. and Mrs.
Hamilton ran a well-known hotel at the First Pond
named the "Kokadjo House" and were of the opinion
that the Indian names of the area were worth saving
as a fitting memorial to the very first inhabitants of

the Moosehead region. The petition was granted and the names changed to Kokadjo.

KOKADJO: Once a bustling community with a hotel and lumber headquarters, it is now a ghost town with only a small general store catering to fishermen and tourists on their way to Ripogenus Dam and Millinocket. The full Indian name is *Kok adjeweemgwa sebem,* so you can see why Mrs. Hamilton's petition shortened it to Kokadjo, even though that is properly the name of a mountain. The full name breaks down in this manner: *Kok,* meaning "kettle," *Wadjo,* "mountain," and *pegwasebem,* "lake," hence "Kettle Mountain Lake." The shortened version, also the Indian name of the more westerly of the Spencer Mountains, is: *kok,* "kettle," and *wadjo,* "mountain," or "Kettle Mountain."

MOOSE RIVER, SAHK HA BEHA TUCK: "More water flowing from it than from any other stream that empties into the lake." The above name was taken from Hubbard's map of 1883, but in his list of place names he gives another Indian name for Moose River, probably applied to the upper river from Wood Pond to its source. Upper Moose River was *Kweueuktonoonk hégan,* "snow-shoe river," so called from that part above Attean Pond where it bends like the frame of a snowshoe. This is the part of the river on which the "Bow" canoe trip is located, including the beautiful Holeb Falls.

BRASSUA LAKE: This name is said to be a corruption of the French name "François," which was often pronounced "Franc-way" by the north woods loggers. Montresor's map of 1761 gives the name of this lake as "Yengiuarouta or the Wooden Shoe."

MI SEREE: A pond and stream that empty into Brassua Lake, often spelled Misery.

ATTEAN POND: The name of a famous Abenaki chieftain.

HOLEB POND: On the upper Moose River. *Pas conga moc,* "branch lake."

DEAD RIVER and MOUNT BIGELOW, TIAOUIADICHT: The Indian names of Dead River and Mount Bigelow are found on Lt. Montresor's map, and I have not been able to learn their meanings. Bigelow Mountain was named for Timothy Bigelow, one of Arnold's officers on the march to Quebec. He was the one sent to explore the mountain and in particular to see whether he could sight Quebec from the summit. He could not, of course.

CHAIN OF PONDS, early name "Lakes of the Height of Land" (1761): This beautiful chain of five ponds, the source of Dead River, did not have an Indian name given on any of my old maps. These ponds are on the old waterway trail to Quebec, and the northernmost pond is only a few miles from the Canadian border at Coburn Gore. I grew up hearing these ponds called "Chaney Ponds," which I supposed to be the correct name until I started reading maps. My father and his friends all called them that, and we visited them often. The fishing and blueberrying were absolutely great at Chaney Ponds!

The five ponds are (starting on the north end):

ROUND POND.

NATANIS POND: This is an Abenaki Indian name of a young woman trapper who lived on the pond. Her cabin was at the narrows and it is at that spot that her grave can be found now. She was found one spring when the ice melted, after being missing all winter. The mystery of what happened to Natanis has never been solved, although foul play was suspected.

LONG POND: This pond is connected to the next pond by a short thoroughfare or connecting stream.

BAG POND: Connected with Long Pond by a short thoroughfare. This little body of water was supposedly called Bag Pond because the lower end is almost closed together.

LOWER POND: This is the last in the chain, and its outlet is the beginning of Dead River. Whoever named these pretty ponds didn't use much imagination. The only Indian name is Natanis Pond and that was because of the interesting story connected with it.

The next group of names, although not in the Kennebec watershed, were places of great concern to some of the travelers along the Kennebec.

CANADA, KANATA (Iroquois): A collection of tents or huts.

QUEBEC, N'KEBAK or KEBHEK: The Indians called this city *N'Kebac* because a certain portion of the lower part was often flooded and remained under water for some time. They also said that the French found the word hard to pronounce so it was changed to the simpler form "Quebec." Joseph Laurent gives *Kebhek* or *Kebek* (old Abenaki), which means "obstructed current, where it is narrow or shut."

Place Names of the Kennebec Valley

THE ST. FRANCIS RIVER, ALSIGONTEGW: The Abenaki name was given to this river by the Indians who
live there. Its meaning is: "River abounding in
shells." Many migrated from Indian villages on the
Kennebec River when they were driven out during
the Indian wars. The Indians of St. Francis (now
Odanak) are called *Alsigontegwiak*. A portage on the
St. Francis River a little above the village is *Makua-
pasik,* meaning "at the red rock." Many Maine captives may have been carried over this portage during
the Indian wars.

CHAUDIERE RIVER, KOKWI SIBO: "Whirlpool
river." *Kokw* is the Abenaki word for "kettle" or
"boiler," so the French gave it the name "Chaudiere," meaning "hot" in French. The word
obviously derives from the fact that it is a rough and
rapid river with lots of boiling and turbulent water.
This river is an important tributary of the St. Lawrence and formed part of the ancient Indian trail
connecting Maine, particularly the Kennebec valley,
with Quebec. It was the route taken by the Jesuit
priests and early explorers. Arnold's ill-fated expedition also used it.

FAMINE RIVER, MANOSA'I SIBO: This is the area
where Indians were starving, hence the name "Famine." Some authors have thought that it received the
name because of the starving condition of Arnold's
army when they passed, but it seems certain that it
had that name long before 1775. Henry Lorne Masta
told about a Jesuit priest (Druillettes) and guides
who lost their way on the Famine and almost died of

387

hunger. Since the last Jesuit priest on the Kennebec River was Father Rasle, who died in 1724, it must have been before that that the river was named.

RIVIERE DU LOUP, O'BAMAS (Abenaki): *O'Bamas* is the term by which the Abenaki Indians designated this river, a tributary of the Chaudiere, which was an alternate route on the old Indian trail, leading to the West Branch of the Penobscot River and Moosehead Lake. Montresor used this route on his way to the Kennebec River in 1761. The name was given because of the great winding and twisting which begins below Hunterstown Mills. The Indian name translates to mean "opposite course or winding," and especially applies to the upper reaches of the river.

RIVER OF SNOW STORMS, TOULIDESIHONTES, modern name NEBNELLIS: I found this fascinating river name on Montresor's map of 1761, and since he traveled with Indian guides from Canada, I believe his place names are authentic. It is a tributary of the Chaudiere River and lies south of the Riviere du Loup, with headwaters near the Maine border not far from Boundary Bald Mountain (Montresor's *Onegnla*).

LAKE MEGANTIC, NAMOKOTTIK or NAMOGWOTTIK (old Abenaki): The Indian name means "lake trout place." Lake Megantic is fed by the Arnold River, called "Seven Mile Stream" by Benedict Arnold in his journal. Arnold almost lost a section of his army in the swamps at the foot of the lake, because Montresor had omitted to enter those and Spider Lake on his map which Arnold was using.

Place Names of the Kennebec Valley

To return to the Kennebec River valley:

THE KENNEBEC RIVER: This river name has been spelled in a great many ways. Some examples are: Kinibecki (1609); Cinebaque (1610); Kinibequi (1611); Quinebequy (1613); Kenebecka (1614); Kenebeke (1616); Kenebeck (1626). The word is quite simple and means "long quiet water," referring to the long stretch without rapids below Augusta. The Abenaki forms for the word "long" are *kine, kini* and *quine. Bague* is the root for quiet or still water, not dead water with no current but level water with no rapids or falls. Mrs. Eckstorm gives this etymology in her *Indian Place-Names* and remarks that early writers made a sorry mess of the word. One went to the Delawares in Missouri for his meaning, "They who thanked." This must be discarded, as most scholars agree that all Indian place names were descriptive of the place. Others have said that it was named for the Abenaki Bashaba Kenebis who lived on Swan Island, but he was alive and selling pieces of Swan Island to the settlers in 1653, fifty years after Lescarbot's map was drawn. It is more likely that the chieftain was named for the river. Indian writers didn't do much better. Nicolar said the word meant "Long Blade." Masta gives "River full or nearly full up to its banks." Joseph Laurent came very close with the acceptable "large lake or deep river." An old Indian friend of Mrs. Eckstorm wrapped the whole thing up when he told her with a straight face: "Kennebec named for people — all dead now."

Kennebec was only one of the river's names. We

have explained that the Indians gave names to small areas that they could easily visualize. The lower part of the river below Merrymeeting Bay was called:

THE SAGADAHOC: The meaning is clear, being the word for "mouth of a river." The root found in the word "rain," *Soglan,* means "that which pours down." Captain John Gyles, official interpreter, gave this meaning in a statement made in 1753. He said that the word *Sagadarock* in Abenaki and the English form *Sagadahock* meant "the mouth or entrance into a river."

The upper Kennebec was called *Arransoak* when Montresor traveled through in 1761, and the middle river from above the falls in Madison to a spot below Skowhegan Falls was named *Nanrantsouak* after the Abenaki village one mile below the falls at Old Point. These two are the original Indian forms of our present English name Norridgewock.

NORRIDGEWOCK: Comes from the Abenaki *Moloujoak* with the connotation of "river flowing deeply." The adverb prefix *Mol ou* means "deeply" and the verb suffix *joak* means "flowing." Many linguists translate this word as "Calm waters between falls." The description is apt as there are falls eight miles up the river and also several miles downriver at Skowhegan. Mrs. Eckstorm suggested "At the rapids," which also fits, with Bombazine Rips close by.

INDIAN POND, SEBA'TICOOK: Indian Pond is on the upper Kennebec River and is where the waters of the East and West Outlets meet to form the larger East

*The Forks of the Kennebec and Dead rivers, seen from the air.
The confluence of the two rivers, known as the Point, is just
below the villages of The Forks and West Forks, where there is a
bridge on Route 201 (out of sight in this view). Photograph by
the author.*

Branch of the river. Officially it is the Kennebec River from the East Outlet at Moosehead to the sea.

The Abenaki name *Seba'ticook* means "logon or sluggish stream" ("logon" is defined as a short body of water with little or no current). Indian Pond suits that description, as in the log drives it was necessary to tow the rafts of logs across the pond by boat. Montresor called it the Lakes of Aronsoak because at that time there were two ponds with a high waterfall between them. The waterfall and short thoroughfare were flowed out when the first dam was built in the early 1800s.

MOXIE (MAXIE?): This is the name of a pond, its outlet stream and the ninety-six foot waterfall on the stream. It enters the Kennebec about four miles upriver from the Forks, and below Kennebec Gorge. I have not learned whether the name is Abenaki, or its etymology. However, residents of the area say the meaning of the word is "Dark Water." Who knows?

THE FORKS, NICKETWO: "Forks of a river." Its name was of course chosen because the village is situated at the forks of the Kennebec River. The confluence of the Kennebec and Dead rivers is just south of the village. When Montresor passed through on his trip to Fort Halifax, he called it "La Fourche," the French translation of the name. Perhaps he had a French guide on that trip?

CARATUNK: All I have regarding the name of this small village in the upper Kennebec valley is a little verse which has come down to us with only the date and initials to identify it.

Rough and broken is the country,
And that gives the town its name
For the Indian name it's called by
And rough and broken mean the same.
The Red man named Caratunk long ago
As up and down they came —
Named all this northern country
For many miles the same.

I.C.M. 1916

MOSCOW: The first name chosen for this town was Bakerstown because several early settlers were Bakers. Joseph Baker from Readfield was the first to arrive, followed by Reuben and Abner Baker, who were twins. These three families provided a sizeable increase in the town's population. The Joseph Bakers had eight children, and the twins had twelve and ten respectively.

This very suitable name, however, was denied because there was already a Bakerstown in Androscoggin County (now Poland). The second choice was Moscow and the incorporation petition was passed with that name.

BINGHAM: An early name of Bingham was Caratunk, named for the falls in Solon; in fact all the territory north of Solon to the Forks was called by that name. In 1812 when the town was incorporated it was named Bingham for William Bingham, who had purchased one million acres of land on the upper Kennebec River in 1786.

SOLON: The first petition for incorporation carried the name of Sumner. However, as there was already a town by that name, the petition was denied. Some time later the name Solon was selected and the incorporation went through in 1809.

As Solon's main scenic attraction and economic asset was the waterfall named by the Indians *Caratunk,* it is surprising that that name was not selected for the town. However, the neighboring township to the north did use it. *Carratoank* or "Devil's Falls" also has the meaning of "something very rough or broken."

CONCORD: This was named for historic Concord, Massachusetts. No Indian name found. It was incorporated as a town in 1821 but was disorganized in 1939. Concord is now an unorganized township.

PLEASANT RIDGE (ROWE POND): This is a plantation on the west shore of Wyman Lake in which the west end of Wyman Dam is situated. Rowe Pond is in Pleasant Ridge. I could not find any information on how it got its name or any Indian connections. The only clue I have is that it is certainly a pleasant ridge and has a beautiful shoreline on Wyman Lake and lovely views out over it. Rowe Pond has a long history as a good fishing spot.

EMBDEN (early Indian name CARRIOTONKA): This township, just north of North Anson on the west bank of the Kennebec River, has had several names since its beginning just after the Revolutionary War. They were, first, *Carriotonka* or *Carratunk,* then Queenstown, Windsor, Emden and Embden. Some of these names show that there was still loyalty for England even after the war of the rebellion. George III and his queen Sophia were on the throne at the time the name was being chosen. The incorporation petition went to Boston with the name "Windsor," the palace where the royal family resided, written in the space provided for the name of the new town. Someone in Boston ran his pen through the name "Windsor" three times, as can be seen on the original document in the state archives, probably muttering "Tories" while doing it. The incorporation papers came back with "Emden" in place of the hated British name.

Carriotonka was the Abenaki name applied to the northern part of Embden near the waterfall. The Norridgewock Indians visited the falls and rough and broken land around them often, especially for the good salmon fishing.

NORTH ANSON (early name SEVEN MILE BROOK): Situated near the mouth of the Carrabassett River, which enters the Kennebec in North Anson after passing through the village. We find the town called "Seven Mile Brook" in early records, because the mouth of the Carrabassett is seven miles north of Old Point. The Indian word *Carrabassett* was the name of a famous Norridgewock chieftain, who was shot down during the massacre at Old Point in 1724 along with Father Rasle, Chief Bomazeen, and others. He has been immortalized in the stirring narrative poem "Carabasset" by Deering.

ANSON: I was unable to find an Indian name for

Anson. It was named Anson after Lord George Anson of a distinguished English family. Before the town fathers settled on its final name it had had several others: Brookfield, Seven Mile Brook Plantation, and Titcomb Town. The last was in honor of the man who surveyed the area and owned large tracts of land there.

STARKS: Was incorporated in 1795, being the one hundredth town in Maine to achieve this status. Its first name was Lower Sandy River Plantation.

When James Waugh, the first settler, arrived in 1772, he found he could not cross the Sandy River, so he turned and went along the south bank. He chose the second lot from the mouth of the river. This was a remarkable piece of land on an intervale of the Sandy containing about one hundred acres of rich soil. The land is just opposite the site of the Norridgewock village at Old Point and the Indians had tilled the land for countless years. Mr. Waugh found the land entirely cleared and filled with the ancient corn hills of the Indians. An interesting note is that descendants of Mr. Waugh still own the original, which has supported several generations of the Waugh family handsomely.

Even with the Indian background of the area, Lower Sandy River Plantation was given an English name on its incorporation in 1795. It was named "Starks" in honor of the hero of Bennington and Bunker Hill for his outstanding service to the country. General John Starks richly deserved the honor.

SANDY RIVER: A tributary of the Kennebec, which

enters the parent river just opposite Old Point in Madison. The Indian name is *Penobsquis umquise-bou* meaning "rocky and sandy river."

MADISON, site of NANRANTSOUAK or Norridgewock Falls, and the Norridgewock Indian village: The early French explorers and Jesuits called the Indian village at Old Point *Nurantsuak,* derived from the Abenaki word *Mol ou joak,* meaning "river flowing deeply." They gave the same name to the waterfalls one mile above the village. When the English arrived on the scene the name was anglicized to Norridgewock. Benedict Arnold's army took one week to carry themselves, their bateaux, and their provisions around the lower and upper falls.

Mr. Masta, in *Abenaki Indian Legends, Grammar and Place Names,* gives the present-day town of Norridgewock as the site of the Abenaki village and falls. He is not the only author, unfamiliar with the area, to have jumped to this conclusion, which is completely incorrect. As Lina Moore McKenney stated in a letter to *Sprague's Journal of Maine History* in 1919:

"There is one point which has always been misunderstood. Old Point is not and never has been in the town of Norridgewock. It is in Madison. Originally the site of the village was on the, so called, one and half mile strip left over when the first surveys were made."

This was a strip of land, one and a half miles in width, lying between the north line of Norridgewock and the south line of Madison, the north line of

Norridgewock being the north line of the Kennebec Patent. Old Point, the site of the Indian village, was on this strip left over when the towns were surveyed. There was a settlement made upon this strip of land in 1773 when Sylvanus Sawyer and Morris Fling, the first settlers of Madison, built cabins there, on the site of the old Indian village.

The falls, of course, were and are in Madison, the upper falls being under the present Madison-Anson Bridge. The lower falls are at the former Hollingsworth & Whitney mills, now owned by Scott Paper Company.

The name of the town was first Norridgewock Falls, with mail being addressed as follows: Madison Bridge, Norridgewock Falls, Maine. Later, before it became a town, the plantation name was Barnardtown for an early landowner. At its incorporation in 1804, the town was given the name "Madison" in honor of the president of the United States.

EAST MADISON: This small village is on the eastern shore of Wesserunsett Lake in the town of Madison. It is located at the outlet on Wesserunsett Stream.

WESSERUNSETT LAKE: Also in Madison, it is best known as the home of the Lakewood Theatre and summer resort. Its original name was Hayden Pond. Lakewood is situated on what was Jedediah Hayden's cow pasture back in 1799. It was also called Madison Pond. The small settlement on the western shore of the pond, which even had a general store in the late 1800s, was called Madison Center. We have in our family an account book that belonged to my grandfather, John Renier, who was postmaster and storekeeper there in the 1880s. The heading reads: Madison Center, Maine.

The name Wesserunsett derives from the word *Wassoulanset* meaning "spearing." In the early days this was a good fishing lake, and that is no doubt why the Wesserunsett Indians camped there. Wesserunsett Stream is a tributary of the Kennebec, entering the river just below Skowhegan near the bend. One of its branches forms the outlet stream of Wesserunsett Lake. The meaning is the same for both lake and stream.

I found a charming poem in the Madison town history which mentions the names of lake and hamlet, but unfortunately it is not dated. It was written by Helen Hilton and dedicated to Mrs. William D. Hayden of Madison Center, Hayden Lake. A short excerpt follows:

Hayden Lake
While standing on yon Solon Heights,
'tis pleasing to the eye,
To look below into the vale where Hayden waters lie.
How placidly and still they lie, embowered among the trees;
But they can dance the minuet to music of the breeze.

How clear and blue the waters are, they photograph the sky
And sun and moon and twinkling stars that habitate on high;
And when the stilly evening comes and nature sinks to rest,
We trace the constellations there, reflected on its breast.

BOMBAZEEN or ABOMAZEEN RIPS: This stretch of white water near the site of the Indian village at Old Point was named for the famous warrior and orator

The Kennebec at Old Point, Madison, Maine, site of the Norridgewock Indian village that was destroyed in 1724. Photograph by the author.

of the Norridgewock tribe. He was killed during the massacre of the Norridgewocks in 1724. When the dam was built at the falls in Madison, the rapids were flowed out so they are no longer as rough as they were before.

NORRIDGEWOCK, NAURANTSOUAK, NORRIDGEWOG: The village of Norridgewock is situated on both sides of the Kennebec River eight miles below Madison. It was settled in 1773 and incorporated in 1788. The town was named for the Norridgewock Indian tribe whose village at Old Point was about eight miles up river. The meaning of the name is: "Little falls with smooth water above and below."

You will note that the explanation of the word does not describe the town of Norridgewock, which has no waterfalls. However, that is explained when we realize that it was not named by the Indians but by the English settlers.

OOSOOLA: J. W. Hanson, in his *History of the Old Towns*, written in 1849, describes this village on the south bank of the Kennebec. At that time there were twin towns with Norridgewock on the north bank and Oosoola on the south side, with houses on both sides of the hill leading east to Fairfield Center. Tradition says that the same name had been applied to Mill Stream by the Indians. Mr. Hanson gives the meaning as "the place where it is very yellow." He thought it referred to the yellow flowers that grew in abundance along the banks of the stream. I believe marsh marigolds did grow there on the marshy banks.

Place Names of the Kennebec Valley

SKOWHEGAN: Skowhegan, formerly Canaan, Bloomfield, and Milburn, took the Indian name always given the falls for their town name in 1836. The Indian spelling as given by Maurault is *Sk ou aigen.* The meaning is "It is pointed." Joseph Laurent agrees with this but gives a slight variation in the spelling — *Skuchigan* or *Skawahigen.* The description is good since the river makes a sharp 90 degree bend about one half mile below the falls, forming a sharp point. Some authors have said the word means "waiting and watching place," and as this was a favorite salmon fishing spot for the Indians it is a possibility. However, I have not seen a breakdown of the Abenaki word *Ka ksk awi higen,* and so must lean toward the one with the most proof.

The story I heard as a girl in the area was surely only an example of folklore. It went like this: When the squaw of the chief of the village was swept over the turbulent falls in her canoe and was lost, the chief and the villagers wailed loudly, "Squaw he gone — Squaw he gone."

FAIRFIELD: This is the southernmost town in Somerset County and lies on the west bank of the Kennebec a few miles north of Waterville. It was incorporated in 1788 and took the name it had had as a plantation. I have been unable to find any particulars about the naming of Fairfield. A very early name was Kendall's Mills, for General William Kendall, a prominent citizen of the town. After 1772 it was known as Fairfield. Other villages in the township were and still are:

SHAWMUT: An Indian name of obscure meaning. This small village three miles upriver from the village of Fairfield was formerly Somerset Mills.

HINCKLEY: This village is eight miles upriver from Fairfield and was the site of a ferry across the Kennebec. The Hinckley Bridge replaced the Pishon Ferry and leads to Canaan and Dexter via Route 23. Pishon is shown on the east bank of the Kennebec on some modern maps.

WATERVILLE: When the first settlers came to the area around Teconnet Falls, they settled on the east side of the river to be under the protection of Fort Halifax, built in 1754. The settlements afterward spread to both sides of the river but were all in the same town, first called Kingfield and then Winslow. By 1800 it was evident that the town should be divided, so Waterville was incorporated on the west bank in 1802 and soon outgrew neighboring Winslow on the east bank.

An important event in Waterville's history was the foundation of a seat of learning. In 1788 Colby College was only an idea in the mind of Dr. Obadiah Williams, who suggested it to Dr. N. Whittaker of Canaan. The first paragraph of Dr. Whittaker's reply follows:

"Sir: Your favor of the 30th of April came to hand last Friday. I have weighed the contents. Am agreeably affected by the noble and important design of erecting a Seminary of learning in these parts, where little skill is required to discern a too hasty return to a state of barbarism."

Place Names of the Kennebec Valley

Dr. Williams' dream became a reality when a charter was granted to the Maine Literary and Theological Institution on February 27, 1813. $3,000 was raised by the town of Waterville in 1816 for the benefit of the college if located there, and the first president, Jeremiah Chaplin, arrived in 1818. The name of the college was changed to Waterville College some time later, and then to Colby College in 1867, in grateful appreciation of the gift of $50,000 presented by Mr. Gardner Colby of Boston.

SEBASTICOOK or SEBESTEGUK RIVER: A tributary of the Kennebec River entering at Winslow, it was one section of a very important travel route used by the Indians and early explorers. Called "the Ah Wangan trail," it was the shortest route from the Penobscot River to Quebec. Though not a literal translation, the best English equivalent is "the short route," according to Mrs. Eckstorm. One theory given by the Indians is that Sebasticook means "Sebattis Stream," *Sebat* or *Sebattis* being an Indian who lived on the river. Another meaning is derived from the very old word *Tchibatigosak* which means "across."

The Sebasticook River fans out over its widespreading valley. The longer branch, which rises in Sangerville and Dover near Moosehead Lake, was known as the main stream. The shorter but more important branch, with its source in Newport, was called the East Branch. Originally only the main river and its East Branch were called the Sebesteguk, "the almost through river," because it was the "river that runs into another," shortest and easiest route to

Penobscot waters.

SEBASTICOOK LAKE, formerly Newport Pond and, still earlier, Great East Pond: Two Indian names are found on old maps: *Nala bongan* and *Sagon-dagon*. *Nalabongan* is an Abenaki name and means "the lake above" or "above the lake," and *Sagon dagon* can be interpreted the same way.

NECADORAM: The word given by Chadwick on his "large crown map" for the main stream of the Sebasticook. This name is used, as far as is known, only on this map. Mrs. Eckstorm points out that since Chadwick could and did spell words in his own way, his place names must be used with caution. She guessed that it could mean "a fork" from *nik* (Rasle gives "forked" from *nikadeoua* or "the better of the two" from *nek* with a long *e*). *Nec-adorum* could be a form of *Neek-awangan*, meaning "the better route." Chadwick and others did call the Penobscot to Kennebec route via the Sebasticook "The Awangan Trail."

WINSLOW, TECONNET, sometimes TICONIC: The earliest name of both Waterville and Winslow was Teconnet, named for the waterfall at this point. Hanson gives the meaning of Teconnet as "a place to cross," although I am not sure where the river could be forded near the falls (where there is now a dam). Another former name for Winslow was Kingsfield. This settlement on the eastern bank of the Kennebec was one of the earliest towns on the river. Fort Halifax was built in 1754 and it has never been without inhabitants since that time. At the incorporation in 1771 the town was given the name Winslow in honor of General John Winslow who had charge of the building of Fort Halifax.

TACONIC FALLS: Another variation of the name of the falls between Winslow and Waterville. The name Taconic was found as far back as 1699 on the map of Guillaume de Rozier.

VASSALBOROUGH: This town on the east bank of the Kennebec River is widely known as the home of Oak Grove Seminary, a school founded by the Society of Friends in 1853. Settlement began shortly after 1754 when Fort Halifax was built a few miles upriver in Winslow, and at that time Sidney, on the west bank of the river, was a part of the town. Many settlers came from Dresden a few miles down river, which was becoming too crowded for some of the more independent-minded pioneers. As more and more people arrived, proceedings were started for the incorporation of the town. The Plymouth Colony procured from the General Court in Boston the passage of four bills of incorporation on the 26th of April 1771. Vassalborough was one of the four, the others being Hallowell, Winslow and Winthrop.

The town was named in honor of Florentius Vassall, a Plymouth Company proprietor, and a landowner in the area. There seems to be no Indian name for Vassalborough but it has a very interesting Indian history. Artifacts indicate that there were Indian villages within the town in Riverside, at Webber Pond, and at the outlet of China Lake. There is a marker on the grounds of Oak Grove Seminary in memory of the Abenaki Indian Sebatis, who joined Arnold's march to Quebec and had a summer camp at Flagstaff. The name of Natanis, said to be his brother, was perpetuated as the name of a golf club.

The first reports we have of Kennebec Indians come from this locality. Raleigh Gilbert spent the night in either Sidney or Vassalborough when he made a trip up the river in 1607, and visited a large Indian village there.

SIDNEY: The year 1792 marked the division of Vassalborough into two towns, Vassalborough on the east side of the river and Sidney on the west. Sidney was named for the English poet, statesman and soldier, Sir Philip Sidney.

NEGWAMKEAG in Vassalborough: This was a spot between two islands, where treacherous currents caused by sunken rocks or a sandbar caused the water to boil and churn. Whether it is an Abenaki word is uncertain; however, Mrs. Eckstorm gives the meaning of the ending *amkeag* as being a Maliseet word for "sandbar."

AUGUSTA, CUSHNOC: This was the head of the tide, which was here stopped by the falls. Colonel Lithgow noted in 1767, "On the eastern side of the Kennebec is a point of land called Cusinock by the native Indians, who said they gave it that name because the tide runs no further up the river. There is no current above." There are at least three variations in spelling of the Indian name, all meaning the same thing: *Koussinok, Cusinok,* and the shorter version *Cushnoc,* shortened and simplified by the early settlers so they could pronounce and spell it more easily.

They all mean the head of tide.

Cushnoc was incorporated as a part of Hallowell in 1771, then set off and incorporated under the name of Harrington in 1797. Harrington was the name of a British nobleman and it was decided to change the name to Augusta later the same year.

The present name of Maine's capital was chosen to honor Pamela Augusta Dearborn, the daughter of General Henry Dearborn, the Revolutionary War officer who began his brilliant career as one of Benedict Arnold's captains on the march to Quebec. After leaving the army he settled in Maine and served two terms in Congress, two terms as state marshal and eight years as Secretary of War under Thomas Jefferson.

GARDINER, COBBOSSEECONTEE: Dr. Sylvester Gardiner, one of the Kennebec Proprietors, was so successful in sending new settlers to this spot on the Kennebec River that he was given a large tract of land comprising what is now the business section of Gardiner. In addition the new town was given the name Gardinerstown in his honor. Later at the time of incorporation in 1778 the name was changed to Gardiner in honor of Robert Hallowell Gardiner.

General Henry Dearborn, for whose daughter the city of Augusta was named, was delighted with the area around present-day Gardiner when he marched with Arnold's army as a twenty-four year old captain in 1775. He returned after the war and bought land on which he lived until he became Secretary of War in 1801. He established a ferry in 1786 and bought the first wagon in town. General Dearborn was without doubt one of Gardiner's most distinguished citizens. A small town on Great Pond across from Rome, incorporated in 1812, was named Dearborn in his honor. It is too bad that this community did not survive, but over the years portions of it were given to the surrounding towns until today the name "Dearborn" has disappeared from the Kennebec County map.

Cobbosseecontee is now the name of a stream and lake near Gardiner, but originally applied only to the mouth of the stream. This was the spot where the Indians fished for sturgeon; they lured the fish with torches and then speared them. *Kabasseh* means "sturgeon," or more exactly the habit of a sturgeon leaping out of the water. *Kantti* denotes something occurring in abundance, so the complete meaning is "a place where many sturgeon are to be found."

HALLOWELL, ancient name MEDUMCOOK or KEE-DUM-COOK: This city was named for one of the Kennebec Proprietors, Mr. Benjamin Hallowell, a wealthy merchant of Boston. It was called "the Hook" when first settled, with the other village in the town being called "the Fort" (Fort Western in present-day Augusta). The name "Hook" was said to be a short form of *Bombahook*. Emma Huntington Nason in *Old Hallowell on the Kennebec* gives the origin of the name. She wrote: "The banks of Bombahook were once a favorite camping ground of the Abenaki Indians; the picturesque plateau at the southern end of the Plains was the place of many lodges; and on the eastern shore of the river, in the northern portion of the territory originally included in the town of Hallowell, there was a large and permanent Abenaki village and if we would understand the history of Hallowell, we must go back to the days when the men of Plymouth dwelt here side by side with the Indians of Koussinok."

The ancient Indian name of Hallowell, perhaps antedating Bombahook, was, according to Col. William Lithgow, *Kee-dum-cook*. When the Indians were asked to explain the name they answered that it was because the river was very shallow there, and gravel and sand appeared across the river at times of low water.

PITTSTON, MEHUMKEAG or NAHUMKEAG: This town was named for one of two men and authorities disagree which one deserves the honor. The bill for incorporation, with Randolph as the name, was passed and delivered to John Pitt, a distinguished Bostonian who was a representative to the legislature. When it was delivered to the town officials, Pittston had been inserted in place of Randolph. However, some think the name was in honor of James Pitts.

The Indian name of Pittston was *Nehumkeag* or *Nahumkeag*. Mrs. Eckstorm gives preference to the second spelling, as the word comes from the Abenaki *nahurmo* meaning "eel." The locative ending *eag* is interpreted as *eak* (Micmac and Maliseet) for "runs out," or "there was eel fishing at the mouth of the stream."

DRESDEN: The township bordering Pittston on the south is Dresden, incorporated in 1794. Its name was said to be the choice of an early settler from Germany, a Hessian doctor named Ernst Frederick Theobald. Another foreigner, from Alsace, vied for the opportunity to choose. He was Dresden's first town clerk and first lighthouse keeper at Seguin and wanted to give the town the name "Fayette." Since Dresden was a part of the original Pownalborough it is surprising that name was not retained. Pownalborough, named for Thomas Pownal, was the shire town of Lincoln County, incorporated on February 13, 1760. John Adams wrote a letter many years later giving his feelings on the matter. "I am sorry that the name of Pownalborough has been changed to Dresden; that of a virtuous and sensible man to that of a scene of frivolity. Pownal was a Whig, a friend of liberty, a lover of his country, and he considered North America part of his country as much as England, Scotland and Ireland."

Pownal's name is retained, however, by the handsome and historic Pownalborough Court House, built by Gershom Flagg of Boston on the bank of the Kennebec River. It served as post office, tavern, meeting place and home of the tavern keeper. Pownalborough was eventually divided into four towns: Wiscasset, Perkins or Swan Island, Alna and Dresden.

WOOLWICH, JEREMYSQUAM: *Jeremysquam* is a part of the present town of Woolwich and comprises the peninsula between Montsweag Bay and Nequasset

Pownalborough Court House in Dresden, Maine, built in 1761.
Photograph by the author.

Stream. It is a difficult name to translate as Indian words do not usually begin with the letter *j*. One form found in a deed of 1734 gives the spelling as "Cheremessequame Neck." This helps slightly as *misquam* means "great neck" in some Indian dialects.

NASKET POINT in Woolwich: This is probably the long narrow point across the Kennebec from Bath. It is the same word as *Naskeag* on the Penobscot River and means "at the end" or "the tip."

MERRYMEETING BAY: "Chisapeak" is the name given to this body of water by the Reverend Joseph Baxter in 1722, according to Allen's *History of Dresden*. This name fits the locale, with the following breakdown: *Che*, "big"; *sepe*, "river"; *ak* (locative): "at the big part of the river."

Nassouac or Naxoat is another name given to Merrymeeting Bay by Father Druillettes, the first white explorer of the river in 1649. He knew the region well, having established a mission at Cushnoc. Mrs. Eckstorm agreed with Dr. N. T. True's etymology of the words. *Nashue*, "midway," and *auke*, "land," combine to make "the halfway place" or "the land between." This interpretation would seem to indicate that the word meant one of the points of land on the bay rather than the bay itself.

There is still another version, this one from Pierpole, the Norridgewock Indian of Sandy River fame. It is *Quabacook*. Many linguists have given this the meaning of "Duck water place" and it would certainly be very descriptive, as the bay is a favorite stop for migrating ducks. However, according to experts

413

qualified to analyze Indian words, there is no part of the name that has anything to do with birds. If the word began with *Mqua,* shortened from *m'wak* or *mugwock,* "bog, swamp, sunken land," we could have the meaning "an expanse of shallow water." Dr. Ganong suggested the meaning "head of a bay," referring to the head of salt water on the Kennebec. He gave the root *wekw.* The student of Indian place names is welcome to make his own choice.

CATHANCE RIVER, a tributary of Merrymeeting Bay, in Bowdoinham: Lewey Mitchell, a Maliseet Indian, gave the following etymology of this word: *kecht,* meaning "principal or main branch," and *nik,* meaning "fork." The analysis fits as the Cathance has two branches, the main river and the smaller West Branch.

SWAN ISLAND, originally known as Swango: It is not certain when the name was shortened to Swan, and, according to several writers, swans were plentiful there in the early days of settlement. However, "Swango" could be derived from *Sowangan,* meaning "bald eagle," and it is entirely possible that there were eagles on the island. In fact, there are a few bald eagle nests nearby even today. Is it possible the original name of Swan Island was Eagle Island?

KEBEC or the CHOPS: *Chops* in old English signified "jaws," and the Chops were the jaws which closed in at the foot of Merrymeeting Bay. The word *Kebec,* or the narrows, means "closed in," the root being *keb* or *kep,* "contracted, plugged, closed in."

ABAGADUSSET POINT and RIVER, Merrymeeting Bay

in Bowdoinham: The etymology of the name Abaga-dusset would indicate that the stream was named first and the point later. The word was spelled in several different ways on early documents, but they were so similar that the meaning would be the same for all. The root, *abag*, means "following a shore parallel." In this case the name would fit the small stream west of the point, which is parallel with the Kennebec River. Another form was Bagadusset, meaning "to shine," from the bright reflections on the water. There was a famous sachem named Abagaduset who lived there during the Indian wars, but it is likely that he took the name from his place of residence.

EASTERN RIVER, Dresden, MUNDOOUSCOOTOOK or MUNDUSCOOTTOOK: This name is somewhat surpris-ing as it starts out with *Nundoo*, meaning "evil spirit or devil," followed by *esk*, "a green growing thing," *tagook* or *tegwe*, "river," and *ook* (locative ending). Putting all these together we come up with "River where the evil spirit's rush grows." We learn from Allen's *History of Dresden* that it is true that an unusual type of rush grows there. It is a species of cattail, which according to Indian folklore has magi-cal powers when used against one's enemies.

BATH and WEST BATH, WHISKEAG: Bath's earliest name was *Sagadahoc*, which was also the name of the river from Merrymeeting Bay to the sea. Later it was called Shaw's Point for an early settler and, later still, Bath.

ANDROSCOGGIN, AMASCONGAN: "Androscoggin" has been written in about sixty different forms as its sound was understood by different explorers and settlers. There have been some wild guesses at the meaning of the name, including "Great Skunk River," and it is possible that some of the residents near its banks in recent times might think that quite appropriate. Another theory has to do with a family named Coggin, so we have Amos Coggin, Andros Coggin, Andrews Coggin, and, even closer to the sound, "Andrus Coggin."

The Indian Pierpole, from Sandy River, said that the original name was Amascongan, meaning "a fishery." "Androscoggin" breaks down to *nahmays,* "fish," and *coggin,* "place for preparing or curing," indicating fish in abundance.

BRUNSWICK, AHMELAHCOGMETERCOOK, PEJEPSCOT: Brunswick, home of Bowdoin College since its founding in 1794, was itself incorporated as a township in 1717. The name Brunswick was adopted at that time, presumably in honor of the family of the king of England. Incorporation as a town came in 1738, it being the fifteenth town in the state. Brunswick became a mill town early, as it was situated on the magnificent Pejepscot Falls, which provided plenty of water power. One passes over these falls when crossing the bridge to Topsham.

Pejepscot describes the river around Brunswick perfectly. The etymology of the word is as follows: *pem,* "extended," *idge,* "rapids," *apsk,* "rock," *scot* or *ook,* "the long rocky rapids." Another interpretation is "crooked like a diving snake," and applies to the portion of the Androscoggin from Brunswick down to Merrymeeting Bay, including the land adjoining on the south. Another Indian name for Brunswick was *Mackquiket.* This may be a corruption of *Maquoit* which means "place where there are bears." *Bunganuc* applies to the western boundary of Brunswick and means "high bank brook."

WEST BATH, WINNEGANCE: A bay and a creek approximately on the town line between Phippsburg and West Bath bear the name Winnegance. The name, however, should apply to the short piece of land between them. This was the old Indian *wunnegan* or *ouinegan,* meaning "carry." This word with *sis* as an ending would mean "short carry." *Sis* is the diminutive. Many old deeds speak of this carry. In 1693 the Gunnison to Pepperell deed reads as follows: "Ye narrow neck of land known by ye name of Winnegance, or carrying place."

GEORGETOWN, ERASCOHEGAN, PARKER'S ISLAND: Three slight variations in the Indian name are Rascohegan, Rasthegan and Reskhegan. It is similar to the Abenaki place name *Skwahegan* (Skowhegan) meaning "a watching place for fish." *Eraskohegan* also bears the meaning "a lookout" or "watching place." It no doubt referred to a spot on the end of the island where sentinels could watch for ships or canoes going up the Kennebec and Sheepscot rivers.

PHIPPSBURG: Originally spelled with only one *p,* Phipsburg. The original spelling is on the incorporation papers and it has never been changed legally. However, from 1890 on it has been spelled Phippsburg. It was named in honor of Sir William Phips of

Woolwich, the first American to be knighted by the king of England, the first royal governor of Massachusetts and one of Maine's most distinguished sons. On the original 1813 petition, however, the name Dromore was written since one area of the town had been called that. Before the petition was passed the name had been changed to Phipsburg.

ROBINHOOD BAY: A large bay in Georgetown, it was named for the famous sachem Robinhood, whose Indian name was Ramegan. Robinhood is the Indian who carried on a thriving business of selling land to the early settlers, in some cases selling the same tract to two or three different purchasers, much to their consternation.

SASANOA: A tidal river which enters the Kennebec at Bath. It has also been called "Back River." In 1607 Captain Gilbert returned from his voyage up the Kennebec by way of the Sasanoa River. It was named for Sasanou, the chieftain whom Champlain met on his voyage up the coast of Maine.

ARROWSIC ISLAND: A large island in the main channel of the lower Kennebec River. Another name for Arrowsic Island comes directly from Father Rasle in a letter dated July 28, 1721. It is *Menaskek* or *Menaskoux*. There is some resemblance to the root *arra,* often found in names of falls and rapids, such as Arantsoak and Nanrantsoak on the upper Kennebec River. Certainly there are swift currents and changing tides past Arrowsic Island.

HOBBOMOCCA POINT, HOCKOMOCK: This point is on Arrowsic Island, very close to upper and lower

Hell Gate with its swirling and boiling cross currents, which are dangerous to small craft and uncomfortable for larger boats. *Hobbomocca* means "Hell" in Indian. The epitaph of John Bonython of Saco illustrates this:

> HERE LIES BONYTHON, THE SAGAMORE OF SACO;
> HE LIVED A ROGUE AND DIED A KNAVE
> AND WENT TO HOBOMOCO.

Bonython figures prominently in Whittier's narrative poem, "Mogg Megone."

To the west of the Phippsburg peninsula, in the town of Harpswell, are two islands whose names commemorate the 1724 Norridgewock massacre. Jacquish Island, south of Bailey Island, is said to be named for Lieutenant Jaques or Jacquish, who lived on the neck opposite in the early 1700's. This man was famous, or perhaps we should say infamous, for having shot and killed Father Rasle at the sack of Norridgewock. Orders had been given to take the Jesuit alive, but Jaques disobeyed them.

There is also a Bombazine Island between Brunswick and Great Island. Bomazeen was the beloved chief of the Norridgewock tribe in August of 1724, and he was also killed on that day, his scalp accompanying Father Rasle's and twenty-six others to Boston.

SAGADAHOC: Formerly the name given to the lower Kennebec River and now the name of the county through which the Kennebec flows on its last few miles to the sea. A very early version was *Sunkda hunk,* meaning "mouth of the river."

419

Place Names of the Kennebec Valley

SEGUIN: An island just off the mouth of the Kennebec River, famous for its lighthouse and as a landfall for ships. The island rises to a height of 145 feet above the water. Captain John Smith spelled it Satquin in 1616, and there were other variations in the spelling. The experts disagree on the meaning of Seguin. I like the explanation of Champlain, who said that when they arrived at the "Riviére du Quinibequy" there was at the opening a rather high island which had been named "the Tortoise." Dr. Ganong, an authority on Indian names, explained that from the east the island does look like a tortoise with its rounded top, and that the name derived from *che-quen-ocks,* pronounced *Siguenoc.* Mrs. Eckstorm advances another theory, that it comes from the modern Abenaki word *sigan* meaning a hump or rounded mass. This is another mystery name and the reader can make his own choice.

We have arrived at the sea, and my list of place names of the Kennebec valley is concluded. In spite of the fact that our practical ancestors discarded many beautiful Indian names for ones like Rum Pond, Mud Lake, Bag Pond, and Misery Stream, there were more than I dreamed I would find.

To end on a light note: Have you ever wondered where the odd-sounding name "Yankee" came from? No, it was not originated by a loyal Confederate just so he would have something to hang "Damn" on. It took a French Jesuit priest to figure this one out. The explanation comes from Maurault's *Histoire des Abenakis.* Translated from the French, it goes like this: When the Monhegan Indian, Samoset, welcomed the Pilgrims at Plymouth with the words, "Welcome Engis, welcome Engis," it sounded to their ears like "Welcome Yankees," so Yankee it has been ever since, thanks to Samoset.

Bibliography

This list includes some of the works consulted in the preparation of this book. It is hoped that the reader will be stimulated to inquire further into the history of the Kennebec River valley, using some of these sources.

Allen, Charles Edwin. *History of Dresden, Maine[,] Formerly a part of the old town of Pownalborough[,] From its earliest settlement to the year 1900.* NP: 1931. Reprinted by Jennie G. Everson and Eleanor L. Everson, 1977. 894 pp.

Allen, William. *The History of the Norridgewock: Comprising Memorials of the Aboriginal Inhabitants and Jesuit Missionaries, Hardships of the Pioneers, Biographical Notices of the Early Settlers, and Ecclesiastical Sketches.* Norridgewock: Edward J. Peet, 1849. 252 pp.

Augusta-Hallowell on the Kennebec. Comp. by WPA Writers' Program. American Guide Series. Augusta, Maine: The Augusta-Hallowell Chamber of Commerce, 1940. 123 pp.

Baker, Charlotte Alice. *True Stories of New England Captives.* New York: Garland Publishing Co., 1976.

Baxter, James Phinney. *The Pioneers of New*

Bibliography

France in New England, with Contemporary Letters and Documents. Albany, N. Y.: Joel Munsell's Sons, 1894. Reprinted by Heritage Books, 1980. 450 pp.

Baxter, James Phinney. *Samuel de Champlain,* address delivered June 25, 1904 at the tercentenary of the landing of Sieur de Monts at St. Croix Island.

Bourne, Edward E. *The History of Wells and Kennebunk[,] From the Earliest Settlement to the Year 1820, At Which Time Kennebunk was Set Off, and Incorporated.* Portland: B. Thurston & Co., 1875. xxiii + 797 pp.

Brown, John Marshall. *Coasting Voyages in the Gulf of Maine,* paper read before the Maine Historical Society, February 18, 1875.

Burrage, Henry S. *The Beginnings of Colonial Maine 1602-1658.* Portland, Me.: Marks Printing House, 1914. xv + 412 pp.

Burrage, Henry S. *Gorges and the Grant of the Province of Maine 1622[:] a Tercentenary Memorial.* NP, 1923. 178 pp.

Cederborg, Hazel. "Joseph Laurent: Grand Chief of the Abenakis" in *New Hampshire Profiles,* Vol. XXII, No. 7 (July 1973), pp. 32-35.

Chadbourne, Ava Harriet. *Maine Place Names and the Peopling of Its Towns.* Freeport, Maine: The Bond Wheelwright Company, 1957. County editions. Franklin and Androscoggin Counties, 50 pp. Kennebec and Somerset Counties, 75 pp.

Charland, Thomas-M. *Histoire de Saint-François-du-Lac.* Ottawa: Collège Dominicain, 1942. 364 pp.

Charlevoix, Pierre de. *Journal of a voyage to*

Bibliography

North-America. Readex Microprint Corporation, 1966.

Chase, Fannie S. *Wiscasset in Pownalborough[:] A History of the Shire Town and the Salient Historical Features of the Territory between the Sheepscot and Kennebec Rivers.* Wiscasset, Maine: 1941. vx + 640 pp.

Church, Thomas. *The History of Philip's War, Commonly Called the Great Indian War, of 1675 and 1676.* 2nd edition, Samuel G. Drake, ed. Exeter, N. H.: J. & B. Williams, 1829. 360 pp.

Codman, John. *Arnold's Expedition To Quebec.* New York: The Macmillan Company, 1901. ix + 340 pp.

Colby, Solon B. *Colby's Indian History[:] Antiquities of the New Hampshire Indians and Their Neighbors.* Center Conway, N. H.: Walkers Pond Press, 1975. 288 pp.

Congdon, Isabelle P. *Indian Tribes of Maine[:] With particular reference to Indian activities in the regions around the present locations of Bath and Brunswick.* Brunswick, Maine: Brunswick Publishing Company, ND. 20 pp.

Cummings, E. C. *The Mission of Father Rasles as Depicted by Himself,* paper read before the Maine Historical Society, December 9, 1892. 67 pp.

Davidson, D. S. "Decorative Art of the Têtes de Boule of Quebec," *Indian Notes and Monographs,* Vol. X, No. 9. Museum of the American Indian Heye Foundation, New York, 1928.

Dethier, Brock. "Bringing Back New Hampshire's

Bibliography

Lost Language" in *New Hampshire Profiles*, Vol. XXVIII No. 7 (August 1979), pp. 105-107.

Eckstorm, Fannie Hardy. *Indian Place-Names of the Penobscot Valley and the Maine Coast*. Number 55, Second Series, in *Maine Studies*. NP: University of Maine at Orono Press, 1978. xxix + 272 pp.

Eckstorm, Fannie Hardy and Mary Winslow Smyth. *Minstrelsy of Maine[:] Folk-Songs and Ballads of the Woods and the Coast*. Boston and New York: Houghton Mifflin Company, 1927. xvi + 390 pp.

Eckstorm, Fannie Hardy. *Old John Neptune and Other Maine Indian Shamans*. Portland, Maine: The Southworth-Anthoensen Press, 1945. A Marsh Island Reprint, University of Maine at Orono, 1980. xii + 209 pp.

Eckstorm, Fannie Hardy. *The Penobscot Man*. Boston and New York: Houghton, Mifflin and Company, 1904. xii + 326 pp.

Favour, Edith. *First Families: Woodland People of Maine and the Canadian Maritimes*. NP: Maine Department of Educational and Cultural Services, Division of Curriculum, 1975. 44 pp.

Fisher, Carleton Edward. *History of Fort Halifax*. Winthrop, Maine: Carleton E. Fisher, 1972. 28 pp.

Fleming, John Daly. *Richmond On The Kennebec*. Richmond, Maine: Richmond Historical Committee, 1966. vii + 198 pp.

Folsom, George. *History of Saco and Biddeford, With Notices of Other Early Settlements, and of the Proprietary Governments, in Maine, Including the*

Bibliography

Provinces of New Somersetshire and Lygonia. Saco: Alex. C. Putnam, 1830. Reprinted by New Hampshire Publishing Company, 1975. 331 pp.

Francis, Convers. "Life of Sebastian Rale, Missionary to the Indians" in *The Library of American Biography,* Second Series, Vol. VII (Boston, 1848), pp. 157-333.

Greenleaf, Moses. *A Survey of the State of Maine, in Reference to Its Geographical Features, Statistics and Political Economy.* Portland: Shirley and Hyde, 1829. Reprinted by the Maine State Museum, 1970. 468 pp.

Hannah Swanton, the Casco Captive: or the Catholic Religion in Canada, and Its Influence on the Indians in Maine. Second edition. Boston: Massachusetts Sabbath School Society, 1839. 60 pp.

Hanson, J. W. *History of Gardiner, Pittston and West Gardiner, with a Sketch of the Kennebec Indians, & New Plymouth Purchase, Comprising Historical Matter from 1602 to 1852; with Genealogical Sketches of Many Families.* Gardiner: William Palmer, 1852. 343 pp.

Hatch, Louis Clinton, ed. *Maine[:] a History.* New York: The American Historical Society, 1919. 3 vol. 936 pp.

Heffernan, John Paul. "Silent Bell" in *Down East,* Vol. XI No. 3 (October 1964), pp. 24-27, 48.

Historic Maine and Indian Mythology. [Paper pamphlet, published by Consolidated Steamship Lines?, ca. 1907.]

Holand, Hjalmar R. *Norse Discoveries and Explo-*

rations in America. New York: Dover Publications Inc., 1969.

Huden, John C., comp. *Indian Place Names of New England.* Contributions from the Museum of the American Indian Heye Foundation, Vol. XVIII, 1962. xiv + 408 pp.

Jackson, Charles T. *Third Annual Report on the Geology of the State of Maine.* Augusta: Smith & Robinson, 1839. xiv + 276 + lxiv pp.

[Johnson, Susannah.] *A Narrative of the Captivity of Mrs. Johnson, Containing an Account of Her Sufferings, During Four Years, with the Indians and French.* New York, 1841. 111 pp.

Jones, Robert Ralston. "The Bell of a Jesuit Mission," paper read before the Maine Historical Society, April 15, 1904. 44 pp.

Josselyn, John. *New-Englands Rarities Discovered: in Birds, Beasts, Fishes, Serpents, and Plants of that Country.* London: G. Widdowes, 1672.

Kelly, John. "Narrative of Mrs. Shute's Captivity" in *Collections, Topographical, Historical, and Biographical, Relating Principally to New-Hampshire.* Vol. I (Concord, 1822), pp. 116-123.

Kershaw, Gordon E. *The Kennebeck Proprietors[,] 1749-1775.* Portland: Maine Historical Society, 1975. xvi + 343 pp.

Kingsbury, Henry D., and Simeon L. Deyo, ed. *Illustrated History of Kennebec County, Maine.* 2 vol. Vol. I contains Nash's Indian History. New York: H. W. Blake & Company, 1892. viii + viii + 1273 pp.

Bibliography

Laurent, Jos. *New Familiar Abenakis and English Dialogues[:] The first ever published on the grammatical system.* Quebec: Leger Brousseau, 1881. 230 pp.

Laurent, Stephen. "The Abenakis: Aborigines of Vermont" in *Vermont History,* Vol. XXIII, No. 4 (October 1955), pp. 286-295, and Vol. XXIV, No. 1 (January 1956), pp. 3-11.

Maine Indians In History And Legends, by the Maine Writers Research Club. Portland, Maine: Severn-Wylie-Jewett Company.

Masta, Henry Lorne. *Abenaki Indian Legends, Grammar and Place Names.* Victoriaville, P. Q.: L'Imprimerie de Victoriaville, Enr., 1932. 110 pp.

Mather, Cotton. *Magnalia Christi Americana or, The Ecclesiastical History of New-England, From Its First Planting in the Year 1620, Unto the Year of Our Lord, 1693.* Hartford: Silas Andrus, 1820. 2 vol.

Maurault, J. A. *Histoire des Abenakis depuis 1605 jusqu'à nos jours.* NP: «La Gazette de Sorel», 1866. x + 631 pp.

McLellan, Hugh D. *History of Gorham, Me.* Portland: Smith and Sale, 1903. 860 pp.

Moorehead, Warren K. *A Report on the Archaeology of Maine[:] Being a Narrative of Explorations in that State[,] 1912-1920[,] Together with Work at Lake Champlain[,] 1917.* Andover, Mass.: The Andover Press, 1922. 272 pp.

Morison, Samuel Eliot. *The European Discovery of America.* New York: Oxford Press, 1971.

Nason, Emma Huntington. *Old Hallowell on the*

Kennebec. Augusta, Maine: 1909. 359 pp.

New England Indians. Comp. by New England Journeys Magazine, 1969.

Nicolar, Joseph. *The Life and Traditions of the Red Man.* Bangor, Maine: C. H. Glass & Co., 1893. v + 147 pp.

North, James W. *The History of Augusta, from the Earliest Settlement to the Present Time: with Notices of the Plymouth Company, and Settlements on the Kennebec; Together with Biographical Sketches and Genealogical Register.* Augusta: Clapp and North, 1870. xii + 990 pp.

O'Brien, Michael Charles. "Grammatical Sketch of the Ancient Abnaki[,] Outlined in the Dictionary of Fr. Sebastian Râle, S. J." in *Collections of the Maine Historical Society,* Vol. IX (1887), pp. 259-294.

Owen, Henry Wilson. *The Edward Clarence Plummer History of Bath[,] Maine.* Bath, Maine: The Times Company, 1936. 547 + xxviii pp.

Parkman, Francis. *Pioneers of France in the New World.* Williamstown, Mass.: Corner House Publishers, 1970.

Penobscot Indian issue of *SALT,* Volume IV, Number 4 (March, 1979), pp. 2-27.

Pierce, Josiah. *A History of the Town of Gorham, Maine.* Portland: Foster & Cushing, and Bailey & Noyes, 1862. Pp. 44-55.

Pike, Robert E. *Tall Trees and Tough Men.* New York: W. W. Norton & Company, Inc., 1967.

Pohl, Frederick J. *The Viking Settlements of North America.* New York: Clarkson N. Potter Inc.

Bibliography

Rasle, Sebastian. Abenaki-French dictionary, Pickering edition. Also English translation by Stephen Laurent, unpublished manuscript in author's collection.

Robbins, Alma Pierce. *The History of Vassalborough, Maine.* NP:ND. 62 pp.

Roberts, Kenneth, comp. *March to Quebec[:] Journals of the Members of Arnold's Expedition.* New York: Doubleday & Company, Inc., 1946. xiv + 722 pp.

Sanger, David, ed. *Discovering Maine's Archaeological Heritage.* Augusta, Maine: Maine Historic Preservation Commission, 1979. 156 pp.

Shea, John Gilmany. *History of the Catholic Missions Among the Indian Tribes of the United States, 1529-1854.* New York: P. J. Kenedy, 1854. 514 pp.

Smith, Justin H. *Arnold's March from Cambridge to Quebec[:] A Critical Study Together with a Reprint of Arnold's Journal.* New York: G. P. Putnam's Sons, 1903. xix + 498 pp.

Smith, Walter Brown. *The Lost Red Paint People of Maine.* Bulletin No. 11, Lafayette National Park Museum, Bar Harbor: 1930.

Spaulding, John H. *Historical Relics of the White Mountains.* Mt. Washington: J. R. Hitchcock, 1855. xi + 104 pp.

Speck, Frank G. *Penobscot Man[:] The Life History of a Forest Tribe in Maine.* NP: University of Pennsylvania Press, 1940. Reprinted by Octagon Books, 1970. xx + 325 pp.

Sprague, John Francis. *Sebastian Ralé[:] A Maine*

Tragedy of the Eighteenth Century. Boston, Mass.: Heintzemann Press, 1906. 162 pp.

Sprague's Journal of Maine History, Vol. 8, Nos. 2 and 4 (1920); Vol. 9, No. 2 (1921); and Vol. 10, No. 1 (1922), on the Maine Indians. Vol. 11, Nos. 3 and 4 (1923), on Arnold's march to Quebec.

Starbird, Charles M. *The Indians of the Androscoggin Valley[:] Tribal History, and their Relations with the Early English Settlers of Maine.* NP: Lewiston Journal Printshop, 1928. 108 pp.

Sullivan, James. *History of the District of Maine.* Boston: I. Thomas and E. T. Andrews, 1795. vii + 421 pp.

Tercentenary of the Landing of the Popham Colony at the Mouth of the Kennebec River[,] August 29, 1907. Portland: Maine Historical Society, 1907. 58 pp.

Trigger, Bruce G., ed. *Northeast,* Volume 15 of the *Handbook of North American Indians,* William C. Sturtevant, general ed. Washington: Smithsonian Institution, 1978. xvi + 924 pp.

Vetromile, Eugene. *The Abnakis and Their History.* New York: James B. Kirker, 1866. 94 pp.

Wheeler, George Augustus, and Henry Warren Wheeler. *History of Brunswick, Topsham, and Harpswell, Maine, Including the Ancient Territory Known as Pejepscot.* Boston: Alfred Mudge & Son, 1878. viii + 959 pp.

Whisler, Frances L. *Indian̄ Cookin.* NP: Nowega Press, 1973. 61 pp.

Whitney, S. H. *The Kennebec Valley.* Augusta:

Bibliography

Sprague, Burleigh & Flynt, 1887. 122 pp.

Wight, D. B. *The Androscoggin River Valley.* Rutland, Vermont: Charles E. Tuttle Company, 1967.

Williamson, William D. *The History of the State of Maine; from Its First Discovery, A. D. 1602, to the Separation, A. D. 1820, Inclusive.* Hallowell: Glazier, Masters & Co., 1832. 2 vol. xii + 660 pp., 714 pp.

Willoughby, Charles C. *Indian Antiquities of the Kennebec Valley.* Number 1, Occasional Publications in Maine Archeology. Published by the Maine Historic Preservation Commission and the Maine State Museum.

Wood, Henrietta Danforth. *Early Days of Norridgewock.* Skowhegan, Maine: The Skowhegan Press, 1933. 124 pp.

Woodrow, Arthur D., ed. and comp. *Metallak[,] the Last of the Cooashaukes[:] with the Life of David Robbins[,] the Story of Molly Ockett[,] the Adventures of Lieut. Segar and the Killing of the Last Moose.* Rumford, Maine: The Rumford Publishing Co., 1928. 103 pp.

Yerxa, Donald A. *The Burning of Falmouth, 1775[:] A Case Study in British Imperial Pacification.* Portland: Maine Historical Society, 1975. Reprinted from the Maine Historical Society Quarterly, Volume 14, Number 3, pp. 119-160.

York, Vincent. *The Sandy River & Its Valley.* Farmington, Maine: The Knowlton & McLeary Co., 1976. 251 pp.

Index

Page numbers printed in italics refer to illustrations.

Color plates I-IV follow page 104; plates V-VIII follow page 216; plates IX-XII follow page 328.

Index

Index

Index

Index

Index

Index

443

Index

Index

Index

Index

Index